PRIVATE POWER, ONLINE INFORMATION
FLOWS AND EU LAW: MIND THE GAP

This monograph examines how European Union law and regulation address concentrations of private economic power which impede free information flows on the Internet to the detriment of Internet users' autonomy. In particular, competition law, sector specific regulation (if it exists), data protection and human rights law are considered and assessed to the extent they can tackle such concentrations of power for the benefit of users. Using a series of illustrative case studies, of Internet provision, search, mobile devices and app stores, and the cloud, the work demonstrates the gaps that currently exist in EU law and regulation. It is argued that these gaps exist due, in part, to current overarching trends guiding the regulation of economic power, namely neoliberalism, by which only the situation of market failure can invite ex ante rules, buoyed by the lobbying of regulators and legislators by those in possession of such economic power to achieve outcomes which favour their businesses. Given this systemic, and extra-legal, nature of the reasons as to why the gaps exist, solutions from outside the system are proposed at the end of each case study. This study will appeal to EU competition lawyers and media lawyers.

Volume 15 in the series Hart Studies in Competition Law

Hart Studies in Competition Law

Private Power, Online Information Flows and EU Law: Mind the Gap

Angela Daly

·HART·

OXFORD · LONDON · NEW YORK · NEW DELHI · SYDNEY

HART PUBLISHING
Bloomsbury Publishing Plc
Kemp House, Chawley Park, Cumnor Hill, Oxford, OX2 9PH, UK

HART PUBLISHING, the Hart/Stag logo, BLOOMSBURY and the Diana logo are
trademarks of Bloomsbury Publishing Plc
First published in Great Britain 2016

First published in hardback, 2016
Paperback edition, 2019

A catalogue record for this book is available from the British Library.

Library of Congress Cataloging-in-Publication Data

Names: Daly, Angela, author.

Title: Private power, online information flows, and EU law : mind the gap / Angela Daly.

Description: Oxford [UK] ; Portland, Oregon : Hart Publishing, 2016. |

Series: Hart Studies in Competition Law ; volume 15 | Includes bibliographical references and index.

Identifiers: LCCN 2016034346 (print) | LCCN 2016035222 (ebook) | ISBN 9781509900633
(hardback) | ISBN 9781509900657 (Epub)

Subjects: LCSH: Antitrust law—European Union countries. | Competition, Unfair—European Union
countries. | Internet—Law and legislation—European Union countries. | Data protection—Law and
legislation—European Union countries.

Classification: LCC KJE6497 .D35 2016 (print) | LCC KJE6497 (ebook) | DDC 343.2407/21—dc23

LC record available at https://lccn.loc.gov/2016034346

ISBN: HB: 978-1-50990-063-3
PB: 978-1-50992-881-1
ePDF: 978-1-50990-064-0
ePub: 978-1-50990-065-7

Typeset by Compuscript Ltd, Shannon

To find out more about our authors and books visit www.hartpublishing.co.uk. Here you will find
extracts, author information, details of forthcoming events and the option to sign up for our
newsletters.

ACKNOWLEDGEMENTS

This book has been many years in the making and many people have aided and supported me in its development.

It is based primarily on my doctoral research at the European University Institute's Department of Law, supervised by Giorgio Monti and Giovanni Sartor, to whom I owe a debt of gratitude. I must also thank my examiners, Christopher Marsden and Lilian Edwards, for their insightful comments and suggestions, which have been incorporated into this book.

From 2013 until 2016 I was employed by the Swinburne Institute for Social Research (Australia) where I also carried out some of this research and was supported in particular by my Director there, Julian Thomas. I also owe thanks to colleagues Amanda Scardamaglia and James Meese for comments on earlier versions of this work.

I also thank Queensland University of Technology, where I have been employed during the final stages of this work, and my supervisor here, Matthew Rimmer. On trips back to Europe I have been accommodated by the Tilburg Institute for Law, Technology and Society, where I am a research associate, and thank those there for enabling me to maintain a strong connection with EU matters.

Finally, to my family and friends who have stood by me and supported me in this endeavour which has taken the best part of a decade from its germination to the publication of this book—thank you.

CONTENTS

ABBREVIATIONS

API	application program interface
BEREC	Body of European Regulators of Electronic Communications
CDN	content delivery network
CJEU	Court of Justice of the European Union
DoJ	Department of Justice (US)
DPI	deep packet inspection
DRM	digital rights management
DSL	digital subscriber line
ECHR	European Convention on Human Rights
ECtHR	European Court of Human Rights
EDPS	European Data Protection Supervisor
EPG	electronic programming guide
FCC	Federal Communications Commission (US)
FTC	Federal Trade Commission (US)
ICANN	Internet Corporation for Assigned Names and Numbers
ISP	Internet Service Provider
NRA	national regulatory authority
NSA	National Security Agency (US)
P2P	peer-to-peer
SMP	significant market power
SSNIP	small but significant non-transitory increase in price
STS	science and technology studies
TFEU	Treaty on the Functioning of the European Union
TPM	technical protection measure
VoIP	Voice over Internet Protocol

TABLE OF CASES

EUROPEAN UNION

EUROPEAN COURT OF HUMAN RIGHTS

UNITED STATES OF AMERICA

Federal Trade Commission Decisions

TABLE OF LEGISLATION

1

Introduction

The phenomenon of the Internet is widely believed to have been a revolution in society akin to that of Gutenberg's printing press 600 years ago. One aspect of this revolution initially was perceived to be the ungovernable, indomitable nature of the Internet, especially as compared to the control that could be exerted over previous communications technology, such as television, print media and the telephone, due to the decentralised nature of the 'network of networks'.

However, after more than 20 years of the Internet being widely available as a public medium, poles of power have emerged, both public (based around the nation-state) and private (based around for-profit corporations), which also interact with each other to produce a corporatised private-public pole of power over the Internet. It is the private aspects of this public-private nexus which is the topic of this book. This private power has manifested in concentrations of power which do not promote and facilitate an optimally free flow of information online for users, compromising their autonomy.

A framework of laws and regulation already exist with the explicit aim, or implicit effect, of governing such concentrations of private power. It is those of the European Union (EU) that are considered here, in particular antitrust/competition law,[1] sector-specific regulation, data protection and human rights. However, it is competition which is the most prominent: absent any ex ante regulation, mono- and oligopolies are prima facie governed by competition law (as a 'legal regime of last resort'); also, EU competition law has strong enforcement measures available for when breaches are detected. Indeed, in only one of this book's case studies is ex ante regulation present, namely telecoms markets, with its presence a legacy of the privatisation and liberalisation of this sector from the 1980s rather than a response to the new challenges posed by the Internet. Given the Internet is used as a communications medium extending beyond a mere economic marketplace, EU data protection law and fundamental rights, in particular privacy and free expression, are also relevant to the book's discussion.

Each chapter of the 'substantive' part of this book forms a case study which provides an example of where existing law and regulation in the EU, namely

---

[1] 'Antitrust' is the US term, whereas 'competition' is used in most other jurisdictions, including the United Kingdom (UK) and European Union. In this book, 'competition' will be the primary term used, except when referring to the American system, in which case 'antitrust' will be used.

competition, sector-specific regulation, data protection and fundamental rights, leave a 'gap' where Internet users' interests, encapsulated in the idea of 'autonomy' explained below, are not protected and instead left exposed to the negative effects of concentrations of private economic power affecting online information flows.

These gaps exist due, in part, to current overarching trends guiding the regulation of economic power, namely neoliberalism. Accordingly, only the situation of market failures can invite ex ante rules. This is also buoyed by the lobbying of regulators and legislators by those in possession of economic power to achieve outcomes which favour their businesses. Given this systemic, and extra-legal, nature of the reasons as to why the gaps exist, some 'quick fixes' from outside the system are proposed at the end of each case study, namely the potential for applying regulation and/or applying 'self-help' solutions, which are mainly technical measures using peer-to-peer design. These extra-systemic solutions are, admittedly, not a complete or perfect solution to the problems of private economic power online, but they do give a glimpse of alternatives which could be deployed on a grander scale to effect positive change for users.

I. This Book's Approach

This book explores how information flows on the Internet are controlled by for-profit corporations at various important 'choke-points' and critiques the EU's existing legal and regulatory framework for being unable to ensure that these flows occur in an 'optimal' way. In practice the corporate 'gatekeepers' of these online information flows at the choke-points are private, for-profit undertakings which have a monopolistic or oligopolistic character. The main argument of this book is that existing EU law and regulation does not adequately address concentrations of private economic power adversely affecting online information flows to the detriment of Internet users' autonomy due to their neoliberal basis.

A 'law in context' approach is taken to the subject of corporate dominance over Internet data flows.[2] More specifically, a critical political economy approach is taken to the study of the EU legal and regulatory frameworks governing concentrations of private power online.[3] This is preferred over a traditional 'black letter' doctrinal approach to the law due to the issues of power, freedom, autonomy and control which are explored in relation to online information flows.

The focus of this book is on Internet markets whose subject matter concerns online information flows. While the Internet is transnational by its very nature,

---

[2] W Twining, 'Law in Context Movement' in P Cane and J Conaghan (eds), *The New Oxford Companion to Law* (Oxford, Oxford University Press, 2008).

[3] F Pasquale, 'Symbiotic Law and Social Science: The Case for Political Economy in the Legal Academy, and Legal Scholarship in Political Economy' (Jotwell Fifth Anniversary Conference, Miami, 2014).

the EU is the book's principal jurisdictional locus since it is one of the two most advanced competition and regulatory regimes in the world, as well as having a highly complex and developed Internet infrastructure, the majority of which is privately-owned (as opposed to being the property of the state). The analysis is comparative in part, drawing as well from the experience of the United States of America (US) where relevant, given its position as having the other most advanced competition and regulation regime globally. In addition, many of the Internet corporations managing online information flows considered here are transnational entities, which operate in both the EU and the US. This also triggers a (partially) comparative analysis since what happens to such a corporation in one jurisdiction in terms of competition investigations and regulatory action can have spillover effects in the other jurisdictions in which that corporation operates.[4]

Internet corporations involved in the management and facilitation of online information flows, by providing either physical or virtual infrastructure through which this information flows between Internet users, are considered. These corporations can be termed 'gatekeepers of information' since through their infrastructure they channel information to users, and they also have the power to switch on or off these flows, as well as manipulate the flows in other ways: thus, they exert control over the information flows.[5] Online information flows have become increasingly important to social and economic aspects of life, given that the data they contain may be the 'new currency' of the information economy, or a business input as important as capital and labour.[6] The rise of 'Big Data' (ie the collection and analysis of large volumes of information), and the associated hype around it,[7] reinforces the importance of data in the information economy, and the crucial role of the entities which control that information and data.[8] Indeed, the transition to the 'Internet of Things', whereby a plethora of objects such as clothes and accessories, coffee machines, and energy meters are becoming Internet-enabled, is likely to cement data gathering and analysing as key functions of the economy but the problems that are generated by control of information are also likely to be amplified as a result of this development.[9] Moreover, the proliferation of devices connected to the Internet culminating in the Internet of Things and the amount of activities in the lives of those in (over)developed Western societies which take place involving the Internet in some way or other cause the distinction between

---

[4] JL Goldsmith, 'Unilateral Regulation of the Internet: A Modest Defence' (2000) 11(1) *European Journal of International Law* 135, 142–45.

[5] K Barzilai-Nahon, 'Toward a Theory of Network Gatekeeping: A Framework for Exploring Information Control' (2007) 59(9) *Journal of the American Society for Information Technology* 1493.

[6] 'Data, Data Everywhere', *The Economist*, 25 February 2010, available at www.economist.com/node/15557443.

[7] S Fox and T Do, 'Getting Real about Big Data: Applying Critical Realism to Analyse Big Data Hype' (2013) 6(4) *International Journal of Managing Projects in Business* 739.

[8] D Boyd and K Crawford, 'Six Provocations for Big Data', 'A Decade in Internet Time: Symposium on the Dynamics of the Internet and Society', Oxford, September 2011.

[9] V Ryan, 'The Internet of Things: Data Goldmine and Social Nightmare', *CTO*, 20 May 2014, available at ww2.cfo.com/it-value/2014/05/internet-things-data-goldmine-social-nightmare/.

online and offline to blur.[10] In an increasingly ambient intelligent environment, more of what used to be 'offline' is now also 'online', which makes this book and the issues it interrogates all the more timely.

Such corporations operating in markets in which data and information gathering is of paramount importance challenge conventional EU competition and regulation analysis, due to facts such as: the nature of their products and services being highly complex and technical; users in some cases paying no monetary sum (although often paying with their privacy)[11] to access the services or products which make up examples of two- or multi-sided markets;[12] and the rise of 'prosumer' peer production to (part-)produce informational products and services.[13] These factors place obstacles in the way of traditional applications of competition law, as well as competition's paternalistic attitudes towards passive consumers and failure to see or deal with the 'non-economic' aspects of issues it encounters.

This book looks at available law and regulation to address the control of online information flows by concentrations of private economic power. Absent specific regulation, competition law is the main legal player, operating as a residual regime to address accumulations of economic power principally through its sanctions for abuse of dominance. There are other legal and regulatory regimes which intersect with parts of the Internet and its information flows but they too leave gaps where Internet corporations are concerned. In any event, these laws also are not designed primarily to tackle corporate dominance resulting from concentrations of private economic power, and for this reason also cannot be relied upon to deal with this issue.

Yet certain other legal regimes, which promote the autonomy of users and are applicable to the scenarios at hand, are considered to determine the extent to which they can solve problems of corporate control of online information flows in the interests of users. EU data protection laws and fundamental/constitutional rights to free expression and privacy are highly pertinent to the governance of online information flows. Furthermore, the objectives of these areas of law converge with the idea of user autonomy, which is central to the argument of this book. Data protection law has the objective of protecting individuals' privacy, which itself protects individuals' autonomy.[14] In Europe, the right to free

---

[10] See S Monteleone, *Ambient Intelligence and the Right to Privacy: The Challenge of Detection Technologies*, EUI Law Working Papers 2011/13 (2011).

[11] J Rule, *Privacy in Peril: How We are Sacrificing a Fundamental Right in Exchange for Security and Convenience* (Oxford, Oxford University Press, 2009); O Tene and J Polonetsky, 'A Theory of Creepy: Technology, Privacy and Shifting Social Norms' (2013) 16 *Yale Journal of Law and Technology* 59.

[12] S King, 'Governing the Ungovernable: The Market, Technology and You' (2014) 15 *Insights* 55.

[13] A Daly, 'Free Software and the Law: Out of the Frying Pan and into the Fire: How Shaking Up Intellectual Property Suits Competition Law Just Fine' (2013) 5 *Journal of Peer Production*.

[14] P Bernal, *Internet Privacy Rights: Rights to Protect Autonomy* (Cambridge, Cambridge University Press, 2014) 9–15; H Nissenbaum, *Privacy in Context: Technology, Policy and Integrity of Social Life* (Redwood City, Stanford University Press, 2009).

expression is conceptualised as centring on the individual, and being based on the ideas of autonomy and human dignity.[15]

There are various related areas which are outside this book's scope. First, the discussion concentrates on exercises of *private economic power*, and thus excludes state-only control of online information flows, such as for the purposes of preventing crime (eg child pornography, terrorism, fraud), addressing copyright infringement and restricting 'adult' material. While the nation-state and private economic power do cooperate with each other for mutual benefit, pure state conduct is excluded from consideration, as well as its 'outsourcing' to private providers.

Secondly, the discussion here centres on whether *current* EU law and regulation, and their application, are capable of addressing the problems caused by the control of online information flows by private economic power, and thus ensure that users' autonomy is preserved and protected. Accordingly, possible conceptual reforms to this law and regulation to promote user autonomy are not considered in great detail. The omission of such discussion is due in part to concerns of space and to the fact that such conceptual reform is also likely to be a longer-term project in terms of time. Instead, a more pragmatic approach is taken to the problems that exist now with these large concentrations of private power online manifesting in commodified information gatekeepers, and how they may be resolved in the short term by existing law, regulation and extra-legal methods. Nevertheless, the reform of existing law and regulation in ways which would promote user autonomy online, and perhaps autonomy for citizens in other areas of life as well, may be a much larger project, part of a broader and more profound societal change which embraces more radical, heterodox, schools of economic theory, such as participatory economics (and participation beyond just the economic sphere).[16]

Thirdly, of current EU law and regulation, consumer protection law is largely excluded from consideration. Consumer protection law may theoretically promote individuals' autonomy through its concern for the weaker parties (ie individuals) in the marketplace. However, in practice redressing this balance has generally involved greater transparency obligations on companies to provide more and accurate information about the products and services they are selling. While more information may be provided about eg non-net neutral conduct from Internet Service Providers, what happens to users' data once it is collected or the existence of restrictions that mobile device providers put on their devices and access to content, this does not go far enough to advance user autonomy. The Unfair Terms in Consumer Contracts Directive (93/13/EEC) does concern the substantive

---

[15] E Barendt, *Freedom of Speech*, 2nd edn (Oxford, Oxford University Press, 2005); V Zeno-Zencovich, *La Liberta d'espressione Media, mercato, potere nella società dell'informazione* (Bologna, Il Mulino, 2004).

[16] See M Albert and R Hahnel, *The Political Economy of Participatory Economics* (Princeton, NJ, Princeton University Press, 1991).

'fairness' of terms in standard form consumer contracts, which are frequently used for digital products and services, and in theory an expansive interpretation of what constitutes 'unfairness' in such contracts may involve invalidating terms which impinge upon user autonomy as defined below. Yet in practice, consumer law has been tardy in its consideration of digital matters compared to other areas of EU law.[17] There is scant Court of Justice of the European Union (CJEU) jurisprudence on unfairness in digital consumer contracts, even though several types of terms commonly used in such contracts would likely fail the current 'unfairness' test, let alone an expanded version of it.[18] Furthermore, many 'consumer protection' issues regarding privacy are already subsumed by the data protection regime in the EU, in contrast to the US which, lacking a similar comprehensive data protection law, has experienced a more activist Federal Trade Commission protect consumer privacy via its authority to police unfair and deceptive trade practices.[19] Thus, consumer protection is not one of the areas of law considered in detail within this book's substantive chapters, but its consideration ought to be incorporated into future reform.

Fourthly, this book contains *illustrative* examples of the gaps left by the current legal and regulatory system in terms of addressing the adverse effects on online information flows for Internet users resulting from concentrations of private economic power. It does not attempt to cover all such examples. Indeed, for instance, the domain names and root server system overseen by the Internet Corporation for Assigned Names and Numbers (ICANN) is outside the scope, even though ICANN may fall into the definition of an online private gatekeeper, or at least a 'public-private gatekeeper'.[20] The reason for this is multifaceted: ICANN and the system it oversees can be seen as *sui generis* in various respects.[21] Despite its global reach and the 'public' nature of some of the power it wields, in terms of legal structure ICANN is currently a private, not-for-profit organisation incorporated under Californian law. The extent to which the law of other jurisdictions, for instance European law, applies to ICANN in any way is far from a settled point.[22]

[17] N Helberger and others, 'Digital Content Contracts for Consumers' (2013) 36(1) *Journal of Consumer Policy* 37.

[18] M Loos and J Luzak, 'Wanted, A Bigger Stick: On Unfair Terms in Consumer Contracts with Online Service Providers' (2016) 39(1) *Journal of Consumer Policy* 63.

[19] D Solove and W Hartzog, 'The FTC and the New Common Law of Privacy' (2014) 114 *Columbia Law Review* 583.

[20] CM Bruner, 'States, Market, and Gatekeepers: Public-Private Regulatory Regimes in an Era of Economic Globalization' (2008) 30 *Michigan Journal of International Law* 125, 132.

[21] E Schweighofer, 'A Review of the Uniform Dispute Resolution Policy of the Internet Corporation for Assigned Names and Numbers (ICANN)' (2001) 6 *Austrian Review of International and European Law* 91, 100.

[22] International or European human rights law would seem not to apply to ICANN: M Zalnieriute and T Schneider, *ICANN's Procedures and Policies in the Light of Human Rights, Fundamental Freedoms and Democratic Values*, report prepared for the Council of Europe DGI (2014) 12. However, EU data protection law may apply to the WHOIS database operated by ICANN, particularly the parts of the database compiled and managed by the European Regional Internet Registry RIPE NCC which is headquartered in Amsterdam. See also Article 29 Data Protection Working Party, *Opinion 2/2003 on the Application of the Data Protection Principles to the WHOIS Directories*, WP 76 10972/03.

Furthermore, even in the US, ICANN has claimed that antitrust law does not apply to its activities, so even in its 'home' jurisdiction it is unclear what aspects of the legal system govern its activities.[23] Another absence is a full consideration of monopolistic social networks such as Facebook, which could also be termed a gatekeeper of information online[24]—or at least a manipulator of that information (and its psychological effect on users), as its controversial 'Emotional Contagion' experiment demonstrates.[25] Facebook and other social networks have been excluded, though, for considerations of space and a wish to avoid repetition, given that the application of relevant law would be largely similar to that detailed in the case study on online search in chapter 3.

II. Intended Contribution

This critical perspective on competition law, sector specific regulation, fundamental rights and data protection regarding the Internet differs from what is standard, and believes another world beyond that envisaged by neoclassical economics and its assumptions, as well as its implementations via neoliberalism, is indeed possible.[26] In legal scholarship and especially scholarship on competition law, the dominant paradigm of neoclassical economics is usually implicitly accepted as being true or good, and the analysis thus follows. This book professes an explicitly normative consideration of the issues, in contrast to 'orthodox' or 'conservative' approaches, which in practice also adopt normative perspectives, even if they often purport (explicitly or implicitly) to be neutral. The explicit normative position taken here is that users' autonomy is promoted above the interests of the centralised state and centralised capital. To what extent this objective could be achieved by a more 'behavioural' approach to EU law and regulation currently being discussed in the literature[27] is unclear, and beyond the scope of this book looking at whether the *current* rules in this area promote user autonomy, although insights from behavioural studies of users may prove helpful for guiding future reform.

In each of this book's case studies, where it is seen that the existing law and regulation is unable to uphold users' autonomy adequately, technical solutions are

---

[23] See L Blue, 'Internet and Domain Name Governance Antitrust Litigation and ICANN' (2014) 19(1) *Berkeley Technology Law Journal* 387; JT Lepp, 'ICANN's Escape from Antitrust Liability' (2012) 89(4) *Washington University Law Review* 931.

[24] J Haucap and U Heimeshoff, 'Google, Facebook, Amazon, eBay: Is the Internet Driving Competition or Market Monopolization?' (2014) 11 *International Economics and Economic Policy* 49.

[25] R Schroeder, 'Big Data and the Brave New World of Social Media Research' (2014) 1(2) *Big Data and Society*.

[26] Following and attempting to further the initiation of a theory which 'would actually be of interest to those who are trying to help bring about a world in which people are free to govern their own affairs'. D Graeber, *Fragments of an Anarchist Anthropology* (Chicago, IL, Prickly Paradigm Press, 2004) 9.

[27] A Alemanno and AL Sibony, *Nudge and the Law: A European Perspective* (Oxford, Hart Publishing, 2015).

instead proposed. This is not done on a technologically deterministic basis (that a 'code' is a better regulator of human conduct than law, markets, norms, etc) but on the basis that these particular technical solutions, often designed explicitly with ideas of privacy, expression and decentralised commons organisation in mind, better uphold the normative value of user autonomy and so form pragmatic alternatives to the offerings of the poles of private economic power identified. As mentioned earlier, these solutions are not total, complete or perfect but do represent an important alternative to the commercial offerings and open up possibilities of paradigm change in the Internet ecosystem.

Optimal free information flows from an Internet-user-centric perspective will be defined, with a particular focus on facilitating users' capacity for autonomous conduct online. Although competition law, and regulation for that matter, are more familiar with 'consumers' (and occasionally 'citizens'), for various reasons which will be explained later, Internet users cannot be fully equated with the 'consumer' of competition law: for them the Internet is more than just an economic marketplace. Why these free flows are valuable for individuals and society, and thus desirable goals, will be explained.

Then, the focus will move to considering the ways in which users' autonomy over free flows of information is threatened by private economic power, which acts as gatekeeper and controls certain important choke-points for information flows. The case studies each concern a particular choke-point, encompassing: the network infrastructure providing Internet access to users; search engines organising web content; mobile Internet ecosystems (devices and application platforms); and cloud providers.

The discussion then examines how far the current EU legal and regulatory system addresses the interference with the free flow of online information by these axes of private economic power, for the benefit of Internet users. Competition law and pertinent sector-specific regulation concerning concentrations of economic power, namely that for telecommunications, will be considered primarily as the parts of the system which are designed to address the problems that economic power can cause, since the corporations under consideration may be considered to be abusing their positions of power in contravention of the rules. Data protection and fundamental rights, especially free expression and privacy, are also considered as subsidiary parts of the legal and regulatory system which might provide some remedy to the interference with free information flows, although these legal regimes have their deficiencies, particularly given that their aims are not primarily to address these concentrations of private power.

The case studies exist along a continuum or spectrum of regulatory intervention, with Internet provision (chapter 3) and Internet search (chapter 4) evidencing the most intervention from EU authorities, with the forthcoming net neutrality regulation and the ongoing competition investigation into Google, respectively. Chapter 6 on cloud computing represents the other end of this scale, with the least legal and regulatory intervention, and is the most prospective case of the four. However, all of the case studies establish that the current legal and regulatory system in the EU does not address fully the negative impact that concentrations of private economic power have over the free flow of information online and thus Internet users' autonomy. Why that is the case, that is to say why these 'gaps' in current law and regulation exist, is discussed and explained, with the neoliberal influence over EU competition law and economic regulation considered in particular as a factor accounting for these gaps.

With the Internet now increasingly the subject of law enforcement and regulatory interventions by governments, including competition investigations, as well as the growing concentration of private for-profit power—while dialectically the Internet holds the potential for more liberated activity by individual users than previous communications media—this book aims to contribute to the academic and policy discussion in various ways.

First, the book aims to demonstrate the limits of the current legal and regulatory approach in the EU to addressing private economic power in a gatekeeping function over online information flows. The discussion and analysis is based upon Buch-Hansen and Wigger's critical political economy approach to EU competition policy, which was originally directed at merger control,[28] and expands upon it by applying it to how the current system in the EU addresses concentrations of private economic power in Internet markets.

The discussion in the following chapters will show that the Internet is capable of being captured by for-profit corporations with the associated accumulation of market power and concentration in online markets, and that this is harmful for not just the 'welfare' of 'consumers' but also for users and their autonomy. Except in the case of Internet Services Providers, there is no ex ante regulation which applies to concentrations of for-profit corporate power exercised online, and it is competition law, in its sanctioning of abuses of dominance, which operates residually to address these accumulations of power.

While competition law can solve some of the problems created by this concentration of private for-profit corporate power through its sanctioning of abuses of dominance, it is not a panacea for all issues involving such an accumulation of private economic power on the Internet, and the approach to thinking of competition law as the only or one of the only permissible checks on this private economic power is misguided. Indeed, it can be seen that an accumulation of market power to form a dominant position in an Internet market can have consequences which are prejudicial to Internet users, but are not adequately captured by competition law. Due to EU competition law's current 'More Economic' approach, its inability to take account of the changed identity of the consumer into user and its difficulties in incorporating 'non-economic' values into its analysis, competition law cannot adequately respond to all of the issues created by such accumulations of private power. Furthermore, in situations where there is no dominant position in

---

[28] H Buch-Hansen and A Wigger, *The Politics of European Competition Regulation: A Critical Political Economy Perspective* (Abingdon, Routledge, 2011).

a given market, the profit-seeking characteristic of online corporations entails that all players (or all major players) in a given market may compete with each other on price and other features, but may all still be acting in a similar way which is prejudicial to users' interests. Thus users lack a 'real choice' of alternatives.

Certain other legal regimes may be applicable to these situations where users' autonomy is being eroded by accumulations of private power, namely fundamental rights and EU data protection law. However, their operation alongside competition law still does not address the entirety of the prejudice and harm suffered by Internet users. In the case of fundamental rights, this is mainly due to the fact they operate primarily vis-à-vis state action rather than that of private entities. Data protection, while applicable to private entities, is limited in its application to 'personal information', and not always well-enforced in practice. As a result, the operation of these existing laws and regulation leaves 'gaps', where the system does not promote autonomy for Internet users vis-à-vis concentrations of private economic power.

The book shows that these 'gaps' in the legal and regulatory system exist because the system does not promote autonomy for users, and is still focussed on their character as consumers vis-à-vis corporations (and citizens vis-à-vis the state). A cognisance of user autonomy is necessary in order to address all the harm that users suffer from accumulations of economic power. However, this book is also critical of the law itself in being able to provide such an adequate outcome, especially where new technologies are concerned, given their very quick rate of change and development. Thus, any legal/policy/regulatory solution, aside from potential substantive inadequacies, may also procedurally be too little, too late. In addition, corporate regulatory capture gives rise to scepticism as to the possibility of regulation being mooted in the first place and its successful adoption and implementation. Moreover, the 'invisible handshake' and the nation-state's interest in the surveillance of Internet users, particularly through privately-owned infrastructure,[29] entails that in practice, full public/state control over the Internet is undesirable, let alone unlikely to happen (eg via expropriations) given the neoliberal currents at play in the EU and beyond.

While there is a need for a new approach in addressing the problems caused by concentrations of private economic power acting as online information gatekeepers for Internet users, advocating for new laws and regulation is not an easily-accomplished solution. This is due to the deep penetration of neoliberal ideas in competition law's 'More Economic' approach and 'light touch' sector-specific regulation in the EU; the lack of 'joined up' coherence throughout the

---

[29] MD Birnhack and N Elkin-Koren, 'The Invisible Handshake: The Reemergence of the State in the Digital Environment' (2003) 8 *Virginia Journal of Law and Technology* 6. Birnhack and Elkin-Koren's 'invisible handshake' would seem to correspond to the alignment of Colander's 'invisible hand' (economic forces) and 'invisible foot' (legal and political forces). See D Colander, *Neoclassical Political Economy: The Analysis of Rent-Seeking and DUP Activities* (Cambridge, Ballinger, 1984).

legal and regulatory framework to marry 'social' and 'economic' objectives; and the regulatory capture of institutions and the lobbying which the intended targets of regulation engage in to avoid being regulated in the first place. Thus, the short-term promotion of user autonomy may be better, or at least more immediately accomplished by users taking matters into their own hands and designing non-hierarchical, non-exploitative online tools and infrastructure, possibly operated on a cooperative basis, rather than prioritising requests for more state intervention such as ex ante regulation. Indeed, peer-to-peer commons-based alternatives are suggested in the substantive case studies as pragmatic options for users unwilling to wait for the benevolence of state and for-profit corporate power to protect and promote their autonomous interests.

III. Outline of the Book

The following chapters are structured into one theoretical chapter and four substantive case studies followed by a concluding chapter. These case studies have been chosen as they illustrate the issues at the core of this book, namely the gaps that the current legal and regulatory system in the EU produces when protecting and promoting users' autonomy vis-à-vis private economic power online.

Before exploring how the case studies play out in practice, chapter 2 provides more background on the book's main argument, that existing EU law and regulation does not adequately address concentrations of private economic power adversely affecting online information flows to the detriment of Internet users' autonomy due to their neoliberal basis. First, the emergence of neoliberalism and its influence over contemporary Internet-related EU laws will be outlined. The Internet is bound up in a dialectic of corporatist control and individual freedom given the historical context surrounding its origins, and the technological affordances it presents to individual users, a dichotomy which will be examined. Then, the idea of user autonomy will be explained, followed by how it interacts with contemporary EU competition law and regulation. Finally, conceptual alternatives to this existing law and regulation are suggested as better ways of achieving user autonomy in practice.

The four substantive case studies comprise situations in which there are concentrations of private economic power in the EU which perform a gatekeeper function over a certain 'choke-point' for online information flows going to and from Internet users. As mentioned above, these case studies are illustrative of what are broader trends in both how Internet markets are set up, and also the gaps left by the application of current law and regulation in the EU. An assessment is made in each chapter of the extent to which these accumulations of private for-profit power online harm user autonomy, and the extent to which pre-existing EU law and regulation can address these issues. In each case, it is found that while current law and regulation go some way to addressing user autonomy concerns, they still leave some aspects of these concerns unaddressed, so there is a 'gap' in the law and regulation where user autonomy is not protected vis-à-vis private power. This is an undesirable state of affairs, yet one which is unlikely to be remedied easily and expeditiously within the current system.

The case studies consist of an examination of Internet provision, search engines, mobile device ecosystems, and cloud computing. These case studies encompass both the physical and virtual infrastructure facilitating Internet users' communications and other activities online, and each form a point at which a gatekeeping function can be performed with regard to the information that users send and receive over the Internet. They are illustrative of concentrations of online private power whose negative consequences for Internet users are not fully addressed by existing law and regulation in the EU, and demonstrate greater trends in the commodification of the Internet, particularly the contemporary and forward-looking chapters on mobile devices and apps, and the cloud, given these are directions that are being pursued with new devices developed as part of the Internet of Things.

In particular, chapter 3 ('Dominance and Internet Provision') looks at issues of dominance in how Internet access services are provided to users. Internet Service Providers (ISPs) offering this access perform a gatekeeping function over online information flows, particularly in the 'last mile' to and from users: they are in a position to censor or otherwise manipulate what users send and receive. These ISPs under consideration are mostly private for-profit corporations, although some of the European ones have emerged out of what used to be state-owned telecoms monopolies, which underwent a process of privatisation and market liberalisation from the 1980s. The ex ante sector-specific regulation of these entities is a legacy of that process, accompanied by competition law. However, as is explored in more detail in the body of the chapter, these have been insufficient to address the rise of 'net neutrality' as an issue for Internet provision, which is born of corporate dominance and encompasses both competition concerns and digital rights issues. While in both the EU and US net neutrality has been a subject of regulatory activity, it can be seen that this activity, where it exists, is 'too little, too late', and so demonstrates the inadequacies of the system in instituting ex ante regulation to address pre-existing legal and regulatory gaps.

Chapter 4 ('Dominance and Internet Search') turns attention to search engines, which perform a major gatekeeping function over information available to users on the Web. They also represent an important example of almost total dominance by one single entity in the EU, namely Google. Google's functioning has been subject to competition investigations for alleged abuses of dominance in both the US and EU, which will be analysed, along with the extent to which the results of these investigations alongside the operation of other relevant areas of law uphold online user autonomy.

Chapter 5 ('Dominance and Mobile Devices') charts the transition to Internet-enabled mobile devices, namely tablets and smartphones, providing a more 'closed' and controlled Internet experience to users. The position of gatekeeping that device vendors and app store operators possess vis-à-vis users is considered, which again raises the (by now familiar) issues of competition and users' digital rights. There have been some competition investigations in this field, which again are examined to determine whether they have resulted in gains for users' autonomy online.

Finally, chapter 6 ('Dominance and the Cloud') is more forward-looking than those which precede it, in examining the migration of various previously offline functions of data storage, software and applications to centralised Internet-enabled cloud providers. Again, cloud providers occupy a gatekeeping position regarding the information users send and receive. The prospective application of competition law and the other relevant areas of law are examined to determine whether these gatekeeping issues can be addressed adequately to protect and promote users' autonomy.

The final chapter summarises the outcomes of the case studies vis-à-vis how dominance of online information flows by concentrations of private economic power is addressed in the interests of user autonomy by the available legal tools in the EU. It will be seen that the case studies together present a situation in which gaps exist in the application of current EU law and regulation to concentrations of private power. While acknowledging that these gaps arise from more deep-seated currents in society that are likely to be too profound to be addressed in the short term, possible next steps for law and regulation will be discussed.

2

The Internet, User
Autonomy and EU Law

This chapter presents the theoretical backdrop to the subsequent case studies by examining the Internet's origins and development as a 'freedom-enhancing' tool, alongside the contemporaneous evolution of EU law and regulation governing private economic power. The concept linking these two streams of discussion is that of 'user autonomy', which is implicated by the Internet's affordances for individuals, and which, it is argued, should also be the legal and regulatory framework's goal when governing Internet matters. However, the trends influencing EU law and regulation from the 1980s, especially neoliberalism, have resulted in these frameworks not being well-equipped to advance user autonomy in the Internet sphere, as will be explained in more detail below.

I. The Internet, Power and Freedom

The Internet emerged into the public realm in the 1990s: an interesting moment for ideology in recent Western history, with the fall of the Soviet Union and the seeming inevitability of liberal democracy's social and economic freedoms.[1] Perhaps this was part of the reason that strong discourses around the Internet's freedom-enhancing aspects permeated the literature and discussion from this time, although this discussion also questioned the nation-state's role in managing the new medium. Indeed, the 'cyberlibertarians' denied the authority, but also the very ability, of the nation-state to control the Internet,[2] and believed they were seeing a 'freeing' of culture and information in the online environment.[3] Subsequently,

---

[1] F Fukuyama, *The End of History and the Last Man* (New York, Free Press, 1992).
[2] JP Barlow, 'A Declaration of the Independence of Cyberspace', *Electronic Frontier Foundation*, 8 February 1996, available at https://projects.eff.org/~barlow/Declaration-Final.html.
[3] E Dyson and others, 'Cyberspace and the American Dream: A Magna Carta for the Knowledge Age', *Progress and Freedom Foundation*, August 1994, available at www.pff.org/issues-pubs/futureinsights/fi1.2magnacarta.html.

the advent of Web 2.0 and the birth of social media were also supposed to usher in a new era of freedom for users.[4]

However, this narrative sits awkwardly with the Internet's origins as a US government-based project associated with 'both the "closed world" of the Cold War and the open and decentralized world of the anti-war movement and the counterculture'.[5] The Internet's predecessor, ARPANET, rose out of a Cold War-era US military programme, yet ARPA money also 'supported the "hackers" at MIT's Artificial Intelligence Lab' including Richard Stallman,[6] who would later become a luminary of the free software movement.

This dichotomy between centralised control and anti-authoritarian decentralisation rooted in the historical events leading up to the creation of the Internet has persisted throughout the Internet's public emergence from the 1990s until the present day. This complex relationship between the Internet, freedom and power will be explored below.

A. The Internet and Freedom

The Internet's freedom-enhancing aspect is evidenced by early Internet users' experience, who viewed it as 'an open public space which was decentralised, diverse and interactive' but gave 'largely uncritical reception ... to the commercialisation of the internet'.[7] Indeed, the absence of government control was lauded, and developed into a socio-political discourse producing various cyberlibertarian manifestos.[8] Due to factors which mostly concerned the lack of obvious content restriction, the Internet's transnational nature, the lack of visible de facto government control over the medium, and the initial lack of prominence of large corporate entities at these layers more visible to users, it appeared that the Internet represented an autonomous space in which users had control over their actions and online destiny. Indeed, some considered that the Internet provided the best outlet so far for individuals' free expression.[9]

These perceptions may have been informed by the fact that during the mid to late 1990s, the Internet even in developed jurisdictions still did not have a high rate of penetration. In addition, corporate involvement at the more 'visible' levels was still limited: e-commerce had not quite yet matured, due to factors such as

---

[4] Y Benkler, *The Wealth of Networks: How Social Production Transforms Markets and Freedom* (New Haven, CT, Yale University Press, 2006).

[5] R Rosenzweig, 'Wizards, Bureaucrats, Warriors and Hackers' (1998) 103(5) *American Historical Review* 1530, 1531.

[6] ibid 1542.

[7] J Curran, 'Rethinking Internet History' in J Curran, N Fenton and D Freeman (eds), *Misunderstanding the Internet* (Abingdon, Routledge, 2012) 41.

[8] Dyson and others, *Cyberspace and the American Dream* (n 3); Barlow *A Declaration of the Independence of Cyberspace* (n 2).

[9] E Volokh, 'Cheap Speech and What It Will Do' (1995) 104(7) *Yale Law Journal* 1805.

this low rate of penetration, online security for credit card payments not being adequate and consumers not having sufficient trust in online corporations. What for-profit corporate involvement there was, however, was not met with much criticism, 'accord[ing] with the ethos of the time … a moment of triumphalism when democracy and capitalism had defeated communism'.[10]

While nation-states such as the US were at least attempting to control the Internet by the mid-1990s by enacting legislation, the corporate axis on the Internet until this point was not acting in a way which was manifestly restrictive of user behaviour, nor were there obvious poles of its dominance being seen. The user experience of the Internet in the 1990s and the legalistic conception of it[11] would suggest that it was an arena without centralised control either from dominant corporate bodies or nation-states, a truly public sphere for debate, culture and human flourishing.

By the 2000s, for 'normal' Internet users without much in the way of technical knowledge, the advent of Web 2.0 was another pivotal moment when their freedom to make and create was facilitated by the Internet. Web 2.0 involved both the running of software programmes online on the Web rather than offline on a computer desktop, and increased and easier access for Internet users to publishing information online (and often the two combined). These web-based applications, allowing information sharing, interoperability, user-centred design and collaboration, catalysed the phenomenon of mass user collaboration on the Internet, especially content generated by users, which opened up to a wider category of people the possibility of creating, participating and disseminating their creations to a vast global audience. From the advent of Web 2.0, users did not need to be equipped with any programming knowledge to create and share information in a public fashion on webpages.

Given Internet users' role in actively producing content and information, with Web 2.0 as a catalyst, the terms 'prosumer' and 'produsage' came to be used to describe this phenomenon.[12] Prior to this, particularly in the 'old media' world, individuals were generally viewed as mere consumers of what others were producing, which was usually done on a centralised scale and in the context of bureaucratic institutions of state or the firm. There have been notable examples of 'prosumption' or 'produsage' before Web 2.0, such as in the free software movement where individuals had existed as both consumer and producers with the fruits of their works subsisting in a non-commodified knowledge commons.[13]

---

[10] Curran, 'Rethinking Internet History' (n 7) 41.

[11] In cases such as *Reno v American Civil Liberties Union*, 521 U.S. 844 (1997).

[12] See D Tapscott, *Digital Economy: Promise and Peril in the Age of Networked Intelligence* (New York, McGraw Hill, 1997), reintroducing the term originally coined by Alvin Toffler; A Bruns, *Blogs, Wikipedia, Second Life, and Beyond. From Production to Produsage* (Bern, Peter Lang, 2008).

[13] G Coleman, *Coding Freedom: The Ethics and Aesthetics of Hacking* (Princeton, NJ, Princeton University Press, 2013).

Yet the Internet's affordances seemed to give many more people the tools to participate as active creators of content and information as well as passive consumers of the same.

The 'mainstreaming' of presumption/produsage via Web 2.0 has given rise to great potential transformations via decentralisation and democratisation in the way that resources are created, organised and managed. An important example of this is what Benkler has termed 'commons-based peer production'.[14] These are decentralised peer collaborative projects such as Wikipedia, where individual users work together for no fee to create the end-product, and over which no traditional intellectual property right is asserted and so the product is free to access and use.[15] This kind of information production is usually not explicitly exclusionary regarding who is entitled to participate in its creation, and is non-hierarchical inasmuch as individuals participating in the project are all on the same level and there is no official manager or owner dictating what must happen. Thus the process is free to join, and the product of the process is free to use and access. In addition, the cooperation among the individuals participating is not dependent on 'either market signals or managerial commands' and so elements of hierarchy are not present.

One significant benefit of these alternative platforms is that they decrease the extent to which individuals can be manipulated by the owners of the facilities on which they depend for communication, thus enhancing an individual's freedom and autonomy from hierarchical bureaucratic power, whether public or private. Yet the current legal and regulatory system is based on this public-private binary, having been formulated in an epoch prior to decentralised, non-proprietary and non-hierarchical information production. As a result, the system contains certain assumptions about the state of the world which no longer necessarily hold true.[16]

B. The Internet and Power

However, despite the cyberlibertarians and then the emergence of commons-based peer production, the freedom-enhancing nature of the Internet has been far from clear cut.[17] Both the state and corporate actors reasserted their presence and power in the Internet ecosystem in various ways, including during the 1990s. Even if it is

---

[14] Benkler, *Wealth of Networks* (n 4); Y Benkler, 'From Consumers to Users: Shifting the Deeper Structures of Regulations Towards Sustainable Commons and User Access' (2000) 52 *Federal Communications Law Journal* 561.

[15] Benkler, *Wealth of Networks* (n 4).

[16] A Daly, 'Free Software and the Law: Out of the Frying Pan and into the Fire: How Shaking Up Intellectual Property Suits Competition Law Just Fine' (2013) 5 *Journal of Peer Production*; Coleman, *Coding Freedom* (n 13).

[17] J Curran, 'Reinterpreting the Internet' in J Curran, N Fenton and D Freeman (eds), *Misunderstanding the Internet* (Abingdon, Routledge, 2012).

true that the Internet was a free(r) space during this time, when states and markets had not fully acknowledged the important of the Internet, '[g]overnments and large multinational firms now have pervasive presences in cyberspace'.[18] This may not be surprising: Wu has observed a tendency over time for predecessor communications technologies which started out with similar decentralised and open philosophies to move towards centralisation and more 'closed design'.[19]

Governments of both liberal democracies and authoritarian regimes, instead of fading out of cyberspace, in fact managed to assert political and legal control over the medium in various ways.[20] Aside from the overall success of repressive regimes such as China to contain their citizens' Internet access to 'permitted' practices,[21] so-called 'liberal democracies', led by the US, have engaged in mass surveillance of their citizens' online activities as well as the online activities of citizens (and leaders) of other countries, including supposed allies,[22] and certain kinds of content censorship have also manifested in these jurisdictions.[23] Although the enforceability of existing laws may be challenged by the Internet's decentralised design and transnational reach, nation-states have been able to regulate what occurs physically in their territory, and so where online companies or users have some kind of physical presence, the existence of assets or infrastructure in a certain jurisdiction could be subjected to local laws, at least in part.[24] While it could be said that some 'ungovernable' (or very difficult to govern) parts of the Internet remain at the edges with decentralised initiatives such as Tor, cryptocurrencies and other activities 'under the radar' in the deep Web,[25] governments' attempts—and indeed successes—in controlling their citizens' Internet experiences would at least dampen how freedom enhancing the Internet actually is.

As regards private power, the emergence of large Internet corporations such as Google and Facebook is contemporary evidence of the (re)emergence of this pole

---

[18] L Solum, 'Models of Internet Governance' in LA Bygrace and T Michaelsen (eds), *Internet Governance: Infrastructure and Institutions* (Oxford, Oxford University Press, 2009) 58.

[19] T Wu, *The Master Switch: The Rise and Fall of Information Empires* (New York, Knopf, 2010).

[20] JL Goldsmith and T Wu, *Who Controls the Internet? Illusions of a Borderless World* (Oxford, Oxford University Press, 2006).

[21] See R MacKinnon, 'Flatter World and Thicker Walls? Blogs, Censorship and Civic Discourse in China' (2008) 134 *Public Choice* 31; B Liang and H Lu, 'Internet Development, Censorship and Cyber Crimes in China' (2010) 26(1) *Journal of Contemporary Criminal Justice* 103; E Morozov, *The Net Delusion: How Not to Liberate the World* (New York, Public Affairs, 2011).

[22] See D Lyon, 'Surveillance, Snowden and Big Data: Capacities, Consequences, Critique' (2014) *Big Data and Society* 1.

[23] See L Edwards, 'Pornography, Censorship and the Internet' in L Edwards and C Waelde (eds), *Law and the Internet* (Oxford, Hart, 2009); TJ McIntyre, 'Child Abuse Images and Cleanfeeds: Assessing Internet Blocking Systems' in I Brown (ed), *Research Handbook on Governance of the Internet* (Cheltenham, Edward Elgar, 2012); H Carrapico and B Farrand (eds), *The Governance of Online Expression in a Networked World* (Abingdon, Routledge, 2015).

[24] Goldsmith and Wu, *Who Controls the Internet?* (n 20).

[25] P Biddle and others, 'The Darknet and the Future of Content Protection' in E Becker and others (eds), *Digital Rights Management: Technological, Economic, Legal and Political Aspects* (Berlin, Springer, 2003); P De Filippi, 'Bitcoin: A Regulatory Nightmare to Libertarian Dream' (2014) 3(2) *Internet Policy Review*; LJ Trautman, 'Virtual Currencies: Bitcoin and What Now after Liberty Reserve, Silk Road, and Mt Gox?' (2014) 20(4) *Richmond Journal of Law and Technology* 1.

of power in the Internet ecosystem. However, the 'privatisation' of the Internet started earlier: by commercial providers 'supplementing the NSFNET backbone with a separate (though connected) national network capacity' and eventually 'the NSF quietly stepped out of the scene by selling off its assets, a process that was completed by April 30, 1995 at which point the Internet was unequivocally a private entity'.[26] The commercialisation of the Internet from the mid-1990s ushered in the development of the online marketplace in its initial, somewhat anarchic, version under limited state control.[27] Running parallel to this was the transition to privatised telecoms utilities in the EU from being state-owned enterprises, the liberalisation of these new markets and the generation of competition within them. The results of both processes, spurred on by similar ideological drivers, has been that the Internet and the infrastructure over which it runs in the EU are highly privatised spheres, with the majority of key actors being for-profit corporations. In addition, concentrations of such private power could be seen from the late 1990s onwards, especially over virtual and physical infrastructure.

While Web 2.0 developments have opened up possibilities for users to create and share content, true, non-hierarchical, non-market commons-based peer production initiatives of the type described by Benkler remain few and far between. Aside from a few successful exceptions such as Wikipedia (which also now has a large managerial class and so may no longer be considered non-hierarchical)[28] these initiatives have not been strong and numerous enough to counter the resurgence of power from corporate and state quarters. Private power has managed to integrate itself into various peer production initiatives. One way has been for companies to collaborate on open source projects such as Open Office. Although traditional intellectual property rights are not asserted over such open source projects, the corporations involved often invest significant sums of money in them, with the motivation usually being that they are able to make profit through (proprietary) associated products and services, eg user manuals, support, etc.[29]

Another way private power has reasserted itself in Web 2.0 has been by providing the very platform over which users coordinate, including the most popular among users such as Facebook, Google's services and Twitter. While some of these platforms began life as small start-ups, due to network effects, economies of scale and scope,[30] and the performance of a 'curatorial' role over the plethora of content and other services available online,[31] some of them have ended up as large players with quasi-monopolistic status in their respective markets.

---

[26] BM Leiner and others, 'A Brief History of the Internet' (2009) 39(5) *ACM SIGCOMM Computer Communication Review*.

[27] Curran, 'Rethinking Internet History' (n 7) 34–42.

[28] See N Tkacz, *Wikipedia and the Politics of Openness* (Chicago, IL, University of Chicago Press, 2015).

[29] G Robles and others, 'Corporate Involvement of Libre Software: Study of Presence in Debian Code over Time' in J Feller and others (eds), *Open Source Development, Adoption and Innovation* (Berlin, Springer, 2007).

[30] A Graham, 'Broadcasting Policy and the Digital Revolution' (1998) 69B *The Political Quarterly* 30.

[31] D Freedman, 'Web 2.0 and the Death of the Blockbuster Economy' in J Curran, N Fenton and D Freeman (eds), *Misunderstanding the Internet* (Abingdon, Routledge, 2012).

Although many of these platforms are free for users to use, in terms of costing them nothing financially, the for-profit corporations which run them make money by monetising the content that these users create using their platforms and services, a process which has been critiqued through the term 'digital labour'.[32] In addition, by participating in these corporately-owned web-based platforms and services, users and their behaviour generate a large amount of data which is stored, analysed and sold on to third parties by the platform owner, a process which has been termed 'economic surveillance'.[33]

While corporations primarily collect this data to use it for their own economic purposes or sell it on to advertisers or other firms, these large pools of user data have also proved useful to law enforcement and security agencies in both liberal democracies and authoritarian regimes. States access this data gathered by corporations either by obliging them to comply with their demands (through using legislative means), by offering incentives for these entities to do so voluntarily, or sometimes, it has been claimed, by hacking into the data stores or introducing secret 'backdoors' into software and hardware. Birnhack and Elkin-Koren have termed collaboration between states and large online corporations 'the invisible handshake' since the average citizen is not usually aware of the extent of this cooperation between the two axes of power, which is often fairly clandestine and 'beyond the reach of judicial review'.[34] Cohen has also remarked on these 'architectures of control' emerging where state and private interests—already deeply and inevitably intertwined—emerge.[35]

Regulation that governments impose on these platforms for surveillance and policing purposes may also contribute to market concentration, given that they increase barriers for potential new entrants into that particular market, which also has the effect of making them easier for governments to regulate, given the smaller numbers of companies able to operate in a particular market.[36] These platforms increasingly fulfil a key role in actively policing user activity for purposes including (but going beyond) national security and serious crime, such as defamation, data protection and copyright.[37]

Thus, despite the origins of the Internet in a publicly-funded project and the cyberlibertarian claims from the 1990s regarding the Internet's enhancement of

---

[32] See T Terranova, 'Free Labor: Producing Culture for the Digital Economy' (2000) 18(2) *Social Text* 33.; T Scholz (ed), *Digital Labor: The Internet as Playground and Factory* (Abingdon, Routledge, 2013).

[33] C Fuchs, 'Critique of the Political Economy of Web 2.0 Surveillance' in C Fuchs and others (eds), *Internet and Surveillance: The Challenges of Web 2.0 and Social Media* (Abingdon, Routledge, 2011).

[34] MD Birnhack and N Elkin-Koren, 'The Invisible Handshake: The Reemergence of the State in the Digital Environment' (2003) 8 *Virginia Journal of Law and Technology* 6.

[35] J Cohen, *Configuring the Networked Self: Law, Code and Everyday Practice* (New Haven, CT, Yale University Press, 2012) 177.

[36] Birnhack and Elkin Koren, 'The Invisible Handshake' (n 34).

[37] See L Edwards, 'The Rise and Fall of Online Intermediary Liability' in L Edwards and C Waelde (eds), *Law and the Internet* (Oxford, Hart, 2009) 47–88; G Sartor and M Viola de Azevedo Cunha, 'The Italian Google-Case: Privacy, Freedom of Speech and Responsibility of Providers for User-Generated Content' (2010) 18(4) *International Journal of Law and Information Technology* 356;

economic and political freedom for users, the reality is that the Internet has become a heavily commodified space which has seen the emergence of for-profit actors performing a 'gatekeeping' function over data flows, both for their own economic benefit as well as for the state's surveillance and law enforcement capabilities.

II. User Autonomy

Yet, it is the Internet's promise or possibility of enhanced individual freedom from bureaucratic structures of production which is important. The Internet has given rise to the more widespread possibility of individuals producing information as well as consuming it, facilitated by its many-to-many structure. While there are axes of hierarchical power which impede the full realisation of this promise, pro-sumers do exist, and in doing so cast doubt on whether the implicitly passive character of consumers traditionally envisaged by the law is appropriate. The Internet thus does provide the potential to enhance user autonomy vis-à-vis both the state and private corporations and includes an increased space for 'non-market' production.

Users can be conceptualised as human individuals ('natural persons' as opposed to 'legal persons') who both produce and consume information over the Internet. There has been some debate over what precisely constitutes a 'user' in the context of copyright law,[38] media and communications scholarship,[39] and science and technology studies (STS).[40] Here, no definitive position is taken as to which approach enumerated in these debates is the correct one: suffice it to say, the objective of this book is to introduce the concept of the individual as *user* into EU competition law and regulation which hitherto has only recognised the individual as *consumer*—an inappropriate and outdated concept given the increased capacity for individuals to produce as well as consume facilitated by the Internet (and other new technologies such as 3D printing).

One argument of this book is that 'user autonomy' is a more appropriate objective for law and regulation to achieve than 'consumer welfare'. This idea of

O Lynskey, 'Control over Personal Data in a Digital Age: *Google Spain v AEPD and Maria Costeja Gonzalez*' (2015) 78(3) *Modern Law Review* 522.

[38] See J Cohen, 'The Place of the User in Copyright Law' (2005) 74 *Fordham Law Review* 347; J Liu, 'Copyright Law's Theory of the Consumer' (2003) 44 *Boston College Law Review* 397; J Meese, 'User Production and Law Reform: A Socio-Legal Critique of User Creativity' (2015) 37(5) *Media Culture Society* 753.

[39] See J Hamilton, 'Historical Forms of User Production' (2014) 36(4) *Media Culture Society* 491; B Griffen-Foley, 'From Tit-Bits to Big Brother: A Century of Audience Participation in the Media' (2004) 26(4) *Media, Culture and Society* 533; J Van Dijck, 'Users Like You? Theorizing Agency in User-Generated Content' (2009) 31(1) *Media, Culture and Society* 41.

[40] See M Bakardjieva, *Internet Society: The Internet in Everyday Life* (Thousand Oaks, CA, Sage, 2005).

user autonomy used here is inspired by Raz's conception of personal autonomy, which sees it as an end in itself, ie deontologically:

> The ruling idea behind the ideal of personal autonomy is that people should make their own lives. The autonomous person is a (part) author of his own life. The ideal of personal autonomy is the vision of people controlling, to some degree, their own destiny, fashioning it through successive decision throughout their lives.[41]

Raz's conception of personal autonomy is not antithetical to state action: indeed, he sees a role for the government to 'take positive action to enhance the freedom of their subjects' (while warning of the dangers of concentrating power in the hands of the few).[42] This idea of autonomy involves the presence of meaningful choice in individuals' lives and them being free from 'coercion, restraint, or excessive undue influence', with 'freedom from manipulation [being] as important in this context as freedom from coercion'.[43]

This idea of autonomy, then, entails that individuals should have real choices as to what happens in their lives and should have the freedom to make those choices—and the state should act to facilitate this. However, the state may not have individuals' autonomy in its own interests, especially in the context of the Internet. Thus autonomy also ought to resist the undue influence of concentrations of power which may manipulate or coerce choices and choice-making, and can have both public (ie state-controlled) and private (ie corporate) character. The malign influence of power with either of these provenances on individuals' autonomy ought to be viewed as suspect.

Although user autonomy is considered according to Raz's deontological view, user autonomy and free online information flows can also be seen to have significance beyond being worthy objectives to pursue in themselves. Free flows of information fit within the conceptualisation of free speech and expression, either explicitly in terms of Article 10 of the European Convention on Human Rights (ECHR) which encompasses the right 'to receive and impart information and ideas', or implicitly in the First Amendment to the US Constitution which protects free speech.[44] Furthermore, free flows of information, or at least political information, for some time has been viewed as a constituent part of a well-functioning (liberal) democracy,[45] and even a hallmark of a more 'radical' digital democratic project such as that of WikiLeaks.[46]

[41] J Raz, *The Morality of Freedom* (Oxford, Oxford University Press, 1988) 369.

[42] ibid 427.

[43] P Bernal, *Internet Privacy Rights: Rights to Protect Autonomy* (Cambridge, Cambridge University Press, 2014) 25.

[44] Although the US Supreme Court's First Amendment jurisprudence has not always been consistent with this notion. See BP McDonald, 'The First Amendment and the Free Flow of Information: Towards a Realistic Right to Gather Information in the Information Age' (2004) 65(2) *Ohio State Law Journal* 249.

[45] L Diamond, *Developing Democracy: Towards Consolidation* (Baltimore, MD, John Hopkins University Press, 1999).

[46] LJ Heemsbergen, 'Designing Hues of Transparency and Democracy After Wikileaks: Vigilance to Vigilantes and Back Again' (2015) 17(8) *New Media and Society* 1340.

There are, however, some limitations to the idea of user autonomy discussed here. Only natural persons (real human beings) and not legal persons (corporations) should be the beneficiaries of user autonomy. Horizontal conflicts of autonomy among individuals are also beyond the scope of this work; such conflicts might include the use of the Internet to vilify others on the basis of their race, sexual orientation, gender and so on, or the conflict between free speech and privacy which might arise in online defamation or the right to be forgotten. Here, instead, the concentration is on the detrimental effects of private economic power in the form of corporations on online information flows.

An ideal of user autonomy in terms of optimal online information flows can be conceptualised as a state of affairs in which users are in control of their data and what is done with it; they are not subject to censorship or illegitimate restrictions on what they can send and receive; they have the fullest capacity possible to produce and disseminate information as well as consume it; and they are not subjected to blanket surveillance of their activities, whether for the benefit of the state or the benefit of for-profit corporations. Accordingly, this is the objective which EU law and regulation should aim to achieve.

III. User Autonomy, Non-Economic Values and EU Competition Law

While copyright law and debates for its reform have recognised the existence of users, this is not the case for EU competition law. Furthermore, the relationship between user autonomy and this area of law is far from clear cut, especially given the problems contemporary competition law has with including 'non-economic' values in its analysis. Here, the relationship between user autonomy and choice in competition law will be explored, before addressing the problems brought by these non-economic values in competition analysis.

A. User Autonomy and Consumer Choice

Some element of autonomy may be found in the concept of choice in competition law: competition law, or competitive markets, should operate to give consumers a choice of products and/or services. This is a far more limited idea of choice and choice-making than that envisaged by Raz above, since there is no great concern with the background conditions against which the choice is made (such as imbalances in power, inequalities of resources and other deficiencies in how that choice is facilitated), so long as there have been no recognised violations of the competitive process, such as the formation of a cartel.

This idea of choice in competition law, however, accords with the illusory nature of choice in consumer capitalist society viewed by Horkheimer and Adorno: even though consumers may be able to choose among products that differ in shape, colour and design, all of these products have the same basis or set of fundamental assumptions.[47] Indeed, this illusory choice produces the spectacle of competition, even if there is not a true alternative to what is on offer, and individuals may also be unable to choose an entirely new category of product and service. Yet competition law is indifferent to the 'basis' or 'fundamental assumptions' which products have and is content with this illusory choice.

Competition law also does not concern itself with monopolies along the lines of Ilich's 'radical' ones, which may also reproduce Horkheimer and Adorno's illusory choice. Radical monopolies are monopolies not in the conventional sense of 'the exclusive control by one corporation over the means of producing (or selling) a commodity of service' which 'restrict the choices open to the consumer', but 'the dominance of one type of product rather than the dominance of one brand' which is produced by 'large institutions' rather than individuals or small groups of people.[48] Illich views a radical monopoly as being dangerous or undesirable because it 'imposes compulsory consumption and thereby restricts personal autonomy'. Radical monopolies might exclude the possibility that other structures than highly centralised private for-profit corporations can provide certain products and services, and individuals can only consume these products and services, rather than innovate themselves, given that they do not have the tools to do so, or are not permitted to have them. This is close to the imagined scenario at the heart of contemporary competition law: that production occurs in bureaucratised structures, and is out of individuals' reach, who must only consume what these structures produce but cannot be empowered to produce themselves.

In any event, even this narrow conception of choice is not dominant within competition analysis since contemporary competition law (in theory anyway) operates to maximise 'consumer welfare' as an objective via the process of competitive markets.[49] This entails that contemporary competition law's objective is not to preserve the competitive process per se in order to offer choice to consumers,[50] although in practice this may amount to rhetoric rather than reality.[51] Both EU and US competition law now share the goal of maximising consumer welfare due to the influence of Chicago School neoclassical economic theory on

---

[47] M Horkheimer and TW Adorno, *Dialectic of Enlightenment: Philosophical Fragments* (Palo Alto, CA, Stanford University Press, 2002) 97.

[48] I Illich, *Tools for Conviviality* (New York, Harper & Row, 1973) 52.

[49] The objective of welfare was introduced by R Bork in *The Antitrust Paradox*, 1st edn (Free Press, 1978) and has subsequently become generally accepted as the goal of competition law and policy. 'Consumer welfare' has been the view of welfare adopted by European and American competition authorities, but Bork himself referred to 'social welfare'. See O Black, *Conceptual Foundations of Antitrust* (Cambridge, Cambridge University Press, 2010) 33.

[50] See O Andriychuk, 'Rediscovering the Spirit of Competition: On the Normative Value of the Competitive Process' (2010) 6(3) *European Competition Journal* 575.

[51] P Akman, '"Consumer Welfare" and Article 82EC: Practice and Rhetoric' (2009) 32(1) *World Competition* 71.

the two systems,[52] though the EU variety diverges in also having the creation and maintenance of the Single Market as an additional goal.[53] One consequence of this approach has been that the accumulation of market power by an entity to arrive at a monopoly situation, as long as it has not been acquired illegally (eg via participating in a cartel), is not in itself a target for competition law. It is only when that dominant position is 'abused' that it is sanctioned under legal regimes such as that of the European Union, where an 'abuse' of a dominant position is prohibited by Treaty on the Functioning of the European Union (TFEU), Article 102.

While 'consumer welfare' itself is a highly disputed term, open to differing interpretations,[54] competition authorities on both sides of the Atlantic carry out their analyses of whether consumer welfare is harmed primarily through the prism of the price for goods and services (including the effect of hypothetical increases and decreases in price on consumers) in order to define markets in the first place and determine how competitive they are. Although other factors can be included in this analysis, such as a decline in quality of goods or services, or restrictions on innovation in a sector, competition analysis uses primarily quantitative methods which are adept at measuring price, and is not so well suited to assessing these other, less easily quantifiable values, especially in scenarios where there is a zero monetary price.[55]

Yet if there is no clear conceptual definition of 'consumer welfare', it may be possible, conceptually at least, to integrate some broader values into its analysis that might give rise to the protection of something approaching 'user autonomy'. However, the incorporation of 'non-economic' values into the competition analysis is neither conceptually nor empirically simple.

B. Non-Economic Values in EU Competition Law

The idea of 'consumer welfare' even within the confines of mainstream competition law is a problematic concept. A precise definition of 'consumer welfare' is difficult to come by, and at first blush it also makes the assumption that consumers are an amorphous mass with the same needs and interests, which does not reflect

---

[52] CA Jones, 'Foundations of Competition Policy in the EU and USA: Conflict, Convergence and Beyond' in H Ulrich (ed), *The Evolution of European Competition Law: Whose Regulation, Which Competition?* (Cheltenham, Edward Elgar, 2006).

[53] SM Ramirez Perez and S van de Scheur, 'The Evolution of Law on Articles 85 and 86 EEC [Articles 101 and 102 TFEU]: Ordoliberalism and its Keynesian Challenge' in KK Patel and H Schweitzer (eds), *The Historical Foundations of EU Competition Law* (Oxford, Oxford University Press, 2013).

[54] JF Brodley, 'Economic Goals of Antitrust: Efficiency, Consumer Welfare and Technological Progress' (1987) 62 *New York University Law Review* 1020, 1032.

[55] MS Gal and DL Rubinfeld, *The Hidden Costs of Free Goods: Implications for Antitrust Enforcement*, UC Berkeley Public Law Research Paper 2529425, NYU Law and Economics Research Paper 14-44 (2015), available at http://ssrn.com/abstract=2529425.

the diversity of consumers in reality. It is true that the conception of 'consumer' in EU law is inclusive of 'customers' and so encompasses intermediate customers as well as final consumers, even if in practice 'customer welfare' does not always coincide with 'consumer welfare'.[56] It also seems that the definition of 'consumer' will depend on the context in which it is being used: describing the objectives of competition law, determining whether competition rules have been infringed, or in reference to those participating in the rules' enforcement.[57] Attempts have been made to distinguish between different kinds of consumers, such as 'marginal' (ie consumers who value the product in a way which is approximate to its current price, and so are very sensitive to price fluctuations) compared to 'infra-marginal' consumers (ie those whose value of the product is a lot higher than its original price and so are relatively insensitive to price fluctuations) or even 'ignorant' and 'knowledgeable',[58] but consumers as a whole are even more heterogeneous than these attempts suggest. Furthermore, although the enumerated objective of competition law is now generally accepted to be the maximising of consumer welfare through competitive markets, there is a gaping lack of empirical evidence to suggest that competition or competition law actually achieves a greater measure of consumer welfare however defined.[59]

While it might be argued that competition law and its consumer welfare standard are simply not *supposed* to mirror entirely the interests and concerns of autonomous users, the situation remains that absent sector-specific regulation, competition law acts as large corporate Internet players' arbiter of last resort. This is accompanied by the Chicago School's ideological arguments that there should be no government intervention aside from correcting market failures, since the market is presumed to be a more efficient allocator of resources than the state. Yet, as Cohen remarks, '[i]dealized models of market choice cannot provide a useful template for evaluating the dynamics of constrained, path-dependent choice that predominated in markets for networked or network-capable information technologies'.[60]

From the perspective of competition law, Internet users are a different category of actor than mere consumers, around whom competition law is constructed.

---

[56] P Akman, '"Consumer" versus "Customer": The Devil in the Detail' (2010) 37(2) *Journal of Law and Society* 315.

[57] A Albors-Llorens and A Jones, 'The Images of the "Consumer" in EU Competition Law' in D Leczykiewicz and S Weatherill (eds), *The Images of the 'Consumer' in EU Law* (Oxford, Hart Publishing, 2016).

[58] WS Comanor, 'Vertical Price-Fixing, Vertical Market Restrictions, and the New Antitrust Policy' (1985) 98(5) *Harvard Law Review* 983, 991–92. The author posits that it is the preferences of marginal consumers which are more important to suppliers of goods and services since they are more sensitive to changes, yet overall societal gains or losses from changes in the product or service depend on the preferences of all consumers, and so changes which reflect the preferences of marginal consumers may well not reflect those of other kinds of consumers such as the infra-marginal.

[59] Black, *Conceptual Foundations of Antitrust* (n 49).

[60] J Cohen, *Configuring the Networked Self* (n 35) 181–82.

Consumers and users may well have overlapping but also different needs and desires, which the concept of 'consumer welfare' that is currently used in competition analysis does not capture. The user does not only care about characteristics of products such as price and quality, but also whether the product comprises more capacity to produce as well as consume. Furthermore, what happens to what the user produces is of high importance, whether it is enclosed as the intellectual property of the web platform used by the user, whether it is shared in a commons or whether it remains under the user's own individual control.

Accordingly, user autonomy is not identical to consumer welfare. Competition law takes a paternalistic attitude towards consumers, who are characterised as largely passive and without the capacity for production. It is true that consumers are considered not to be entirely passive in competition analysis inasmuch as their ability to switch to competitors' products and services is considered, as well as the barriers they face to exit. However, this kind of activity encompasses a very small area of autonomy for individuals and does not go far enough to conceptualise them as having the ability to create as well as consume. Competition law's regard paid to individuals' ability to choose and switch to alternative products and services from competitors may well be considered one of Illich's radical monopolies inasmuch as this may constitute one type of product which competition law does not envisage consumers making themselves.

In addition, competition law taking into account 'other' 'non-economic' values—essentially those not currently captured by consumer welfare despite pertaining to aspects of the economy—in its analysis may be easier said than done.[61] It is true that Townley has called for EU competition law to have as its task ensuring 'the well-being of its peoples',[62] which would involve goals beyond efficiency. Furthermore, the incorporation of 'social values' into 'economic' areas of law has also been discussed in the context of trade.[63] Yet until recently, the main interaction of EU competition law and 'social' concerns, especially human rights, was comprised by debates around procedural fairness in the course of enforcement.[64]

However, of late two factors have shifted the debate on EU competition law and 'social' or 'non-economic' values: the rise of Big Data and its interaction with competition analyses; and the EU's Charter of Fundamental Rights coming into force.

---

[61] RJG Claassen and A Gerbrandy, 'Rethinking European Competition Law: From a Consumer Welfare to a Capability Approach' (2016) 12(1) *Utrecht Law Review* 1.

[62] C Townley, *Article 81 EC and Public Policy* (Oxford, Hart Publishing, 2009) 50.

[63] See A Lang, *World Trade Law After Neoliberalism* (Oxford, Oxford University Press, 2011).

[64] See A Andreangeli, *EU Competition Enforcement and Human Rights* (Berlin, Edward Elgar, 2008); P Nihoul and T Skoczny (eds), *Procedural Fairness in Competition Proceedings* (Berlin, Edward Elgar, 2015).

C. Data, Democracy and Competition

The European Data Protection Supervisor (EDPS) initiated a public debate on the role of data in competition analyses of online markets in the EU with a 2014 Preliminary Opinion on the subject.[65] It is true that data plays a role of pivotal importance in the Internet ecosystem: it is an input and output of computer processing, and flows of data are what the network carries. Thus, control over the data inputs, outputs and flows has competition consequences as well as those for free expression and privacy.

The EDPS considered that the collection and control of very large amounts of personal data are a source of market power for large players in European Internet markets, and may even constitute 'essential facilities' in certain circumstances, such that a refusal of access to such data may constitute an abuse of dominance. This is not a new issue as such: access to a dominant competitor's data, protected by intellectual property, has been addressed already in certain cases such as *Magill* and *IMS Health*.[66] However, the EDPS also considered that it may be necessary to incorporate violations of the right to data protection into the concept of consumer harm in the context of competition enforcement, for instance, when a dominant entity is restricting users' freedom of choice and control over their personal data, such as when they are offered a product for zero monetary price yet 'pay' with the collection of their data and data about their behaviour.[67]

This suggestion of incorporating other values such as data protection, and the idea of user autonomy, into competition analysis, and 'consumer welfare' in particular, is not novel. As mentioned above, Townley has critiqued the sole use of the 'economic' approach including vis-à-vis consumer welfare as omitting other valuable societal goals because they are 'too difficult' to quantify.[68] In addition, Stucke has remarked that competition policy can go beyond promoting economic efficiency, and in fact disperse economic and political power and promote individual freedom, arguing for a 'blended approach' to competition goals.[69] Yet Stucke does not explain very adequately what this would mean across the board of competition investigations and issues, and it seems just to be a different interpretation of economic policy objectives in the scope of competition law, such as protecting small and medium businesses.

---

[65] European Data Protection Supervisor (EDPS), 'Privacy and Competitiveness in the Age of Big Data: The Interplay Between Data Protection, Competition Law and Consumer Protection in the Digital Economy' (Preliminary Opinion), (2014) EDPS/2014/06.

[66] Joined Cases C-241/91 and C-242/91 *Radio Telefis Eireann and others v Commission* [1995] ECR I-743; Case C-418/01 *IMS Health v NDC Health* [2004] ECR I-5039.

[67] EDPS, 'Privacy and Competitiveness in the Age of Big Data' (n 65) 32.

[68] C Townley, 'Which Goals Count in Article 101 TFEU?: Public Policy and Its Discontents' (2011) 9 *European Competition Law Review* 441.

[69] M Stucke, 'Reconsidering Antitrust's Goals' (2012) 53 *Boston College Law Review* 551, 590.

Historically, competition law has not always been underpinned by the neoclassical economic thought leading to its contemporary 'economic' or quantitative analysis. Even within the history of competition law, accumulations of private power have been put under suspicion for reasons beyond what the final product or service looks like and costs. For instance, the German economic movement ordoliberalism considered it the state's role to ensure that the (otherwise) free market fulfils its theoretical potential, and competition as opposed to mere exchange was pivotal in achieving this. If the state does not act in this way, not only would the market economy suffer and not produce optimal results, but that private corporate power was also to be checked due to its potential to undermine the (democratic) political process and government, since economic power could translate into political power. Ordoliberals saw the threat to individual liberty as not only emanating from the government, but also from powerful economic institutions. Competition law had a different role from the current mainstream conception, which was not aimed at achieving optimal consumer welfare or efficiency, but instead at preserving individual freedom against threats from private power, and competition in itself is crucial, an end in itself rather than a mere means to an end.[70] The ordoliberals were not anti-capitalists critical of all sorts of private power, but something more along the lines of critics of unchecked private power and proponents of a social market economy,[71] with a 'strong state' that would be effective in its ability to discharge effectively its duties and responsibilities regarding, inter alia, the economy, such as providing order and facilitating competition.[72] For ordoliberals, thus, competition is not something that occurs naturally in markets, but a process that must be created and maintained by the state. In addition to ordoliberalism, the development of antitrust law in the US, especially prior to the Second World War, pointed to a distrust of the accumulation of private power beyond merely economic reasons, since this could become stronger than the democratic state itself, and the danger was identified in contemporary American society as the concentrated economic power which had arisen since the Great Depression and included cartels.[73]

These views of competition law would give it a more overtly political role than its contemporary manifestation. In practice, this could mean that competition law would intervene in the market on more occasions than it does now, and for reasons that would not be strictly economic, or on the basis of other, non-quantitative

---

[70] M Vatiero, 'The Ordoliberal Notion of Market Power: An Institutionalist Reassessment' (2010) 6(3) *European Competition Journal* 689.

[71] MA Peters, 'Foucault, Biopolitics and the Birth of Neoliberalism' (2007) 48(2) *Critical Studies in Education* 165.

[72] N Goldschmidt and H Rauchenschwandtner, *The Philosophy of Social Market Economy: Michel Foucault's Analysis of Ordoliberalism*, Freiburg Discussion Papers on Constitutional Economics 07/4 (2007) 8–9.

[73] TA Freyer, *Antitrust and Global Capitalism, 1930–2004* (Cambridge, Cambridge University Press, 2006) 22.

evidence, employing something like the UK's former 'public interest' test in competition law.[74] Critics could point to such interventions being less predictable and more arbitrary than those which are currently used, giving less legal certainty to market players. Yet, as Endicott notes, law is necessarily vague, because it necessarily uses abstract terms,[75] and here such abstract terms may be these qualitative values that competition law should tackle.

In any event, in Europe (and the US for that matter) neoliberalism, not ordoliberalism or anti-corporatism, is the dominant tendency in competition law and policy. Neoliberalism has come to be used since the 1980s to refer to a resurgence of nineteenth century *lassiez-faire* economic liberalism.[76] Neoliberalism, inspired by neoclassical economic theories, has promoted economic liberalisation, fiscal austerity, free trade, open markets and the privatisation of previously nationalised industries and public services and deregulation/regulation in the most unobtrusive way possible vis-à-vis the functioning of the free market.[77] It has been a guiding current in EU policy (and accordingly the law and regulation produced by this policy) over at least the last 20 years if not longer,[78] and competition and sector-specific regulation have been influenced by its ideas.[79] Buch-Hansen and Wigger have argued that EU competition law has undergone a 'neoliberal transformation' which has been primarily in the interests of transnational globalised capital rather than in the interests of other social groups, challenging the established view that it is consumers (and their 'welfare') who are purported to be the main beneficiaries of competition.[80]

Thus, the critique of private economic power for being problematic for democracy and individual ('political') freedom, as well as for what consumers pay and the quality of products and services, is no longer prominent within the competition discourse, nor incorporated into the current 'More Economic' approach, as

---

[74] See A Scott, 'The Evolution of Competition Law and Policy in the United Kingdom' in P Mehta (ed), *The Evolution of Competition Laws and Their Enforcement: A Political Economy Perspective* (Abingdon, Routledge, 2011) 189–213.

[75] T Endicott, 'Law is Necessarily Vague' (2001) 7(4) *Legal Theory* 379.

[76] See T Boas and J Gans-Morse, 'Neoliberalism: From New Liberal Philosophy to Anti-Liberal Slogan' (2009) 44(2) *Studies in Comparative International Development* 137; S Clarke, 'The Neoliberal Theory of Society' in A Saad-Filho and D Johnston (eds), *Neoliberalism: A Critical Reader* (London, Pluto Press, 2005) 50–59.

[77] D Harvey, *A Brief History of Neoliberalism* (Oxford, Oxford University Press, 2005).

[78] See KW Rothschild, 'Neoliberalism, EU and the Evaluation of Policies' (2009) 21(2) *Review of Political Economy* 213; S Bernhard, 'From Conflict to Consensus: European Neoliberalism and the Debate on the Future of EU Social Policy' (2010) 4(1) *Work Organisation, Labour and Globalisation* 175; DS Grewal and JS Purdy, 'Introduction: Law and Neoliberalism' (2014) 77(4) *Law and Contemporary Problems* 1.

[79] C Hermann, *Neoliberalism in the European Union*, DYNAMO Thematic Paper (2005).

[80] H Buch-Hansen and A Wigger, *The Politics of European Competition Regulation: A Critical Political Economy Perspective* (Abingdon, Routledge, 2011). In the US, an empirical study suggested that antitrust policy did not actually improve consumer welfare in practice: RW Crandall and C Winston, 'Does Antitrust Policy Improve Consumer Welfare? Assessing the Evidence' (2003) 17(4) *Journal of Economics Perspectives* 3.

a result of the neoliberal influence over this area of law. In the likely event of no major changes being made to competition law's methodology in the near future, the current version of competition law is not so well-equipped to take into account more qualitative factors, as a regime which operates using mainly quantitative data to establish relevant markets, market shares and other phenomena. Measuring the extent to which user autonomy, or some subset of that such as data protection or personal freedom, is promoted or harmed would seem to be more a qualitative than quantitative exercise, and generally one that will not be measured in financial terms. For non-economic objectives it may be more expedient to use law and policy aside from competition law to achieve them, since using competition law to do so can be costly and ineffective.[81] Competition law has a particular ideology and aims,[82] which may well not be sufficiently conceptually supple to bend to these situations. Yet still, competition law may be looked to in situations where there is an accumulation of private economic power that threatens individuals' 'political' as well as 'economic' freedom merely because it is the one regime *available* in the circumstances, but not because it is a wonderfully *appropriate* part of the law for dealing with such situations.

D. Fundamental Rights and Competition

In both Europe and the US, judicial and administrative bodies are under duties to apply the law in ways which are not incompatible with fundamental rights[83] and the Constitution, respectively.[84] Indeed, fundamental rights and the Constitution have primacy over other laws in their respective legal systems.[85] In the EU, the coming into force of the Charter of Fundamental Rights has shifted the discussion of non-economic values in competition law, since these rights are addressed to the EU's institutions and bodies and Member States' national authorities when implementing EU law. Along with more traditional human rights, the Charter elevates data protection to a right, but it is unclear how these rights interact with other

[81] Townley, *Article 81 EC and Public Policy* (n 62).
[82] WH Page, 'Ideological Conflict and the Origins of Antitrust Policy' (1991) 66(1) *Tulane Law Review* 1.
[83] Due to the European Convention on Human Rights to which all EU Member States are parties; and the Charter of Fundamental Rights of the European Union which is binding on EU institutions. The question of the EU's accession to the ECHR is an ongoing issue at the time of writing after the CJEU's Opinion in late 2014 that such accession was incompatible with EU law. See Opinion 2/13 of the CJEU, 18 December 2014, available at http://curia.europa.eu/juris/document/document.jsf?text=&docid=160882&pageIndex=0&doclang=EN&mode=req&dir=&occ=first&part=1&cid=480235.
[84] See *National Federation of Independent Business v Sebelius*, 567 US ___ (2012), 132 S Ct 2566, Roberts CJ at 31–32.
[85] DH Ginsburg and DE Haar, 'Resolving Conflicts Between Competition and Other Values: The Roles of Courts and Other Institutions in the US and the EU' in P Lowe and M Marquis (eds), *European Competition Law Annual 2012: Public Policies, Regulation and Economic Distress* (Oxford, Hart Publishing, 2014).

areas of EU law such as competition.[86] Currently, discussion on how this interaction will play out is theoretical since there have been no concrete incidents since the Charter's coming into force where EU competition law has had to encounter fundamental rights. Yet there is some speculation on what shape this interaction may take.

One consequence of the existence of the Charter and its rights may entail that the judiciary or administrative body cannot ignore these rights when investigating or adjudicating competition cases, or at very least should not produce an outcome which is incompatible with these rights. Since rights are not solely economically-based, then this would inevitably involve dealing with non-economic values. However, taking account of rights may prove institutionally difficult given the 'explicitly technocratic remit' of many EU telecoms regulators (some of which also have competition investigatory powers) and even for those with no legislative impediment to taking account of human rights, their organisational culture may preclude the consideration of rights in practice—or at least take those responsible out of their professional comfort zone.[87] Costa-Cabral and Lynskey argue that data protection values could be taken into account in a competition analysis of a product or service's 'quality', such as by assessing the 'quality' of competitors' data use policies, an assessment for which data protection can serve as a 'normative yardstick'.[88]

There are some indications of what this kind of approach in competition law would look like from the 'constitutionalisation' phenomenon in some EU Member States' domestic private law, namely the UK, Netherlands and Germany.[89] This has involved the application of fundamental rights in certain disputes between private parties in contract and tort, such as in situations where there are several possible interpretations of these laws, the court should follow the interpretation which best upholds the parties' fundamental rights. To the extent that the promotion of user autonomy would include the promotion of rights such as free expression, privacy and freedom of assembly, then it may be advanced through similar means in competition law. By analogy, if there are several possible applications of competition law to a particular scenario, then the competition authority should proceed

---

[86] C Kuner and others, 'When Two Worlds Collide: The Interface Between Competition Law and Data Protection' (2014) 4(4) *International Data Privacy Law* 247; F Costa-Cabral and O Lynskey, *The Internal and External Constraints of Data Protection on Competition Law in the EU*, LSE Legal Studies Working Paper 25/2015, available at http://ssrn.com/abstract=2703655.

[87] I Brown and CT Marsden, *Regulating Code: Good Governance and Better Regulation in the Information Age* (Cambridge, MA, MIT Press, 2013) 142.

[88] Costa-Cabral and Lynskey, *The Internal and External Constraints of Data Protection on Competition Law in the EU* (n 86) 17.

[89] See T Barkhuysen and SD Lindenbergh, *Constitutionalisation of Private Law* (Leiden, Brill, 2006); S Grundmann (ed), *Constitutional Values and European Contract Law* (Alphen aan den Rijn, Kluwer Law International, 2008); and C Mak, *Fundamental Rights in European Contract Law: A Comparison of the Impact of Fundamental Rights on Contractual Relationships in Germany, the Netherlands, Italy and England* (Alphen aan den Rijn, Kluwer Law International, 2008).

with the application which best upholds data protection, or free expression or autonomy.

While this method could be incorporated into competition analyses without too much legislative upheaval (although possibly some practical issues that could be solved by closer coordination between eg data protection authorities and competition authorities), as will be seen in the following chapters, the problem may be that competition law does not apply to a given circumstance in the first place: either there is no finding of dominance, or even if there is dominance, there is not a recognised abuse, even if those circumstances harm user autonomy.

Thus, a suspicion of anti-competitive abuse, which absent a merger situation necessitates either a dominant position or evidence of collusion, is still a necessary prerequisite for triggering a competition investigation and analysis, regardless of what other values may be incorporated into that analysis. For this reason, it may remain that this is not the most effective way of securing data protection, or any other desirable (non-economic) value, regardless of any move to 'constitutionalise' competition law or using data protection measures as a measure of 'quality'. In any event, 'the pursuit or consideration for other non-economic goals under competition law is at odds with neo-liberalism',[90] and so likely to give rise to much regulatory tension if competition bodies find themselves under pressure to apply non-economic values that may be encompassed by human rights.

The dominance of the 'More Economic' approach in contemporary EU competition law, underpinned by quantitative analyses of consumer welfare and premised on neoclassical economics, entails that reform to encompass the non-economic aspects of user autonomy would not be simple. Indeed, as already mentioned, a discussion of the possible paths competition law reform could take is outside the scope of this book. Aside from the possible constitutionalisation of competition law through applications and interpretations in accordance with the protection of fundamental rights, any further move towards the incorporation of 'non-economic' values, such as those promoting user autonomy, individual freedom and/or democracy, into the current competition law analysis of consumer welfare is likely to be difficult if not impossible in practice.

IV. Private Power and Fundamental Rights

EU competition law is not the only part of the legal and regulatory framework being examined in the following chapters' case studies for its ability to achieve user autonomy when confronted with private economic power over online information flows. Fundamental rights are another important area which, as mentioned in the Introduction, can act to protect autonomy, especially free expression

---

[90] F Feretti, *Competition, the Consumer Internet, and Data Protection* (Berlin, Springer, 2014) 94.

and privacy. However, the extent to which these rights apply to infringements by private entities is not clear-cut, especially with the ascendancy of neoliberalism over the last few decades.

The relationship between fundamental human rights and neoliberalism is contested and complex.[91] One view is that economic liberalism and human rights in general have a productive and strong relationship, and both can be achieved through similar methods.[92] In this view, human rights can also be seen as a 'civilising' force vis-à-vis transnational capitalist globalisation, correcting it if things go awry.[93] Another view would be that fundamental rights are not inherently capitalist or neoliberal, and can be guided by, for instance, anti-statist anti-capitalist anarchist ideology to enhance individual autonomy beyond (bureaucratic) capitalist and socialist conceptions.[94] In any event, the practical application of fundamental rights has been shaped by neoliberal norms. Fundamental rights are mainly enforceable vis-à-vis the nation-state despite there being certain transnational accumulations of capital which are more powerful than certain countries, and also despite the very real violation of individuals' rights that these corporations' business practices can entail in certain circumstances.[95]

Data protection stands out as an area of EU law which seems to have a theoretical basis in fundamental rights (namely privacy), yet which applies to private entities and not just the state and its emanations. While EU data protection law thus conceived would appear not to fit into the neoliberal paradigm, its nature is actually hybrid: it has a fundamental rights component but also an economic basis in seeking to facilitate free trade in personal data within the EU internal market.[96] Moreover, Lynskey views data protection as a 'permissive' legal regime which allows the collection of personal data so long as certain criteria are met, 'ostensibly endors[ing] the commodification of personal data'.[97] Otherwise, data protection can be seen to exist to correct a market failure, namely the lack of privacy protection of personal information that market forces alone would entail.[98]

---

[91] S Moyn, 'A Powerless Companion: Human Rights in the Age of Neoliberalism' (2015) 77 *Law and Contemporary Problems* 147.

[92] EU Petersmann, 'Time for a United Nations "Global Compact" for Integrating Human Rights in the Law of Worldwide Organizations: Lessons from European Integration' (2002) 13 *European Journal of International* Law 621, 621–22. See also EU Petersmann, 'Human Rights and International Trade Law: Defining and Connecting the Two Fields' in T Cottier, J Pauwelyn and E Burgi (eds), *Human Rights and International Trade* (Oxford, Oxford University Press, 2005).

[93] D Kinley, *Civilising Globalisation: Human Rights and the Global Economy* (Cambridge, Cambridge University Press 2009) 1–3.

[94] S Turner, 'Anarchist Theory and Human Rights' in N Jun and S Wahl (eds), *New Perspectives on Anarchism* (Lanhan, Lexington Books, 2010).

[95] See S Deva, 'Human Rights Violations by Multinational Corporations and International Law: Where From Here?' (2003) 19 *Connecticut Journal of International Law* 1; D Kinley and J Tadaki, 'From Talk to Walk: The Emergence of Human Rights Responsibilities for Corporations at International Law' (2004) 44(4) *Virginia Journal of International Law* 931.

[96] O Lynskey, *The Foundations of EU Data Protection Law* (Oxford, Oxford University Press, 2015).

[97] ibid 238.

[98] A Acquisti, 'Privacy and Market Failure: Three Reasons for Concern, and Three Reasons for Hope' (2012) 10 *Journal on Telecommunications and High Technology Law* 227.

Moreover, data protection law is not always well-enforced in practice.[99] Part of this lack of enforcement involves the lack of transparency around data collection and use, the 'black boxes' into which data goes, which challenge effective regulation.[100] Indeed, the argument has been made that existing laws and their enforcement (which itself is patchy across Member States) have only a marginal effect on real-world data processing practices.[101] Furthermore, neoliberal forces can be seen at work in the large amount of industry lobbying employed to influence the recent reform of EU data protection law, in a way which would minimise the effect of these reforms on these companies' business practices.[102]

V. Regulating for User Autonomy

In light of these deficiencies with existing areas of law, some commentators have discussed how a more expansive idea of what is termed here 'user autonomy' might be applied to the normative governance of the Internet. For instance, Benkler is of the view that the Internet should be regulated in a way which enables a wide distribution of the capacity to produce and disseminate information.[103] Furthermore, Elkin-Koren and Salzberger advocate that markets on the Internet should be evaluated 'not only like any other market by the criteria of efficiency, but also as a public sphere, commons or mechanism for private and collective actions'.[104] Frishmann has also argued that the Internet should be managed as a 'commons', and the debate should be around the question of what kind of Internet environment is demanded by society as a whole rather than the narrow view of competition and neoclassical economics-driven regulation.[105] Finally, Brown and Marsden have advocated that both human rights and economic efficiency concerns be taken into account when regulating the Internet in order to take account of individuals' production as well as consumer functions—what they term 'prosumer law'.[106]

---

[99] G Greenleaf, 'Global Data Privacy in a Networked World' in I Brown (ed), *Research Handbook on Governance of the Internet* (Berlin, Edward Elgar, 2012).

[100] See F Pasquale, *The Black Box Society: The Secret Algorithms that Control Money and Information* (Cambridge, MA, Harvard University Press, 2015).

[101] BJ Koops, 'The Trouble with European Data Protection Law' (2014) 4(4) *International Data Privacy Law* 250.

[102] See WG Voss, 'Looking at European Union Data Protection Law Reform Through a Different Prism: The Proposed EU General Data Protection Regulation Two Years Later' (2014) 17(9) *Journal of Internet Law* 1.

[103] Benkler, 'From Consumers to Users' (n 14).

[104] N Elkin-Koren and EM Salzberger, *Law and Economics of Cyberspace: The Effects of Cyberspace on the Economic Analysis of Law* (Berlin, Edward Elgar, 2004) 27.

[105] B Frischmann, *Infrastructure: The Social Value of Shared Resources* (Oxford, Oxford University Press, 2012) 317–27.

[106] Brown and Marsden, *Regulating Code* (n 87) 20.

Yet in practice, ex ante Internet regulation has been approached differently. These existing approaches to Internet regulation can broadly be grouped into three categories: 'traditional' state-led regulation; industry self-regulation; and multi-stakeholder co-regulation.[107] The experience so far with these different regulatory categories does not inspire confidence that user autonomy will be upheld if ex ante regulation is employed.

Industry self-regulation is the process 'whereby an industry-level organization sets rules and standards relating to the conduct of firms in the industry' either on a 'voluntary' basis or with some degree of government mandate.[108] While self-regulation can be more 'efficient' than state-led regulation, it has been heavily critiqued for the unlikelihood that market participants will actually act in the best interests of society overall rather than their own business interests. As Braithwaite puts it, '[s]elf-regulation is frequently an attempt to deceive the public into believing in the responsibility of an irresponsible industry [and s]ometimes ... a strategy to give the government an excuse for not doing its job'.[109]

State-led regulation may be seen as more democratically legitimate inasmuch as the public interest may be better represented by the state rather than just the self-interest of business, and the regulators may be democratically accountable to the legislature or even directly to the electorate. In theory, thus, ex ante state-led regulation of private economic power may be seen as another means of promoting user autonomy in Internet markets, and may be preferred to a reform of competition law.

However, state-led regulation also has its weaknesses, and in the EU its application to concentrations of private economic power, particularly in the communications sector, has been influenced by neoliberalism. Telecoms services were formerly run by state-owned monopolies in each EU Member State, but since the 1980s have been subjected to a process of privatisation, with the liberalisation of telecoms markets which have opened the telecoms incumbent up to competition, reflecting neoliberal ideology.[110] In most EU Member States, the nation-state has gone from having a very large amount of control over telecoms by owning and operating the monopoly provider, to a much-reduced role in their operation, as the arbiter of the conduct of the privatised players.[111] In the wake of these

---

[107] ibid 2.

[108] N Gunningham and J Rees, 'Industry Self-Regulation: An Institutional Perspective' (1997) 19(4) *Law and Policy* 364.

[109] J Braithwaite, 'Responsive Regulation for Australia' in P Grabosky and J Braithwaite, *Business Regulation and Australia's Future* (Griffith, Australian Institute of Criminology, 1993) 93.

[110] S Simpson, *Pervasiveness and Efficacy in Regulatory Governance: Neo-Liberalism as Ideology and Practice in European Telecommunications Reorganisation*, European Consortium for Political Research Standing Group on Regulatory Governance Second Biennial Conference, '(Re)Regulation in the Wake of Neoliberalism: Consequences of Three Decades of Privatization and Market Liberalization', Utrecht, June 2008.

[111] While it is true that some EU nation-states still retain some level of ownership in the incumbent telecoms provider, the expectation is that such ownership will eventually be relinquished in favour of full privatisation.

developments, ex ante regulation is only imposed to aid these markets in becoming competitive, such that when they are deemed competitive, market-based solutions to problems will suffice. Regulation should only apply when markets are not competitive, and then should 'fade out'. Competitive markets do not require ex ante regulation unless there is a market failure, and regulation can be introduced only to address that failure, and not for other reasons, eg social policy. Indeed, there are many arguments advanced *against* regulation where there are no 'market failures' and even counsel to forbear from regulation even where there *are* market failures, because of, for instance, the adverse impact regulation may have on innovation, particularly in high tech markets.

One systemic problem of state-led regulation is the possibility of 'regulatory capture'—that the regulator does not regulate in some notion of the 'public interest' but is subject to 'capture' by the economically powerful and so its regulatory output reflects those interests.[112] While it is true that regulatory theory has moved beyond a 'pure interest-group driven analysis' to take account of institutional design, for instance,[113] regulatory capture is still attempted (and can be successful) in practice, including in the EU.[114] Brown and Marsden note 'widespread' capture of regulators and legislators in the field of copyright law, especially as applied to the Internet, as well as other 'government failures' in regulating the Internet such as the 'overregulation' of censoring content.[115]

These problems detract from the likelihood of ex ante state-led regulation being successful in advancing Internet users' autonomy in the face of accumulations of private economic power. These corporations are likely to lobby to ensure that such regulation is not enacted since it would impose further obligations on them and curtail lucrative business practices. Examples of this happening in practice have been the corporate lobbying around net neutrality and the forthcoming General Data Protection Regulation. While both of these measures, as will be seen later, would go some way to advancing users' interests, corporate lobbies, and their Member State allies, have ensured that they are not overly invasive of many practices which inhibit user autonomy.

Furthermore, even where ex ante state-led regulation may be enacted which *would* go some way at least to enhancing users' autonomy, the time taken to arrive

---

[112] See R Coase, 'The Economics of Broadcasting and Government Policy' (1966) 56(1/2) *American Economic Review* 440; GJ Stigler, 'The Theory of Economic Regulation' (1971) 2 *Bell Journal of Economics and Management* 3.

[113] See R Baldwin and others, 'Introduction: Regulation—the Field and the Developing Agenda' in R Baldwin and others (eds), *The Oxford Handbook of Regulation* (Oxford, Oxford University Press, 2010).

[114] See Corporate Europe Observatory, *The Record of a Captive Commission: The 'Black Book' on the Corporate Agenda of the Barroso II Commission* (Brussels, 2014), available at http://corporateeurope. org/power-lobbies/2014/05/record-captive-commission.

[115] Brown and Marsden, *Regulating Code* (n 87) 2. Farrand has also examined lobbying in EU copyright law formation: B Farrand, 'Lobbying and Lawmaking in the European Union: The Development of Copyright Law and the Rejection of the Anti-Counterfeiting Trade Agreement' (2015) 35(3) *Oxford Journal of Legal Studies* 487.

at this stage may be so long that the regulation becomes too little, too late. This is precisely the case with the EU's net neutrality regulation explored in more detail in the following chapter. Net neutrality was first raised as a possible policy issue in the early 2000s, yet it has taken more than ten years to arrive at the point where ex ante regulation will be imposed on ISPs. Business practices and technology have moved on considerably in the last ten years but the proposed regulation does not address them fully. The 'light touch' model of economic regulation seems to have created a situation in which there is extreme caution on the part of European organs aside from the Parliament to introduce such ex ante regulation vis-à-vis concentrations of private economic power, and so in practice it may not be a very efficacious route to protecting and promoting user autonomy.

The multi-stakeholder co-regulatory model can be conceptualised as a regulatory 'third way' which is neither state-led regulation nor industry self-regulation, and which explicitly involves consumers as part of the institutional setting for regulation, for which it claims more legitimacy as compared to these other forms of regulation.[116] In practice, co-regulation can take various forms, but what they have in common is 'the fact that the regulatory system is made up of a complex interaction of a general framework of legislation and a self-regulatory body'.[117]

Multi-stakeholder co-regulation encompasses nation-states, industry, as well as other stakeholders, typically from the 'technical community' and civil society. While this may aid the legitimacy of the regulatory process, the presence of these participants in the regulatory process may also be critiqued, particularly those from civil society not being representative of the citizenry more generally and thus raising questions of effectiveness, accountability and legitimacy, or civil society groups only being included as a window-dressing exercise, a criticism which has been levelled at the multi-stakeholder process in ICANN.[118] Furthermore, the multi-stakeholder fora currently in existence tend to emphasise 'governance' rather than 'regulation' or 'legislation' as such and form more of a 'conversation' around the issues under consideration rather than the formation of enforceable norms, with a notable example of this being the annual Internet Governance Forum whose impact (or lack thereof) can be called into question.[119] The extent to which these multi-stakeholder processes may represent user autonomy is limited in two dimensions: the deficiencies in representation these stakeholders encompass; and the lack of enforceable norms these processes may produce in practice—or that the enforceable norms which are produced may reflect government and business interests more than civil society's.

---

[116] CT Marsden, *Net Neutrality: Towards a Co-Regulatory Solution* (London, Bloomsbury, 2010) 164.

[117] ibid

[118] See M Mueller, *Networks and States: The Global Politics of Internet Governance* (Cambridge, MA, MIT Press, 2010).

[119] ibid.

Finally, given the state's evident interest in the surveillance of users, and the constitutional convenience of this surveillance being carried out by private entities, strong regulation, whether state-led, self-regulation or co-regulation, which protects and promotes user autonomy (and in particular the data privacy aspects thereof) is unlikely to be implemented in practice. Users may have to look elsewhere than the law for realistic and immediate ways in which their autonomy can be advanced in the Internet sphere.

VI. Better Ways of Achieving User Autonomy?

If law and regulation are deficient in the ways enumerated above, then users may consider turning to extra-legal solutions in order to enhance their online autonomy.

Benkler's model of non-hierarchical, non-market 'commons-based peer production' is not dominant in the Internet ecosystem, but '[its] logic radically contradicts that of capital' and thus can be looked to as an alternative to the status quo for achieving user autonomy.[120] In building this alternative, Bauwens acknowledges different schools of thought around the commons, including those approaches which are compatible with capitalism, but instead of opposing those approaches per se, advocates 'efforts to make the commons more autonomous from profit-maximizing entities and the system as a whole'.[121] In making the commons more autonomous from the current (neoliberal capitalist) system, individuals become more autonomous from both bureaucratised state and corporate power—a point recognised by Benkler himself in more recent writing.[122]

This goes beyond the 'infrastructure as a commons' argument advanced by Frischmann, who advocates commons *management* (although not ownership) for the Internet and communications networks—a resource management principle which entails that the resource is available to all within a community on a non-discriminatory basis. Individuals' autonomy, however, can be better served by infrastructure which is not only managed on a commons basis but also owned and controlled by the peers themselves on a fragmented, decentralised basis.[123] For instance, mesh networks and community clouds are technical solutions offered

[120] J Rigi, 'Peer Production as an Alternative to Capitalism: A New Communist Horizon' (2012) 1 *Journal of Peer Production.*
[121] M Bauwens, 'From the Theory of Peer Production to the Production of Peer Production Theory' (2012) 1 *Journal of Peer Production.*
[122] Y Benkler, 'Practical Anarchism: Peer Mutualism, Market Power and the Fallible State' (2013) 41(2) *Politics and Society* 213.
[123] Although this may be difficult to conceptualise for Western legal systems which attribute property ownership to sole individuals or formalised legal persons. See M Dulong de Rosnay, 'Peer to Peer as a Design Principle for Law: Distribute the Law' (2015) 6 *Journal of Peer Production.*

which can operate both under commons management and under commons ownership and control.[124]

Thus, as a result of the deficiencies in the existing legislation and regulatory approaches in the EU, user autonomy, when faced with concentrations of private economic power performing gatekeeping functions over online information flows, may best be pursued and advanced outside of legal and regulatory structures. The alternative methods suggested are 'code-based', ie infrastructure, software, online intermediaries and other tools. Unlike Lessig, 'code' in this sense is not considered in a technodeterministic fashion, which arguably has its own roots in neoliberal/neoclassical ideas of economic rationality.[125] Instead, the technical solutions suggested are designed with a particular view of society and technology in mind, one which adheres to the idea of user autonomy, by preserving privacy, enabling expression and resisting both corporate and state control. The code-based solutions suggested, as will be seen, are embodiments of users' own autonomy through peer production on a commons basis, as well as being designed to promote their own autonomy, particularly through the use of peer to peer design.

It is acknowledged that these value-imbued code-based alternatives to law and regulation are not perfect in their enhancement of user autonomy; there may be barriers to participation for users, such as a lack of technical expertise. However, they are *better* options than law and regulation in the sense that they are immediately available and already embody user autonomy values. For the moment, this is to be preferred to waiting for law and regulation, possibly, to reform in a way which promotes user autonomy. As already mentioned, this may be a longer term project which may require more profound societal change. Thus, in the meantime, technical solutions, even if imperfect, present the most feasible and pragmatic way of achieving user autonomy.

VII. Conclusion

This chapter has set the theoretical backdrop for the following chapters comprising the substantive case studies. First, the Internet's origins and development, surrounded by discourses around its freedom-enhancing qualities, have been outlined and contrasted with the emergence of poles of power in that environment. The concept of 'user autonomy' was introduced as the goal which the legal and regulatory system should seek to achieve given the Internet's affordances for individuals. The main legal regimes in the EU governing private power online were explored, and the argument made that they are conceptually flawed due to

---

[124] See P De Filippi and F Treguer, 'Expanding the Internet Commons: The Subversive Potential of Wireless Community Networks' (2015) 6 *Journal of Peer Production*.

[125] See V Mayer Schonberger, 'Demystifying Lessig' (2008) *Wisconsin Law Review* 713, 737.

neoliberal influence in achieving the goal of user autonomy. Instead, immediate extra-systemic solutions are suggested as alternatives to achieving user autonomy. The kind of attributes these solutions ought to have to best uphold and protect user autonomy are outlined: ideally they should be infrastructure and services managed and owned on a decentralised commons basis.

From here, the substantive, empirical part of this book will commence. The four case studies forming the next four chapters will provide practical demonstrations of this chapter's theoretical arguments regarding how existing EU law and regulation's application to private power online is insufficient to achieve user autonomy.

3

Dominance and Internet Provision

Internet providers, whether fixed or mobile, occupy a position of control over information flows going to and from their customers, the users. The Internet was originally set up as a 'dumb' network using 'end to end connectivity' in its design, which did not interfere with the packets of information passing over the network, with the 'intelligence' being built into the starting- or end-point of the data, ie the device on which the information originated or for which it was destined. However, developments such as deep packet inspection (DPI), which allows network operators to monitor in real time the content of the data packets passing over their infrastructure, and content delivery networks (CDNs) which allow large content providers to bypass Internet backbone networks when sending their content to users, have ushered in profound changes to how data flows over the Internet, with evident consequences for these users and their autonomy.

This chapter examines Internet access providers and their markets, and will have a particular focus on the net neutrality debate, which concerns the extent to which Internet access providers should be able to 'manage' traffic travelling through their networks. Net neutrality implicates issues of competition, particularly for vertically integrated Internet access providers which also have content-producing/-distributing subsidiaries, but also has other consequences for users' ability to impart and receive information online, for users' privacy, and for the concentration of Internet content in large players which can afford to use content delivery networks and/or make deals with Internet access providers.

While some commentators have considered that existing competition and sector-specific telecoms regulation, particularly in the EU, would be sufficient to address net neutrality concerns, others have argued that only new ex ante regulation will solve the problems. After much debate, in 2015 both the US and EU adopted ex ante net neutrality regulation: a rare instance of further ex ante regulation being considered to address problems of private economic power online with an adverse effect on users' autonomy. This is the only case study in this book where further ex ante regulation has been seriously considered, and subsequently adopted, by policy-makers.

In theory, this might be a development to be welcomed, but in practice the time taken to arrive at this point may render the regulatory measures ineffective or at least only partially effective. The experience with the further regulation of Internet provision to address net neutrality concerns demonstrates the shortcomings of regulation, and suggests systemic problems in turning to regulation as a means of protecting users' autonomy.

I. Technical and Market Developments in Internet Access Provision

Internet users buy access to the rest of the network from a provider, which is usually a telecommunications company (whether mobile or fixed line or both) but can also be a cable TV operator, and Internet access via fibre optic cables has been growing in prevalence. In the EU, Internet access via DSL (digital subscriber line, ie fixed line telecoms) is the most popular technology, although in certain Member States, cable Internet has retail market shares of around 40 per cent.[1] The situation in the US differs inasmuch as cable has been the main form of Internet access, followed by DSL, and while fibre optic access remains a small part of the market, its share is growing.[2]

Although users may wish to access content and programs from other Internet customers of the same provider, they are also highly likely to wish to access data from the customers of other providers, including in other countries beyond their own. In order to access that data, Internet access providers make agreements with each other, negotiated in private, to send and receive data from their customers, and the customers of the other providers with which they have agreements. This results in individual users experiencing 'universal connectivity' to all parts of the Internet.

Formerly, the web of connection among Internet providers took a hierarchical form,[3] with the largest networks interconnecting with each other in the form of 'peering' arrangements,[4] while they charged smaller networks for data transit. The large networks which were capable of peering with each other became known as the 'Internet backbone'.

This more or less represented the topography of the Internet at the time of two major mergers involving MCI WorldCom concerning Internet backbone providers in the late 1990s which raised concerns over competition in the Internet backbone and how smaller networks interconnected with it. These concerns in particular

---

[1] L Hou and others, 'Can Open Internet Access be Imposed upon European CATV Networks?' (2013) 37(10) *Telecommunications Policy* 970.

[2] IHS Technology, 'Broadband Internet Penetration Deepens in US; Cable is King' (9 December 2013), available at https://technology.ihs.com/468148/broadband-internet-penetration-deepens-in-us-cable-is-king.

[3] A D'Ignazio and E Giovannetti, 'Antitrust Analysis for the Internet Upstream Market: A Border Gateway Protocol Approach' (2006) 2(1) *Journal of Competition Law and Economics* 43.

[4] N Economides, 'Chapter 9: The Economics of the Internet Backbone' in S Majumdar and others (eds), *Handbook of Telecommunications Economics Volume 2* (Amsterdam, Elsevier, 2005) 380.

involved the 'bottleneck' position that these 'Tier 1' backbone providers occupied, with the associated competition concerns regarding how they could influence the transmission of data and accordingly the prices paid by smaller networks which were not large enough to peer with them. The initial merger to form MCI World-Com was approved subject to divestitures by authorities in both the EU and US,[5] but the second merger, between MCI WorldCom and Sprint, was opposed by the authorities and subsequently abandoned since it would have created an entity so large that it could act independently of competitors and consumers in the Internet backbone market.[6] Although there were some dissenting voices, such as Econo-mides, in the aftermath of these decisions regarding the hierarchical nature of the Internet backbone, being based on the top tier networks that peer with each other being at the top of that hierarchy,[7] technical and commercial developments in the years since those merger decisions have altered this characterisation of the net-work of networks, and the hierarchical arrangement and terminology is no longer an accurate picture of the Internet.[8]

In the interim, certain developments have changed the Internet's topography from a hierarchy to a more complex picture of relations among the interconnected networks which make up the Internet. This has salient consequences for online information flows in terms of identifying where bottlenecks, and thus gatekeepers, now lie, which would seem no longer to be with the backbone providers as feared in the context of the MCI WorldCom mergers, but instead with retail access pro-viders, as they have a valuable commodity, namely their customers, who content and services providers want to reach. Accordingly, this has been driven by the tran-sition to broadband Internet from slower dial-up access, and the new real-time services that could be delivered over it such as Voice over Internet Protocol (VoIP) and video streaming, as well as the emergence of certain Web 2.0 user-generated content aggregators which wish to access these users. All of this has contributed to three principal developments which have changed the network topology from the previous hierarchical model.

First, 'multihoming' has become more prevalent, which entails smaller Internet Service Providers (ISPs) (which would not be able to provide 'universal connec-tivity' themselves and so under the hierarchical model would have had to pay the top tier providers for data transit) entering into agreements which allow them to use more than one backbone provider. In this way, the ISP can control how traffic

---

[5] US Department of Justice Press Release, *Justice Department Clears WorldCom/MCI Merger after MCI Agrees to Sell its Internet Business* (15 July 1998), available at www.justice.gov/atr/public/press_releases/1998/1829.htm; Case IV/M.1069 *WorldCom/MCI (II)*, Commission Decision 99/287/EC [1999] OJ L116/1.

[6] Case COMP/M.1741 *MCI WorldCom/Sprint*, Commission Decision 2003/790/EC [2003] OJ L300/1.

[7] Economides, 'Chapter 9: The Economics of the Internet Backbone' (n 4).

[8] L De Nardis, 'Governance at the Internet's Core: The Geopolitics of Interconnection and Internet Exchange Points (IXPs) in Emerging Markets', 40th Research Conference on Communication, Infor-mation and Internet Policy, Arlington, September 2012, at 4.

will be routed over these networks, such as by sending the traffic over the route that costs the least or is the quickest at that point in time. Furthermore, many large websites and online content or service providers also 'multihome' by using more than one ISP in order to transmit their own data. In addition to these multiple agreements with backbone providers, smaller ISPs have also been observed to interconnect and 'peer' with each other rather than relying solely on buying transit from top tier providers, particularly in Europe.[9]

Secondly, the rise of 'real-time entertainment' such as video on demand or VoIP services being delivered over IP networks and the corresponding desire to ensure a certain quality of service for customers has been a driver of the development of CDNs. This has generated incentives for major online content providers to seek to gain access to users by deploying their own CDNs at both top tier and lower tier networks. One consequence of the deployment of CDNs is that content providers which are large, rich and popular enough can ensure the speedy provision of their data to users through deploying their networks via agreements with ISPs, while less-visited sites use slower, traditional Internet hosting for the delivery of their content.[10]

The growth of this kind of prioritised traffic has increased the prevalence of peering among ISPs and agreements between CDNs and ISPs, thus diminishing the strictly hierarchical structure of the network which was defined in the merger decision above.[11] As a result, concerns about dominance can no longer be limited to network providers at the top of the hierarchy, ie the top tier networks.

Finally, the creation of DPI has also signalled a significant change for online data flows. DPI is a technology deployed at the level of Internet provision to determine the content of the data packets that are travelling through the network at a point in the network which is not an end-point (eg user's computer terminal), and based on that information, the network operator can manipulate the route of that packet accordingly (speed it up, slow it down, remove it, introduce other packets). This represents a major development from predecessor technologies since DPI permits the possibility to analyse and discriminate Internet traffic in real time using one piece of equipment.

The use of DPI and CDNs for Internet traffic prioritisation has given rise to the net neutrality debate. The focus of the debate has tended to be on the proposed regulation of packet prioritisation via DPI rather than the deployment of CDNs, even though both techniques have the same effect of ISPs prioritising certain content by delivering it quicker than online content whose owner has not paid extra for these services. Both techniques contribute to the situation of certain

---

[9] J Liebenau and others, *European Internet Traffic: Problems and Prospects of Growth and Competition*, London School of Economics White Paper (2013) 3, available at http://eprints.lse.ac.uk/50930/.

[10] M Palacin and others, 'The Impact of Content Delivery Networks on the Internet Ecosystem' (2013) 3 *Journal of Information Policy* 304.

[11] ibid.

information flowing across the Internet being favoured and certain information being disfavoured or even blocked entirely, thus affecting free information flows online.

II. Net Neutrality Explained

Net neutrality, although a contested term, can be said to be a principle proposed for user access to the Internet, which would prevent ISPs from discriminating between different kinds of Internet traffic, regardless of the amount of bandwidth the traffic takes up, and from restricting content, sites or platforms (at least those which are legal).

Due to the Internet originally being set up on the basis of 'end-to-end connectivity' and the network not traditionally interfering with the packets of information passing through it, all information sent (and received) was 'equal'. This scenario is described as 'net neutrality', which was the 'default' for the Internet prior to the development of DPI and CDNs. Although this type of neutrality has had its complexities,[12] different applications and types of information are treated in the same 'agnostic' way by network operators, even if 'better' treatment for some may have been desirable from the user's perspective.

In practice, non-net neutral behaviour can take various shapes, with differing consequences:

— First, an ISP could refuse to carry content from a certain provider unless the provider pays extra, effectively threatening to block access to that content by its users.
— Alternatively, it could still carry the content but slow it down or interfere negatively with the quality of service that that content receives, while not blocking it entirely.
— Another scenario would be a content provider and ISP voluntarily (ie without coercion or the threats of blocking) coming to an agreement that would prioritise content from that provider over other types of Internet traffic, with the effect being that either other content is delivered more slowly than before, or that other content outside of this agreement is not delivered more slowly than before, but is delivered more slowly in comparison to the prioritised content.
— A further scenario would be an ISP blocking or degrading a particular class of data in the same way, eg all data coming from VoIP services or peer to peer file-sharing services.

---

[12] T Wu, 'Network Neutrality, Broadband Discrimination' (2003) 2 *Journal of Telecommunications and High Technology Law* 141, 149.

— Yet another scenario would be an ISP which is vertically integrated with a content or application provider favouring that content, eg by speeding it up.
— Finally, in the context of volumetric pricing (by which users pay ISPs for Internet access at a pre-determined speed and have a maximum download quota, with either lower speeds and/or additional charges on a per MB basis if this quota is exceeded), non-net neutral conduct may be considered to be access to certain information, content or applications online which does not 'count' towards this quota, thus making this data more attractive to users.

III. Problems Arising from Network Management Practices

The practices of the actors involved in the provision of Internet access to users and engaging in non-net neutral conduct implicate various issues for users' autonomy.

A. Competition Concerns

Internet provision can be conceptualised as a two- or multi-sided market, a frequent characteristic of Internet markets. Users are on each side of the market, but on one side they are uploading data and on the other side they are downloading data with the ISP providing a conduit through which these information flows travel, thus acting as a gatekeeper over these flows. One competition concern is that that ISPs could leverage this power that they have in controlling what data their customers can access by threatening to block or otherwise interfere with the data packets coming from certain content providers unless they pay for this special access. Users may suffer harm inasmuch as their choices are impeded by the ISP: they may have to pay more to access it, or it may not be accessible at all.

These concerns would be raised in particular for ISPs which already have a dominant position in the market or 'significant market power' (SMP), since they would have an interest in determining what information is accessible to their customers for their own business purposes. Such network management practices may encompass refusing passage to certain kinds of information coming from certain sources, or favouring the content or application provided by a vertically integrated subsidiary by giving it quicker or otherwise better passage to its Internet access customers.[13]

If there is a competitive market, then in theory a consumer with an ISP that is in some way manipulating what she is sending and receiving will switch to another

---

[13] See N Economides, '"Net Neutrality", Non-Discrimination and Digital Distribution of Content Through the Internet' (2008) 4(2) *I/S: A Journal of Law and Policy for the Information Society* 209.

which is not doing so, assuming there is consumer demand for this.[14] However, if the market is not competitive, if all ISPs see this conduct as advantageous for them, or if it is difficult to switch ISPs, then there is a problem.

However, ISPs' non-net neutral conduct has been justified according to the rationales of competition, to promote investment and consumer welfare: on the one hand, they claim that they need to act in this way to deal with congestion on the network or as a way of raising funds for further investment in infrastructure so as to prevent congestion; and, on the other, that a lack of net neutrality regulation will give them the freedom to develop innovative products and services which will be of ultimate benefit to users.[15] Nevertheless, innovation is an argument which cuts both ways, with net neutrality proponents also arguing that regulation is actually necessary in order to promote innovation.[16]

The default position of net neutrality entails that content providers do not need to pay individual ISPs an additional amount, including ISPs they do not use for their own connection, to access those ISPs' customers in order to deliver them content. However, certain content providers wish to have privileged access to a certain ISPs' customers and so are willing to pay for this quicker or better quality connection, either via their data packets being speeded up by the ISP or via a CDN, or both. Indeed, these 'non-neutral' pricing practices have been justified as being necessary for ISPs to invest in the network infrastructure and develop new and innovative products and services.

In addition, there is increasing vertical integration and consolidation in Internet markets, between Internet access providers and providers of online content and applications, either in the form of mergers or in the form of existing players entering new markets. These trends exacerbate competition concerns since they provide even more incentives to players to prioritise content and services from their own subsidiaries and discriminate against competitors providing similar offerings.

B. Free Expression

Net neutrality and the debate around it are born of technical developments and changed business practices in the Internet sphere, but also of an increasing recognition of ISPs as performing the function of an information gatekeeper. This recognition has taken the shape of ISPs being ordered by governments such as in the UK to block illegal content, such as child abuse images, information related to

---

[14] B van Schewick, *Internet Architecture and Innovation* (Cambridge, MA, MIT Press, 2010) 259–64.

[15] See G Sidak, 'A Consumer-Welfare Approach to Network Neutrality Regulation of the Internet' (2006) 2(3) *Journal of Competition Law and Economics* 349; HJ Singer and RE Litan, 'Unintended Consequences of Net Neutrality Regulation' (2007) 5(3) *Journal on Telecommunications and High Technology Law* 533; and CS Yoo, 'Network Neutrality and the Economics of Congestion' (2006) 94 *Georgetown Law Journal* 1847.

[16] See van Schewick, *Internet Architecture and Innovation* (n 14) 270–73, 289–93.

terrorism and content which (allegedly) infringes copyright. While these are not net neutrality issues per se, ISPs' wish to operate non-net neutral networks for their own business purposes may see them engaged in a greater private enforcement role in these other areas, which they may not find so desirable due to the regulatory burdens that may be imposed.[17]

In any event, the net neutrality debate has been primarily framed as an 'economic' one, with its solution being competitive markets for Internet provision, content, services and applications.[18] This does not paint the full picture of what is at stake. The control that ISPs exert over their customers, on the one hand, and other players such as content providers which wish to access those customers, does not only have 'economic' consequences: it also has a profound impact on what users can send and receive over their Internet connections, and thus is 'explicitly normative and political'—affecting users' autonomy online.[19]

Specifically, one danger lies in ISPs blocking or filtering content which is otherwise legal for purposes which would not be termed anticompetitive. This could include blocking content which is harmful to the ISP's 'brand' without being illegal, or deemed controversial in some way. Indeed, even in developed Western jurisdictions with guarantees of free expression, instances of these scenarios have actually occurred in practice.[20]

Outright blocking of otherwise legal content and services would constitute an egregious impediment to the free flow of information online, and accordingly the freedom to send and receive information, which is usually conceptualised as falling under legal protections of free expression, such as European Convention on Human Rights (ECHR), Article 10. However, the right to free expression has usually been conceived of as a right enforceable against nation-states rather than private entities such as many ISPs (although there are still those with shares owned by the state in the EU). This leaves at least an uncertainty, and at most a lacuna, in the law when users' rights to free expression are infringed by private corporations.

Even network management practices which do not amount to the outright blocking of online content or services are of concern for optimal online information flows and users' free expression. The prioritisation of certain content or services, especially via agreements between ISPs and online content and service providers, poses particular problems. Unless these agreements can be termed

---

[17] R Frieden, 'Internet Packet Sniffing and Its Impact on the Network Neutrality Debate and the Balance of Power Between Intellectual Property Creators and Consumers' (2008) 18(3) *Fordham Intellectual Property, Media and Entertainment Law Journal* 633.

[18] J Sluijs, 'From Competition to Freedom of Expression: Introducing Art 10 ECHR in the European Network Neutrality Debate' (2012) 12(3) *Human Rights Law Review* 509.

[19] CT Marsden, *Net Neutrality: Towards a Co-Regulatory Solution* (London, Bloomsbury, 2010) 19.

[20] For instance, in Canada, the telecoms company and ISP Telus blocked its users' access to the Telecommunications Workers' Union of Canada's website during an industrial relations dispute between the parties. See C Doctorow, 'Phone company blocks access to telecoms union's website', *Boing Boing*, 24 July 2005, available at http://boingboing.net/2005/07/24/phone-company-blocks.html.

anticompetitive in some way, then they will not otherwise be regulated in the absence of ex ante net neutrality rules. However, these arrangements could disadvantage other content and services not included in such an agreement, either by slowing them down or by creating a different kind of Internet access where it is cheaper (or otherwise more attractive) for users to be restricted to only accessing this prioritised content. Thus, deep pocketed entities will entrench their powerful positions, making it more difficult for alternatives to sustain themselves or to be set up in the first place.

While some of these practices might engender competition concerns, they also raise the spectres of media pluralism and the digital divide. Media pluralism in particular may be considered to be an 'old media' phenomenon, based on limited spectrum for broadcast media and a large amount of resources being required for all media to operate in print or via broadcast. The Internet and low-cost digital technology may have removed these impediments to pluralism, although capacity constraints have emerged as one of the justifications for implementing non-net neutral traffic management practices. Whether based on technical restrictions or commercial advantage, limitations in what users can receive, especially if what they *can* receive are the products and services of large corporations, signals a return to a modified version of media pluralism as a topic of concern.[21]

Prioritisation of content also poses concerns for the digital divide, ie the socio-economic inequality relating to the Internet and information and communication technology. Smaller content or service providers may be priced out of the 'fast lanes', and users may be enticed with free or low-cost offers of restricted Internet access to content and service providers which have paid a premium for their services to be offered in this way, with 'full' Internet access costing more, which may be too much for some.[22]

C. Privacy and Confidentiality

Users' privacy is an issue raised indirectly in the context of the net neutrality debate since the use of DPI technology allows ISPs to monitor data about users' behaviour on the Internet, including sensitive data. DPI permits the content of data packets travelling across the Internet to be known by network operators, compromising users' privacy and the confidentiality of their communications.

Indeed, various controversies surrounding DPI involved the perceived invasion of privacy that its use entailed.[23] Even if privacy is an incidental concern for the

---

[21] K Karppinen, 'Rethinking Media Pluralism and Communicative Abundance' (2009) 11 *Observatorio (OBS*) Journal* 151.

[22] N Barratt and LR Shade, 'Net Neutrality: Telecom Policy and the Public Interest' (2007) 32(2) *Canadian Journal of Communication* 295, 299.

[23] Especially the secret Phorm targeted advertising trials in the UK. See I Brown and CT Marsden, *Regulating Code: Good Governance and Better Regulation in the Information Age* (Cambridge, MIT Press, 2013) 148.

net neutrality debate, the use of DPI encompasses an unnecessary monitoring of data, including personal information. This contributes to a state of data proliferation rather than minimisation which endangers users' privacy and the protection of their data.

Furthermore, certain non-net neutrality conduct not involving DPI, such as outright content blocking, may be considered to be a possible infringement of the right to privacy enshrined in ECHR, Article 8, which includes a right to respect for one's correspondence as well as 'private and family life'.[24]

IV. Existing European Law and Regulation

The net neutrality regulation adopted by the EU in late 2015 will be considered below. Here, the existing EU law and regulation which applies to scenarios where there is a deviation from net neutrality is outlined. Telecoms in the EU are already subject to sector-specific ex ante regulation, supplemented by competition law. Furthermore, human rights norms may also have a bearing on how these situations are currently addressed.

A. Regulation

The EU's telecoms regulatory framework, since the Commission's 1987 Telecoms Green Paper, has promoted intra-platform competition in the form of stimulating competition at the retail, consumer-facing level for fixed line telecoms through reforms such as local loop unbundling, rather than inter-platform competition between different technologies such as cable and copper wires which has been a feature of the US regulatory landscape. EU telecoms regulation has also pursued a 'technology neutral' policy, not overly concerning itself with the type of technology used to deliver services, but more the extent to which markets are competitive. If a market is not competitive, then ex ante regulation will be applied, with the idea that this regulation will no longer be needed once competition has been achieved, and market-based solutions will suffice. Indeed, neoliberal ideology giving rise to this approach has been a 'deeply pervasive' force in driving European telecoms regulation over the last few decades.[25]

---

[24] BJ Koops and J Sluijs, 'Network Neutrality and Privacy According to Art 8 ECHR' (2012) 3(2) *European Journal for Law and Technology*.

[25] S Simpson, 'Pervasiveness and Efficacy in Regulatory Governance: Neo-Liberalism as Ideology and Practice in European Telecommunications Reorganisation', European Consortium for Political Research Standing Group on Regulatory Governance, Second Biennial Conference, '(Re) Regulation in the Wake of Neoliberalism. Consequences of Three Decades of Privatization and Market Liberalization', Utrecht, June 2008.

The current regulatory framework is comprised of a suite of instruments adopted in 2002, which were amended in 2009. The result has been that national regulatory authorities (NRAs) impose ex ante obligations on entities which have significant market power (SMP) in relevant markets, as identified by the European Commission. Wholesale broadband markets have been identified as those where SMP exists, and for which NRAs should use ex ante regulation to address competition problems. However, user-facing retail broadband markets have not been included in the SMP list, and it seems that broadband provided over cable networks is also excluded.[26]

When there is SMP in a market, NRAs can impose obligations on undertakings with SMP which concern transparency and non-discrimination in relation to interconnection and access; and access to and use of specific network facilities.[27] Yet NRAs are also empowered to impose certain other obligations even where there is no SMP in a market: they can impose access and interconnection obligations on undertakings controlling access to users 'to the extent that is necessary to ensure end-to-end connectivity';[28] and have the power to set minimum quality of service requirements in order to prevent the degradation of service and the hindering or slowing down of traffic over networks.[29] In addition, entities operating in communications networks are subject to transparency obligations regarding the services they provide to consumers,[30] and operators of public communications networks must negotiate access and interconnection with each other.[31]

Although some of this existing telecoms regulation in the EU might go some way to protecting net neutrality interests of users, it does not protect against all the prejudicial effects of non-net neutral conduct by ISPs. The regulation is highly economics-oriented, its more weighty obligations do not apply to most ISPs, and in any event some of the provisions that might protect against the adverse effects of non-net neutral conduct are optional for NRAs and seem not to have been enforced in practice. The likelihood of the Commission designating the retail broadband market as one exhibiting deficiencies of competition is remote, as is the likelihood of all national regulators implementing the interconnection obligations.

B. Competition in Fixed Line Internet Markets

It has been recognised for some time that competition rules apply to undertakings in the EU telecoms sector, notwithstanding the ex ante regulation.[32] Despite

---

[26] Hou and others, 'Can Open Internet Access be Imposed upon European CATV Networks?' (n 1).
[27] Access Directive (2002/19/EC), arts 9–13.
[28] ibid art 5(1)(a).
[29] Citizens' Rights Directive (2004/38/EC), art 22.
[30] ibid art 20.
[31] Access Directive, art 4.
[32] Since Case 41/83 *Italy v European Commission* [1985] ECR 510.

the attempts to introduce competition and weaken the market power of the incumbents in the markets for broadband Internet provision and other telecoms services, there have still been significant issues in the domestic markets of certain European Member States involving abuses of dominance in the forms of 'margin squeeze',[33] predatory pricing[34] and the hindering of access to the network[35] by the incumbent vertically integrated telecoms providers.

These cases show significant market power is still wielded by the owners of the local loop and this does have an effect on the final prices and choice that Internet users in Europe experience. However, these more 'classical' cases of anticompetitive conduct do not go to the heart of the issue of net neutrality. European competition authorities have not been particularly active in investigating ISPs' network management practices such as blocking, prioritising or degrading access to certain content and applications, while they have been more alert to more straightforward anticompetitive behaviour in broadband Internet markets. Indeed, to date there has been no case brought before the European Commission or courts on the basis of Treaty on the Functioning of the European Union (TFEU), Article 102 which implicates at least the overt competition aspect of net neutrality.

The closest the European Commission has come to tackling net neutrality through competition law was an investigation into Orange, Deutsche Telekom and Telefonica regarding their negotiation of wholesale Internet connections with parties such as large online content providers and Internet backbone providers for international access and interconnection.[36] However the Commission closed the case, stating that the telecoms operators' conduct did not appear to breach EU competition law due to excluding competitors from the Internet transit market or Internet content markets.

Why network management practices have not been investigated by competition authorities may well be due to this conduct not necessarily constituting a violation of EU competition law. Certain network management practices, if carried out by a provider with a dominant position in the relevant market, might be judged abusive under TFEU, Article 102. If the provider does not have a dominant position, then this conduct is unlikely to be anticompetitive. Collective dominance remains possible, but unlikely in the EU telecoms sector.[37]

It seems that the scenario in which anticompetitive conduct is most likely to be found is when there is a provider with a dominant position in the Internet

---

[33] Such as Case C-280/08 *Deutsche Telekom AG v European Commission* [2010] ECR I-9555; and Case COMP/38.784 *Wanadoo Espana v Telefonica*, Commission Decision of 4 July 2007 [2007] OJ C86/6.

[34] See eg Case COMP/38.233 *Wanadoo Interactive*, Commission Decision of 16 July 2003.

[35] Case COMP/39.525 *Telekomunikacja Polska*, Commission Decision of 22 June 2011.

[36] European Commission, 'Antitrust: Commission confirms unannounced inspections in Internet connectivity services' (memo, 11 July 2013), available at http://europa.eu/rapid/press-release_MEMO-13-681_en.htm?locale=en.

[37] A de Streel, 'Remedies in the Electronic Communications Sector' in D Geradin (ed), *Remedies in Network Industries: EC Competition Law vs Sector-Specific Regulation* (Mortsel, Intersentia, 2004) 75.

wholesale market. It is possible a provider may have a dominant position in a retail market, but this is less likely. Thus it would seem that many network management practices by retail ISPs are likely to be permissible, and that while non-net neutral conduct by wholesale ISPs may not be permissible in theory, in practice it may not be investigated.

C. Free Expression

In Europe, free expression is protected by ECHR, Article 10. This is supplemented by constitutional rights in some Member States' domestic jurisdictions, and is also included in Article 11 of the EU's Charter of Fundamental Rights.

Yet, ECHR, Article 10 is an obligation primarily pertaining to contracting states, and is usually conceived of as a negative freedom, although there have been cases in which it has produced a horizontal effect between private parties.[38] The European Court of Human Rights (ECtHR) has also explicitly recognised the right of individuals to send and receive information on the Internet, and that Article 10 may apply to restrictions on Internet access, or, even more narrowly, access to a certain online platform.[39]

It is possible that this jurisprudence may be applied to instances of network management in non-net neutral ways which restrict an individual's freedom to send or receive information on the Internet, when the management is being done by a private ISP. Yet whether such network management practices by ISPs would infringe users or content providers' Article 10 rights seems highly context-specific and it is difficult to predict how the ECtHR might rule on such scenarios in light of its precedent.

Certainly, the most egregious network management practices for the right to receive and impart information would encompass blocking, and perhaps the degradation of quality of service of particular content to an extent equivalent to, or approaching, blocking. Sluijs considers that an infringement might only be recognised if *all* expression is blocked by an ISP.[40] Also, it is unclear whether a certain class of applications or content or services being blocked (or severely degraded) by ISPs might prompt intervention by the ECtHR, such as P2P filesharing networks.

Other problematic network management practices, such as the prioritisation of certain content, are also less likely to constitute a breach of the right to receive information given the user is still able to receive information, albeit perhaps at a slower speed. However, the ECtHR might be willing to intervene if ISPs' network management practices constituted an interference with media plurality, with

---

[38] *Khurshid Mustafa and Tarzibachi v Sweden*, Application no 23883/06, ECtHR, 16 December 2008.
[39] *Ahmet Yildirim v Turkey*, Application no 3111/10, ECtHR, 18 December 2012.
[40] Sluijs, 'From Competition to Freedom of Expression' (n 18).

the intervention possibly in the form of calling on the particular nation-state to stimulate plurality.[41]

Thus it would seem that in the EU, while the right to free expression under ECHR, Article 10 may in certain specific circumstances go some way to protecting net neutrality, it is unlikely to do so on every occasion that net neutrality is infringed.

The Council of Europe has looked at the issue of net neutrality for some years; its Committee of Ministers issued a Declaration on the subject in 2010,[42] followed by a Recommendation in early 2016.[43] While neither are binding on Member States, the Recommendation comprised strong language on net neutrality, stressing that there should be no deviations from the principle except in cases of traffic management based on alleviating congestion, network security or a court or administrative order.

D. Privacy

In terms of the privacy concerns raised incidentally through the use of DPI in facilitating non-net neutral conduct by ISPs, the European Data Protection Supervisor (EDPS) delivered an Opinion on the matter.[44] He stated that the use of DPI by ISPs to inspect the content of communications interferes with the right to the confidentiality of communications, but in principle the existing privacy and data protection framework in Europe is appropriate to guarantee the right to confidentiality. Nevertheless, he counselled close monitoring of the situation, and advocated legislative measures to address this which should give users a 'real choice' especially through forcing ISPs to offer non-monitored Internet connections.

ISPs are permitted, via the E-Privacy Directive (2002/58/EC), to process personal data of users 'for the purpose of the transmission of a communication',[45] but this is subject to some conditions, including a prohibition on ISPs engaging in 'listening, trapping, storage or other kinds of interception or surveillance of communications' without users' consent except where they have other obligations

---

[41] Such as in *Centro Europa 7 Srl and Di Stefano v Italy*, Application no 38433/09 [2012] ECHR 974, ECtHR.

[42] Council of Europe, Declaration of the Committee of Ministers on net neutrality of 29 September 2010, available at https://wcd.coe.int/ViewDoc.jsp?id=1678287.

[43] Council of Europe, Recommendation CM/Rec(2016)1 of the Committee of Ministers on protecting and promoting the right to freedom of expression and the right to private life with regard to network neutrality of 13 January 2016, available at https://wcd.coe.int/ViewDoc.jsp?Ref=CM/Rec%28 2016%291&Language=lanEnglish&Ver=original&BackColorInternet=C3C3C3&BackColorIntranet= EDB021&BackColorLogged=F5D383.

[44] European Data Protection Supervisor, 'Net Neutrality, Traffic Management and the Protection of Privacy and Personal Data', Opinion of 7 October 2011, available at www.edps.europa.eu/EDPSWEB/ webdav/site/mySite/shared/Documents/Consultation/Opinions/2011/11-10-07_Net_neutrality _EN.pdf.

[45] E-Privacy Directive (2002/58/EC), art 6.

to do so such as for national security reasons.[46] ISPs must also comply with data protection laws. However, the CJEU in *Scarlet v SABAM* held that ISPs could not be forced to monitor all of their customers' traffic for possible copyright infringements as this was a disproportionate interference with their rights to privacy, data protection and free expression.[47] While the circumstances in that case involved ISPs monitoring not for their own benefit, but for the benefits of third party intellectual property rights holders, there may be some precedent established if a similar case was brought regarding the privacy aspects of ISPs' network monitoring practices if they were indeed engaging in the total monitoring of their customers' communications.

The problem, however, may lie in the detection of such practices in the first place, and so appropriate enforcement of privacy and data protection vis-à-vis ISPs' network monitoring practices can only occur once there is sufficient knowledge that the problem exists.

Koops and Sluijs have considered the application of ECHR, Article 8 to non-net neutral conduct by ISPs, concluding that only in a narrow set of circumstances might this conduct constitute an infringement, where there is outright blocking, but whether this will be an actual infringement will be highly case-specific and depend on factors including the kind of traffic managed, the duration and scope of network management and the extent to which public authorities were involved.[48]

V. Net Neutrality Regulation

The EU debate around whether specific regulation is necessary for net neutrality gained momentum and has recently resulted in ex ante net neutrality rules. This follows some individual Member States having proceeded with law and regulation on network management at the domestic law. In 2012, the Netherlands and Slovenia legislated on net neutrality, with narrow exceptions under which a deviation from net neutrality is permitted.[49] Other countries such as France have non-binding guidelines on net neutrality.[50]

---

[46] ibid art 5.

[47] Case C-70/10 *Scarlet Extended v Societe belge des auteurs, compositeurs et editeurs (SABAM)* [2012] ECDR 4.

[48] Koops and Sluijs, 'Network Neutrality and Privacy According to Art 8 ECHR' (n 24).

[49] An unofficial translation of the law into English is available in D van der Kroft, 'Net Neutrality in the Netherlands: State of Play', *Bits of Freedom*, 15 June 2011, available at www.bof.nl/2011/06/15/net-neutrality-in-the-netherlands-state-of-play/; Mitar, 'Net Neutrality in Slovenia', *Wlan Slovenia*, 16 June 2013, available at https://wlan-si.net/en/blog/2013/06/16/net-neutrality-in-slovenia/.

[50] ARCEP, *Neutralite de l'internet et des reseaux: propositions et orientations* (2010), available at www.arcep.fr/uploads/tx_gspublication/net-neutralite-orientations-sept2010.pdf. All translations from this report into English are author's own.

For some time, the European Commission had considered that the existing telecoms package, as detailed above, was sufficient to address net neutrality concerns.[51] However, in contrast, the European Parliament at the same time had passed resolutions supporting a more active approach towards net neutrality.[52]

The turning point in the EU's net neutrality debate can be traced to the emergence of data from the Body of European Regulators for Electronic Communications (BEREC) in 2012, which found that there was widespread interference with peer-to-peer (P2P) networks and VoIP on fixed and mobile networks in the EU.[53]

In the following year, the European Commission proposed a draft Regulation which included provisions on net neutrality, which essentially would have created two classes of services: 'internet access services' which are subject to a net neutrality principle; and 'specialised services' which were not subject to this principle.[54] The draft then went to the European Parliament, which, consistent with its previous record of endorsing strong net neutrality principles, adopted various amendments to the original text, which comprised: a stronger definition of net neutrality for 'internet access services'; narrowed the definition of 'specialised services' and the circumstances in which they can be provided; and also entailed that ISPs could not discriminate between 'functionally equivalent services or applications'. The Latvian Presidency of the EU Council during early 2015 also made proposals for modifying the Regulation's text, which seemed to depart from strong net neutrality principles.[55] In the end, after trilogue discussions, the EU institutions settled on the final text of the net neutrality provisions in late 2015, which entered into force in April 2016.[56]

---

[51] European Commission Press Release, *Agreement on EU Telecoms Reform Paves Way for Stronger Consumer Rights, an Open Internet, a Single European Telecoms Market and High-Speed Internet Connections for All Citizens* (5 November 2009), available at http://europa.eu/rapid/pressReleasesAction.do?reference=MEMO/09/491.

[52] European Parliament, Resolution on the Open Internet and Net Neutrality in Europe, P7_TA(2011)0511 (7 November 2011), available at www.europarl.europa.eu/sides/getDoc.do?pubRef=-//EP//TEXT+TA+P7-TA-2011-0511+0+DOC+XML+V0//EN.

[53] Body of European Regulators of Electronic Communications Press Release, BEREC *Preliminary Findings on Traffic Management Practices in Europe Show that Blocking of VoIP and P2P Traffic is Common, Other Practices Vary Widely* (9 March 2012), available at berec.europa.eu/doc/2012/TMI_press_release.pdf.

[54] Proposal for a Regulation of the European Parliament and of the Council of 11 September 2013 laying down measures concerning the European single market for electronic communications and to achieve a connected content, and amending Directives 2002/20/EC, 2002/21/EC and 2002/22/EC and Regulations (EC) 1211/2009 and (EU) 531/2012, COM(2013)627 final, art 23(1)–(3).

[55] See European Digital Rights Initiative and Access, *Comments to the Consolidated Text on Net Neutrality in the Regulation Concerning the Open Internet Proposed by the Latvian Presidency on February 25th 2015*, available at https://edri.org/files/20150225TSM.pdf.

[56] Regulation (EU) 2015/2120 of the European Parliament and of the Council of 25 November 2015 laying down measures concerning open Internet access and amending Directive 2002/22/EC on universal service and users' rights relating to electronic communications networks and services and Regulation (EU) 531/2012 on roaming on public mobile communications networks within the Union.

The net neutrality proposals, which have been agreed to by the three legislative institutions of the EU, comprise the following:

— End-users will have the right to access, distribute and use (legal) information and content, services and applications of their choice.[57]
— There must be equal treatment of all Internet traffic by Internet providers, without discrimination, restriction or interference, subject to 'reasonable traffic management measures' which cannot be based on commercial considerations.
— In particular, providers must not block, slow down, restrict, degrade or discriminate between specific content, applications or services, except as necessary for complying with legislation, for preserving the integrity and security of the network and for preventing and addressing network congestion.
— Specialised services are permitted for specific content, applications or services where optimisation is necessary, but they can only be offered by providers if network capacity is sufficient to provide them in addition to any Internet access services; they are not usable or to be offered as a replacement for Internet access services and must not be to the detriment of the availability or general quality of Internet access services for users.
— There are also a number of transparency measures governing what information providers must disclose in contracts.[58]
— There is also an assurance, that the quality of 'internet access services' will not be hampered by the provision of innovative services such as IPTV and telemedicine which share the same infrastructure; these 'specialised services' may only be offered where there is sufficient capacity for them, and their provision should not affect the availability or quality of generic Internet services.

These net neutrality provisions would address some of the gaps left by the existing law and regulation vis-à-vis Internet providers' network management. For instance, they would ensure that providers of 'internet access services' are not to block, slow down, degrade or discriminate against specific content, applications or services, and this would apply regardless of whether the provider had a dominant position or not.

Yet certain ambiguities and uncertainties still remain, especially regarding how the rules will be implemented in practice by the NRAs at the Member States' domestic level. Particular areas for concern remain around the specialised services (particularly when these can be said to be 'necessary'), zero-rating (which is not explicitly mentioned in the Regulation), and what precisely constitutes traffic

---

[57] ibid art 3.
[58] ibid art 4.

management and congestion.[59] It remains to be seen whether and how these terms will be clarified in guidance that BEREC should issue in the coming months.

This eventual approach taken by the EU to net neutrality seems user-centric, even at potential costs to business, and the willingness to impose further obligations on ISPs certainly cannot be termed a neoliberal move. However, much of the promise of this user-centricity will be tested in the national implementations. Certain Member States, such as the UK, have continued to pursue a 'light touch' approach to net neutrality couched in economic language.[60] The extent to which the UK would embrace a more rights-based approach in practice remains to be seen.

Moreover, the proposed Regulation as it stands, while it may be of benefit to European Internet users, may also be seen as a step 'too little, too late'. The extent to which it addresses content delivery networks is unclear; certain services provided by CDNs may fall into the category of 'specialised services' and therefore not be subject to net neutrality principles. This demonstrates some of the failings of regulation as an option for promoting user autonomy online: while net neutrality has been raised as an issue more than ten years ago, it has taken many years for the EU to arrive at this point where ex ante regulation is being considered, meanwhile technology and business practices have moved on. It would be politically difficult now to ban CDNs given their widespread use.

In addition, the Regulation is unlikely to promote large structural change in how the Internet is provided in the EU: corporate for-profit ISPs are likely to resist the attempt to impose further regulation, and albeit users will have more consumer rights against them, they are still likely to form a 'radical monopoly' over Internet provision.

VI. Technical Solutions

While it remains to be seen how adequate the net neutrality Regulation adopted by the EU is in terms of promoting user autonomy, users for some time have had more immediate solutions to the problems of private power posed by large for-profit entities providing Internet access. These technical solutions to some of the problems underlying the net neutrality debate present quicker and arguably more effective means of ensuring user autonomy and optimal online information flows. While each solution has its weaknesses, if used in combination, especially

---

[59] See H Jarvinen, 'Net Neutrality: The European Parliament has Decided Not to Decide', *EDRi*, 27 October 2015, available at https://edri.org/net-neutrality-european-parliament-decided-not-to-decide/.

[60] See CT Marsden, 'Net Neutrality Regulation in the UK: More Transparency and Switching' (2014) *Journal of Law and Economic Regulation*.

encryption with community mesh networks, then they can be effective to uphold user autonomy.

A. Data Encryption

The encryption of data that is being sent or requested over the Internet would challenge ISPs' efforts to monitor such data flows and act on the content of that data for non-net neutral purposes. Incidentally, data encryption may also facilitate free expression and the protection of privacy in the face of attempts at surveillance and censorship for whatever purpose (economic, ideological or other). However, data encryption may just facilitate an 'encryption arms race' between encryption and decryption technologies[61] and so not provide a total solution to net neutrality issues, especially the efficient delivery of content over the network. Encryption will also not mask the volume of the data being sent or received. There is also some evidence that certain ISPs will slow down all encrypted traffic. Encryption also does not ensure that the underlying infrastructure is managed, controlled or owned on a commons basis.

B. P2P File-Sharing

P2P files-haring networks have effectively been demonised as facilitating copyright infringement even though they are used for a variety of purposes, some of which infringe copyright but others of which are completely legitimate. However, as a result of lobbying by the content industry, access to them has been stymied through legislative means, 'voluntary' ISP self-regulation codes and court orders, and blocking and 'throttling' by ISPs. This is convenient for centralised content providers and ISPs since it shuts down what can be an effective and decentralised content distribution system via the Internet which might make CDNs redundant or at least less necessary to facilitate the effective delivery and storage of content. Indeed, P2P content distribution/streaming networks could ensure that bandwidth is no longer a major obstacle to effective services. They can do this by distributing content or fragments of content across the participating peers' computers, with the fragments being streamed in order to the requesting user according to the peers closest to the user, and in doing so can economise on bandwidth.[62] However, due to the lobbying and legal action against P2P networks, large content providers retain their control over online distribution and strengthen the case for online traffic prioritisation. The legal uncertainty around P2P networks also makes them a less attractive option for users.

---

[61] CT Marsden, 'Net Neutrality and Consumer Access to Content' (2007) 4(4) *SCRIPTed* 407, 422.
[62] I Ha, SS Wildman and JM Bauer, 'P2P, CDNs and Hybrid Networks: The Economics of Internet Video Distribution' (2010) 17(4) *International Telecommunications Policy Review* 1, 7.

C. Community Mesh Networks

A further technical solution to net neutrality issues, particularly control and monitoring by the ISP itself, can be found in mesh networking. Mesh networking consists of each node of the network relaying data for the network, and all nodes cooperating in the distribution of data in a peer-to-peer fashion. Mesh networks are usually (but not always) wireless and decentralised, and their main deployment so far has been in emergency situations to provide telecommunications infrastructure. Many mesh networks are community-based, thus owned and operated by their users, and so providing an alternative, commons-based P2P option to using ISPs' networks.

Community mesh networks can potentially advance user autonomy since they typically have no central regulatory authority and can be conceptualised as a private decentralised intranet: one must connect to the network in order to monitor its traffic, resisting censorship and surveillance by gatekeepers.[63] Thus, 'mesh networking represents an alternative perspective to traditional governance models based on top-down regulation and centralized control'.[64]

As regards the net neutrality debate, mesh networks represent a potential means of sidestepping reliance on the radical monopoly of centralised corporate ISPs for network access, and thus their network management practices.

Yet some of these mesh networks have also faced regulatory hurdles: in France they have been excluded from using public broadband networks financed by taxpayers by unaffordably high fees and faced restrictions on access to spectrum.[65] Nevertheless, community mesh networks do represent an alternative to the 'radical monopoly' of large, centralised for-profit ISPs providing Internet access in a possibly non-net neutral fashion.

VII. Conclusion

This chapter has examined the situation of corporate control over Internet provision through the lens of the net neutrality debate over the extent to which corporate ISPs should be permitted to manage the Internet traffic passing through their networks. The current legal and regulatory situation in the EU has been presented,

---

[63] Center for a Stateless Society, *Entrepreneurial Anti-Capitalism: Radical Mesh Networks* (29 May 2014), available at http://c4ss.org/content/27704.

[64] P De Filippi, 'It's Time to Take Mesh Networks Seriously (and Not Just for the Reasons You Think)', *Wired*, 2 January 2014, available at www.wired.com/opinion/2014/01/its-time-to-take-mesh-networks-seriously-and-not-just-for-the-reasons-you-think/.

[65] P De Filippi and F Treguer, 'Expanding the Internet Commons: The Subversive Potential of Wireless Community Networks' (2015) 6 *Journal of Peer Production*.

with the neoliberal, light-touch regulatory trends discouraging interference with telecoms markets and giving prominence to competition law as a principal tool for addressing whatever problems remain.

However, the rise of net neutrality as a subject of debate demonstrates the failings of this model from the perspective of users, since it would seem that only entities with market power acting in certain non-net neutral ways may warrant regulatory intervention. Furthermore, this model does not address the free expression problems created by non-net neutral conduct, nor the prospect of advancing digital divides and declining media pluralism in such circumstances. In addition, 'real' alternatives such as those incorporating P2P design are not supported by the current model, so Illich's 'radical monopoly' can be said to exist for the most part in Internet provision in the EU aside from a few European ISPs which are still (partially) state-owned, and even then there is a top-down, centralised approach to Internet provision in these public entities as well.

Although the EU's net neutrality Regulation is to be welcomed in terms of concentrating on the harm to Internet users that non-net neutral conduct can entail, they may be conceptualised as being 'too little, too late', given technology has moved on and processes which may not be covered by the Regulation, namely content delivery networks, have similar consequences to ISPs acting in a discriminatory way vis-à-vis traffic which is already on their own networks.

In order to address content delivery networks as well as ISPs' discrimination, interconnection agreements may provide another object for regulation.[66] Certainly these agreements could be subject to greater transparency as a first step.[67] More 'invasive' regulation could encompass obligations on ISPs, especially large ones, to accept traffic bound for their own customers, ie users without payment.[68]

If bandwidth and quality of service are issues for the delivery of content and services online, then there are other options involving decentralised peer to peer design. P2P file-sharing has been demonised in the public narrative as facilitating illegal conduct but this obscures the technical advantages of P2P design, as well as the user-autonomy-enhancing aspects. P2P solutions such as file-sharing services and mesh networks represent a potentially radical alternative for the Internet infrastructure which would resist economic or other concentrations of power, and thus enhance users' autonomy.

Ultimately though, it is this more radical solution of user-owned and -operated community mesh networks, together with encryption, which present the most autonomy-enhancing option for users.

---

[66] See J Speta, 'An Appropriate Interconnection Backstop' (2014) 12 *Journal on Telecommunications and High Technology Law* 113.

[67] D Clark and others, 'Interconnection in the Internet: Policy Challenges', 39th Research Conference on Communication, Information and Internet Policy, Arlington, September 2011.

[68] KD Werbach, 'Only Connect' (2007) 22(4) *Berkeley Technology Law Journal* 1233.

4

Dominance and Internet Search

Search is an especially important part of the Internet ecosystem, since it is one very important way in which information on the World Wide Web is made legible and findable for users. The rise of applications or 'apps' and online app stores for Internet-enabled mobile devices may be beginning to challenge search engines as a way of making sense of and finding information on the Web, but they do not (yet) encompass the entirety of that information, nor do they try to do so, although they are another gateway through which users can access information. In any event, large search engines have also developed their own apps, dulling this challenge to their primacy.

This chapter looks at search engines, their online markets and has a particular focus on US and EU market leader, Google.[1] Google is the focus since it has dominated online search (and its associated market of online advertising) over the last ten years in much of the EU, and accordingly has been the subject of a major competition investigation into the alleged abuse of its dominant position in online search and advertising markets. The effect of Google's information monopoly is more than just economic, but, as will be seen, these non-economic concerns are not addressed by competition law, nor other areas of the law—leaving a 'gap' where user autonomy is not adequately protected or promoted.

I. Problems in the Market for Search

Google, as a dominant search engine, presents various problems for online information flows. There are some 'classical' competition problems stemming from dominance, such as the potential leveraging and bundling of services, as well as some more novel issues, such as how competition law can interact with the use of supposedly 'neutral' algorithms and the relationship between the user data that is collected, the protection of that data and privacy, and competition in the market. However, an economically dominant, private, for-profit player such as Google can also use its dominant position in a way which has 'non-economic' consequences

---

[1] This chapter expands upon A Daly, 'Dominating Search: Google Before the Law' in R Konig and M Rasch (eds), *Society of the Query Reader* (Amsterdam, Institute of Network Cultures, 2014).

for users, inasmuch as users do not pay higher prices (especially since Google's search is offered free of charge to them, subsidised by advertising and data collection and analysis), but do experience issues of biased information filtering and infringements of their privacy and data protection which go beyond what competition law considers to be the economic realm.

A. Expansionist Tendencies

Google's expansionist tendencies have also been observed as problematic. Search is just one part of an ecosystem owned by the same company, and often products and services interact with each other. This gives rise to the potential for Google to leverage a dominant position in one market, such as search, into other markets in which it is active. This can harm Google's competitors at any part of the value chain economically.

However, there are also broader concerns about the emergence of an incredibly large for-profit entity such as Google. Google's core business may be online search and advertising but it has expanded into numerous other areas, from its acquisition of Internet of Things company Nest to the building of a fibre-optic network in parts of the US and its mass digitisation of books. Concerns are raised about the influence of this accumulation of power on the politics (and political economy) of information and technology, and society more generally. Furthermore, thanks to the 'invisible handshake' between data-gathering corporations such as Google and the nation-state, laid bare in Snowden's NSA revelations, large and pervasive entities such as Google are co-opted to monitor their users' conduct for the state's benefit, with more contextualisation provided by collecting data about users from Google's myriad products and services.

This acquisition of other companies in media and technology markets seems to have contributed to Google emerging as a leading player in online search and advertising. While EU and US authorities investigated two mergers involving Google, they were eventually approved. Yet some of Google's acquisitions which were either not scrutinised, or scrutinised but then approved, were subsequently the subject of competition investigations, such as YouTube and Android. US authorities are seen as having a record of being less suspicious of mergers which may lead to exclusionary effects than their EU counterparts due, inter alia, to a non-interventionist ideology coming from the neoliberal Chicago School and implemented during the Reagan administration,[2] but the adoption of the 'More Economic' approach in EU merger control can be seen as a move towards similar 'rigorous' economics-based merger analysis. The result of this is that in theory, conglomerate mergers in the EU will usually not give rise to anticompetitive

---

[2] EM Fox, 'US and European Merger Policy, Fault Lines and Bridges: Mergers that Create Incentives for Exclusionary Practices' (2002) 10 *George Mason Law Review* 471.

effects (according to this method of analysis) or these effects will be offset by 'efficiency gains', eg in the form of cost savings.[3]

Two major mergers involving Google were analysed in both the EU and US before eventually being approved: Google's acquisitions of DoubleClick and Motorola Mobility. In the DoubleClick merger, the European Commission found that Google and DoubleClick were not competing in the same markets despite both being active in Internet advertising. The US Federal Trade Commission (FTC) also approved the Google DoubleClick merger, but Commissioner Pamela Jones Harbor dissented from the majority view and expressed concerns about how Google's acquisition of data from DoubleClick as a result of the merger would affect the entire online market.[4] This criticism was echoed by the European Data Protection Supervisor, who believed that the Commission had given insufficient regard to this combination of datasets, with the possibility that the merged entity could provide new services not envisaged when the data was originally submitted by users, thereby 'neglecting the longer term impact on the welfare of millions of users'.[5] However, the European Commission's treatment of this merger demonstrated a lack of concern for privacy within the context of 'consumer welfare'—an approach which may have to be modified now in the wake of the EU's Charter of Fundamental Rights, and the possible constitutionalisation of competition law this may provoke.

The Motorola Mobility merger involved Google's purchase of a smartphone and tablet computer developer. In the Commission investigation, the danger was raised of Google's acquisition of Motorola Mobility and its patents allowing Google to engage in exclusionary conduct, thus strengthening its market power in mobile search and search advertising.[6] Specifically, this could be done by Google only licensing the patents it has gained from the merger to other mobile equipment manufacturers on the condition that they install Google's mobile services and potentially also forcing them to set the mobile services as default, or by offering the manufacturers more favourable terms for licensing the patents if they install Google's mobile services. This concern was dismissed, not because it was not a real fear, but because Google already had this capacity pre-merger to impose its own services on manufacturers and network operators through the licensing of its Android operating system, and in fact there are already agreements which force manufacturers which want to pre-install Google mobile services on the equipment

---

[3] O Budzinski and K Wacker, *The Prohibition of the Proposed Springer-Prosiebensat.1-Merger: How Much Economics in German Merger Control?*, University of Marburg Papers on Economics (2007), available at http://ssrn.com/abstract=976861.

[4] P Jones Harbour, *Dissenting Statement In the Matter of Google/DoubleClick*, FTC File No 071-0170 (2007) 4.

[5] European Data Protection Supervisor (EDPS), *Privacy and Competitiveness in the Age of Big Data: The Interplay Between Data Protection, Competition Law and Consumer Protection in the Digital Economy* (Preliminary Opinion), EDPS/2014/06 (2014) 30.

[6] Case COMP/M.6381 *Google/Motorola Mobility*, Commission Decision of 13 February 2012 [2012] OJ C75/01, 34.

to set Google search as the default search engine and pre-install a minimum suite of core Google mobile services.[7]

It seems that by the point of this merger, Google had already expanded sufficiently that even before the purchase of Motorola Mobility it had the ability to impose its own services on network operators and handset manufacturers, and so the effect of this further expansion was negligible on the power Google had already amassed. Google's activity in the device market will be discussed in more detail in chapter 5, but interestingly Google's use of the Motorola Mobility patents formed part of its settlement with the FTC.

Google's ever-expanding size and portfolio can be conceptualised as exactly the kind of private power accumulation which concerned the ordoliberals. Indeed, Google's vast (and ever-growing) concentration of power encompasses the political as well as the economic.[8] This influence may pose problems for the democratic process and democratic oversight over such an accumulation of power.

B. Access to Information

Search engines play a pivotal role in locating and filtering information relevant to users.[9] Yet both users and advertisers can face economic and non-economic problems with the way in which search engines operate as gatekeepers of information.

Access to information is a user problem since search engines are portals though which they experience the Web. If a user does a search, and information which (all things being equal) should come up in the results page does not appear, and the search engine has had an active role in ensuring that information does not appear, then this can be characterised as a censorship of sorts (or editorial control of another sort). Furthermore, even if certain information is not entirely blocked from the results pages, if it can be seen to be 'relevant' yet does not appear on the first page, or perhaps even on the first five pages, then it may effectively be unavailable to users who generally will not go beyond these first few pages of results, thus being relegated to the 'periphery'.[10] If the market for search engines is dominated by one entity or a small group of entities, as is the case with Google, then the user may not be able to obtain the results she wants, and have her searches restricted either according to the economic interests and/or the ideological bearing of the dominant player.

---

[7] ibid 35–37.

[8] C Fuchs, 'A Contribution to the Critique of the Political Economy of Google' (2011) 8(1) *Fast Capitalism*; T Hamburger and M Gold, 'Google, once disdainful of lobbying, now a master of Washington influence', *Washington Post*, 13 April 2014, available at www.washingtonpost.com/politics/how-google-is-transforming-power-and-politicsgoogle-once-disdainful-of-lobbying-now-a-master-of-washington-influence/2014/04/12/51648b92-b4d3-11e3-8cb6-284052554d74_story.html.

[9] N Elkin-Koren and EM Salzberger, *Law and Economics of Cyberspace: The Effects of Cyberspace on the Economic Analysis of Law* (Berlin, Edward Elgar, 2004) 71.

[10] MA Zook and M Graham, 'The Creative Reconstruction of the Internet: Google and the Privatization of Cyberspace and DigiPlace' (2007) 38(6) *Geoforum* 1322.

The problem that advertisers using search engines face is one of visibility: they want their products and services to be as visible as possible to users searching for relevant terms. However, there are commercially-driven reasons why Google might manipulate search results, especially the results comprising other entities' advertisements. Google has a host of other services apart from simple search, prominent among which are price comparison services. Google may want its own price comparison sites to appear higher in the results than those of its non-vertically integrated price comparison competitors. If the market is dominated by one player, as is the case with Google, then advertisers have no or little realistic choice of using other platforms.

C. Bias

Problems with bias in how search engines give their results have been identified in academic literature from computer science and politics. Search engines, including Google, like to claim that their results are generated in a 'technical' or 'mechanical' way and so are untainted by favouring certain results beyond their 'relevance' to the search, but the methods they use to determine results are designed in particular ways which have this effect, whether intentionally or not, and involve the value judgements of humans regarding how to collect and present the data.[11]

From a computer science perspective, Vaughan and Thelwell found that search engines are biased in favour of sites coming from the US (at least compared to the other countries examined in the study), and this was not to do with language (ie the use of English) but instead a site's 'visibility', namely the number of other sites that link to it seems to be a source of bias: in general, the more sites already indexed by the search engine that link to a site, the more of that site will be covered by the search engine.[12] Furthermore, Edelman's study of Google's search results suggests that Google has manually adjusted its own links to its other products and services so as to appear at the top of algorithmic search results.[13] In addition, Introna and Nissenbaum argue that search engines systematically exclude (both by design and accidentally) certain sites and certain types of sites in favour of others and systematically make some more prominent at the expense of others, which they argue is a political issue.[14]

While competitive pressures could limit search bias, it is particularly problematic for 'online information credibility and accessibility' where there is a dominant

[11] E Goldman, 'Search Engine Bias and the Demise of Search Engine Utopianism' (2006) *Yale Journal of Law and Technology* 111, 113; M Lao, *'Neutral' Search as a Basis for Antitrust Action?*, Harvard Journal of Law and Technology Occasional Paper Series (2013) 3.
[12] L Vaughan and M Thelwall, 'Search Engine Coverage Bias: Evidence and Possible Causes' (2004) 40(4) *Information Processing and Management* 693.
[13] B Edelman, *Hard-Coding Bias in Google Algorithmic Search Results* (15 November 2010), available at www.benedelman.org/hardcoding/.
[14] LD Introna and H Nissenbaum, 'Shaping the Web: Why the Politics of Search Engines Matter' (2000) 16(3) *Information Society* 169.

search engine leaving consumers without meaningful choices.[15] Certain manifestations of bias, such as the search engine favouring its own products in different markets, could constitute anticompetitive behaviour, although as will be seen later in this chapter, this is not a clear-cut issue. In any event, the problematic effects of bias, while not necessarily anticompetitive, are likely to be exacerbated by a concentrated market and a lack of real choice for users.

D. Privacy and Data Protection

Privacy concerns over users' information and search engines have become prominent in recent years, especially given the diversification of Google into other areas beyond search and advertising which allows it to collect an even larger about of data about users. This is also exacerbated by the Snowden revelations that the data collected by major Internet companies, including Google, can be accessed by government agencies, including those of foreign states such as the US's National Security Agency (NSA), without warrants being issued.

Google has been the subject of data protection concerns and regulatory action in various EU Member States.[16] In particular, Google's modification of its Privacy Policy in 2012 gave rise to a host of complaints and investigations by national data protection authorities in Europe.[17] The authorities in Spain and France have already issued Google with fines for using personal data collected from one of its services with its other services, due, inter alia, to Google not seeking adequate consent for its activities from these users.[18]

However, there is criticism of the level of fines that can be imposed on the finding of a data protection breach, namely that they are so low in level and not always enforced that large firms may find it more profitable to breach the laws and pay the fines rather than to follow the law in the first place.[19] Indeed, much higher fines (more in line with fines for anti-competitive conduct) form part of the new General Data Protection Regulation.

---

[15] E Goldman, 'Revisiting Search Engine Bias' (2011) 38(1) *William Mitchell Law Review* 96, 101.

[16] N Lomas, 'Google Pays Another Tiny Fine in Europe, $1.4M, for Street View Privacy Concerns', *TechCrunch*, 4 April 2014, available at http://techcrunch.com/2014/04/04/google-street-view-fine/; Z Whittaker, 'Germany Fines Google for "Unprecedented" Street View Wi-Fi Data Breach', *ZDNet*, 22 April 2013, available at www.zdnet.com/germany-fines-google-for-unprecedented-street-view-wi-fi-data-breach-7000014337/.

[17] P Sayer, 'Google Must Defend Privacy Policies to 6 European Agencies', *TechHive*, 7 April 2013, available at www.techhive.com/article/2033375/google-must-defend-privacy-policies-to-6-european-agencies.html?tk=rel_news.

[18] B Manolea, 'Google was Fined by French and Spanish Data Protection Authorities', *European Digital Rights Initiative*, 15 January 2014, available at http://edri.org/google-fined-french-spanish-data-protection-authorities/.

[19] P Ducklin, 'How Effective are Data Breach Penalties? Are Ever-Bigger Fines Enough?', *Nakedsecurity*, 26 April 2013, available at http://nakedsecurity.sophos.com/2013/04/26/how-effective-are-data-protection-regulations/.

The US approach to data protection has generally been one of self-regulation, although growing concerns around data protection have led the FTC to respond from a consumer protection perspective, such as its settlements with Facebook, Google and Twitter over consumer privacy, its lobbying for legislative intervention regarding 'data brokers', ie entities which compile and trade data about consumers, and its forceful push of the 'do not track' mechanism.[20] Nevertheless, the lack of EU-US convergence was thrown into sharp relief during the EU's process of formulating its new General Data Protection Regulation, which has been subjected to an unprecedented amount of lobbying from the US in order that the final text of the Regulation did not subject US companies handling EU citizens' data to what they saw as overly strenuous conditions.[21] The divergence between the EU and US approaches to data privacy has also been evidenced by the recent Court of Justice of the European Union (CJEU) decision in *Schrems*, invalidating the 'Safe Harbor' agreement facilitating personal data transfers from the EU to the US due to the inadequacy of US data protection practices.[22]

The current configuration of incentives for Internet companies is detrimental to users' privacy and data protection since it encourages the collection and monetisation of their information, alongside the 'trade' of these protections by users for free services.[23] Indeed, this problematic scenario was mentioned by the European Data Protection Supervisor in the Preliminary Opinion on the interplay between data protection, competition and consumer protection in the context of Big Data mentioned earlier. He considered that the collection and control of very large amounts of personal data are a source of market power for large players in European Internet markets, yet access to these datasets by competitors may be stymied by data protection rules that require data subjects' consent for such a new use (or adherence to other legitimate grounds), and 'this is a substantial hurdle under data protection law'.[24] Thus, adherence to data protection law may facilitate what would otherwise be anticompetitive conduct over the use and control of users' personal data.

II. Search Engines and Market Developments

Search engines initially appeared soon after the creation of the World Wide Web as a means to organise and catalogue websites and information. The experience

---

[20] T Vega and E Wyatt, 'US agency seeks tougher consumer privacy rules', *New York Times*, 26 March 2012, available at www.nytimes.com/2012/03/27/business/ftc-seeks-privacy-legislation.html?pagewanted=all&_r=0.

[21] 'US Privacy Groups Believe US Officials Lobby to Weaken EU Privacy', *European Digital Rights Intiative*, 13 February 2013, available at http://history.edri.org/book/export/html/3215.

[22] Case C-362/14 *Schrems v Data Protection Commissioner*, CJEU, 6 October 2015.

[23] S Vezzoso, 'The Interface between Competition Policy and Data Protection' (2012) 3(3) *Journal of Competition Law and Practice* 225.

[24] EDPS, *Privacy and Competitiveness in the Age of Big Data* (n 5) 31.

with the initial search engines during the 1990s and early 2000s demonstrated a competitive market during this period, characterised by first mover advantages which declined over time and whose continuance were dependent on innovating to provide a superior product, suggesting low barriers to entry and strong competition.[25] Indeed, the last two decades have seen the rise and fall of many players in the search engine market.[26] This suggests that the markets for search engines are characterised by Schumpeter's 'creative destruction', and that competition is for the market rather than within the market.[27]

Furthermore, search engine markets can be described as 'two-sided'. On one side are Internet users searching for information on the Web, and on the other side are advertisers which pay for their adverts to be displayed in search results. The largest, generalised search engines, including Google, do not charge users to use the service, and instead their revenue comes solely from the advertisers. In addition, the market for search engines has been observed to exhibit network effects which potentially encourage concentration.[28] An increase in users adds value for advertisers since more people will see their advertisements, and an increase in advertisers using the platform causes users to experience increased value as well since each additional advertiser hands over more funding to the search engine to provide free services for users, as well as the continuing development and refinement of the search engine itself.

Although the search engine market appeared to be competitive in the 1990s and into the early 2000s, this would no longer seem to be the case. The market appears to be more consolidated now than before and there are various reasons for this development from competition to Google's dominance. Van Couvering posits that this concentration is due to search provision being capital-intensive, requiring large investment in hardware, software and connection capacity.[29] With the huge growth of the Internet since the 1990s, perhaps at one time search engines could be set up and operated without such large capital costs, but search engines currently need this investment in capacity in order to get off the ground. Furthermore, the introduction of 'paid-performance ads' (the paid advertising that appears in specific parts of search engine result pages when users search for certain terms) has strengthened the position of search providers since they provide this service which targets advertising more precisely to consumers' interests than the blanket advertising which was previously used, and search engines control

---

[25] N Gandal, *The Dynamics of Competition in the Internet Search Engine Market*, University of California Berkeley Competition Policy Center Working Paper CPC01-17 (2001), available at http://papers.ssrn.com/sol3/papers.cfm?abstract_id=502823.

[26] A Diker Vanberg, 'From Archie to Google: Search Engine Providers and Emergent Challenges in Relation to EU Competition Law' (2012) 3(1) *European Journal for Law and Technology*.

[27] PA Geroski, 'Competition in Markets and Competition for Markets' (2003) 3(3) *Journal of Industry, Competition and Trade* 151.

[28] KL Devine, 'Preserving Competition in Multi-Sided Innovative Markets: How Do You Solve a Problem Like Google?' (2008) 10(1) *North Carolina Journal of Law and Technology* 59

[29] E Van Couvering, *New Media? The Political Economy of Internet Search Engines* (International Association of Media and Communications Researchers, Porto Alegre, July 2004).

the paid-performance advertising networks Google AdWords and Yahoo! Search Marketing.[30]

In this context, Google emerging as a market leader can be attributed to its early innovation in providing a 'better' search service than that which was currently on offer to users, through developing a better search algorithm which relied on reputation (measured by links) as well as text matching to provide the most relevant results. Google also built on its increasing experience of search to deliver even more relevant advertising through more precise paid results than other search engines had been offering.[31]

This observation as to the development of paid-performance ads and the more precise targeted advertising implicitly suggests the growing importance of user data collection by search engines, which also presents problems for privacy and data protection, as mentioned above. The collection of information about users and their behaviour is also a barrier to entry in the online search and advertising markets since this accumulation of data is used to entrench the position of the leading search engines. Although the market for search in the past was characterised by low entry barriers and frequent new entrants, the current state of the market alongside the pivotal importance of the collection, analysis and sale of user data demonstrates that entry barriers are higher than they were previously.[32]

Furthermore, Google has been able to entrench its leading position in the market for search also due to offering other 'free' services to users, such as Gmail and Google Docs.[33] In this way, users are introduced into the Google ecosystem, giving Google a huge amount more data about its users and their preferences which it can then use to improve its search function, obtain more opportunities to target advertisements more accurately, and reinforce its commercial strength.

III. EU Investigation into Google

The initial legal solution to any problems arising from Google's dominant position is found in competition law, since unlike ISPs discussed in the previous chapter, search engines are not subject to any sector-specific ex ante regulation in the EU. Google has been investigated for alleged anticompetitive conduct in both the US and EU regarding the functioning of its search and advertising business.

The European Commission opened its investigation into Google in November 2010 for an alleged abuse of dominant position contrary to Treaty on the

---

[30] ibid 17.

[31] Devine, 'Preserving Competition in Multi-Sided Innovative Markets' (n 28) 7.

[32] N Newman, 'Search, Antitrust and the Economics of the Control of User Data' (2014) 30(3) *Yale Journal on Regulation* 10.

[33] M Cave and HP Williams, 'Google and European Competition Law', 39th Research Conference on Communication, Information and Internet Policy, Arlington, September 2011, at 4.

Functioning of the European Union, Article 102.[34] This investigation is the largest and most significant competition investigation into Google to date and is still ongoing at the time of writing.

A. Complaints Against Google

The European Commission's investigation was launched in 2010 after complaints were received from Google's competitors (price comparison site Foundem, ejustice.fr (a French legal search engine) and German shopping site Ciao (owned by Microsoft), whose services are known as 'vertical search') that Google was treating them unfavourably in its search results (both 'organic' or unpaid results, and the 'sponsored' or paid results), and was discriminating in favour of its own versions of these services. In 2012, the Commission issued a communication inviting Google to offer commitments to remedy the Commission's concerns about anticompetitive behaviour.

There appear to be four parts to the Commission's investigation into Google:

1. Google is alleged to have lowered the rank of the unpaid search results of services which competed with it (in particular, vertical search services providing users with specific online content such as price comparisons), and to have accorded preferential placement to the results of its own versions of these services in order to foreclose its competitors.[35]
2. Google is alleged to have lowered the 'Quality Score' for the sponsored links of such competing vertical search engines (the Quality Score influences the likelihood of an advert being displayed by Google and the ranking of that advert in the search results, and is a factor in determining the price paid by advertisers to Google).
3. Google is alleged to have imposed exclusivity obligations on its advertising partners which prevented them from placing certain types of competing adverts on their own websites with the aim of foreclosing competing search engines (it is also alleged that Google imposed this obligation on computer and software vendors).
4. Google is alleged to have placed restrictions on the use of online advertising campaign data by competing advertising platforms.

The first two categories of complaint will be the focus of this analysis since they relate directly to how Google operates its user-facing search engine, as opposed to the latter two complaints which concern how Google operates its online advertising services. In addition, these latter two complaints have been addressed by commitments from Google that it will remove exclusivity requirements in search

---

[34] European Commission, *Antitrust: Commission Probes Allegations of Antitrust Violations by Google* IP/10/1624 (30 November 2010).

[35] This was also one of the complaints against Google prompting the FTC investigation.

advertising agreements with publishers and it will remove restrictions on the ability for search advertising campaigns to be run on competing platforms.[36]

B. Is Google Behaving Anticompetitively in Europe?

(i) Relevant Market and Market Share

Traditional competition analysis first requires that the relevant market is defined. Some guidance on market definition can be provided from the European Commission's two merger decisions involving Google, as well as the current investigation.

In the EU, markets are defined based on the substitutability of the product or service at hand from the consumer's point of view and geographical area. However, in the new media and technology environment, market definition has been recognised as being a more complex endeavour, both due to the transnational nature of digitised products and services proving challenging for geographic definition, as well as the actual conceptual defining of the products and services at hand, along with their substitutability. Furthermore, elements such as 'free pricing' and the existence of a two-sided market which are common on the Internet complicate matters even more, for instance making the test for defining the market (the small but significant non-transitory increase in price (SSNIP) in the EU) more complex.

As mentioned earlier in this chapter, Google's online search and advertising business can be conceptualised as a two-sided market. However, some attempts to define this partially zero-price two-sided market have run into problems, for instance in *Kinderstart v Google*,[37] where the US District Court did not consider 'search' as a relevant market as it was a free services for consumers.[38] Yet, this can be criticised as a concentration only on price and not on the other, non-price measures of competition, such as product attributes, service and innovation—or quality. Antitrust analysis can also consider the free product together with its 'companion' products which make money and in practice subsidise the free offering.[39] Changes to practices around the free product can affect the benefits or costs for the companion.

There are differing views on search and advertising substitutability: Manne has implicitly criticised a narrow market definition in this case, by naming alternatives to search engines from an advertiser's point of view as ranging from advertising in print publications, television, or using social networking sites for promotion.[40]

---

[36] European Commission, *Antitrust: Commission Obtains from Google Comparable Display of Specialised Search Rivals*, IP/14/116 (5 February 2014). However, at the time of writing, the Commission has issued a supplementary Statement of Objections regarding Google's advertising practices so the matter may not be over yet. European Commission, *Antitrust: Commission takes further steps in investigations alleging Google's comparison shopping and advertising-related practices breach EU rules*, IP/16/2532 (14 July 2016).

[37] *Kinderstart v Google*, 2007 WL 831806 (ND Cal).

[38] The Court also did not recognise the market for search advertising as a relevant market.

[39] DS Evans, 'Antitrust Economics of Free' (2011) *Competition Policy International* 17.

[40] G Manne, 'The Problem of Search Engines as Essential Facilities: An Economics and Legal Assessment' in B Szoka and A Marcus (eds), *The Next Digital Decade: Essays on the Future of the Internet* (Washington DC, TechFreedom, 2011) 419.

Some research suggests that for advertisers, there is a degree of substitutability between online and offline advertising.[41] In any event, in the EU it is demand substitutability which is of the utmost importance.[42] The issue of market definition has come up in the merger cases involving Google. In the Commission's scrutiny of the DoubleClick merger, it was suggested that the relevant market should encompass the provision of advertising space in all types of media and not just online, but the Commission in its decision rejected that definition given that there is a general perception that online and offline advertising are different markets. In the later *Microsoft/Yahoo!* decision, the Commission followed its analysis in DoubleClick and decided that online advertising was its own separate market from offline advertising.[43]

In the context of Google's search engine operating in a two- or multi-sided market, there are at least two approaches that could be taken to search and advertising in a competition investigation: they can either be viewed together as part of a 'business ecosystem', or the investigation can be focussed on one of the products/services and take the complementary product into consideration when assessing market power.[44] The former approach ensures that all competitive constraints are taken into account, while the latter approach minimises errors such as false negatives and false positives. For multi-sided platform businesses, the preferred approach is to recognise that competition takes place with other multi-sided platforms, and the market consists of these firms as well as firms operating on each side of the platform which impose competitive constraints. Indeed, the European Commission took this approach in its *Microsoft Yahoo!* Decision, where it defined the relevant market as 'online search and advertising'.

The other markets of relevance are those for video streaming and vertical search (which may be further subdivided). Another relevant market may actually be that for user data, or some variant such as 'monetisation of users' information to advertisers'.[45]

Google is the market leader in the overall EU market(s) for online search and advertising, based on either proportion of searches that are conducted through Google (for no monetary cost to users) or its proportional share of advertising revenue (which is where Google gets its funds).[46] The company's market share

---

[41] A Goldfarb and C Tucker, 'Search Engine Advertising: Channel Substitution When Pricing Ads to Content' (2011) 57(3) *Management Science* 458.

[42] European Commission, Notice on the definition of relevant market for the purposes of Community competition law [1997] OJ C372/03, para 14.

[43] Case COMP/M.5727 *Microsoft/Yahoo!*, Commission Decision of 18 February 2010.

[44] Evans, 'Antitrust Economics of Free' (n 39) 18–23.

[45] F Thepot, 'Market Power in Online Search and Social Networking: A Matter of Two-Sided Markets' (2013) 36(2) *World Competition* 195, 218.

[46] There are different methods of calculating shares of the search engine market in Europe, which are subject to various criticisms, but Google seems to come out in all of them as possessing a dominant position in this market.

in Europe is around 90 per cent,[47] which would be classified as 'near monopoly' according to the Commission's past practice.

(ii) Competitive Constraints

Google likes to claim that its competitors are only a click away when on the defensive from allegations that it operates an abusive monopoly. Google does face competition from other general search engines offered by Bing and Yahoo, as well as subject-specific vertical search engines and video streaming services. Nevertheless, there are various barriers to entry for new potential competitors and barriers to expansion for current competitors, which suggest that Google does have market power as well as having a leading market share.

Two- or multi-sided markets such as those in which Google operates usually exhibit features such as network effects and externalities which contribute to the establishment of market power. Furthermore, the enormous amount of user data gathered and analysed in the functioning of Google's search service creates significant barriers to entry by giving Google advantages that cannot be replicated by potential entrants and it allows Google to move easily into neighbouring markets such as vertical search.[48] Due to Google's advanced algorithm, portfolio of related products and services, and its accumulation of user data across these products and services, it would be difficult for a completely new entrant to provide services as advanced as Google's.

A greater threat to Google may come from its established rivals, but in the absence of them developing services, particularly search, as effective as Google's, which they have not managed to do so far, then it is unlikely they will overtake Google. In the context of Internet markets characterised by creative destruction and platform competition, it might be an entity which is not currently competing with Google in the markets already defined which actually may pose the largest threat to Google. In that case, other vertically integrated online platform operators such as Facebook (which itself has a very large repository of very personalised information about its users and their preferences) and Apple may actually be more of a threat to Google rather than the other search engine providers. Facebook had developed its own Graph Search product, which integrated Bing's general search engine with other results based on information in a Facebook user's social network connections.[49] This did provide a potential competitive constraint on Google's search and advertising ecosystem, but Facebook seems now to have

---

[47] StatCounter Global Stats, *Top 5 Desktop, Tablet and Console Search Engines in Europe from 2013 to 2016*, available at http://gs.statcounter.com/#search_engine-eu-yearly-2013-2016.

[48] N Newman, *The Cost of Lost Privacy: Search, Antitrust and the Economics of the Control of User Data* (2013), available at http://ssrn.com/abstract=2265026; N Zingales, 'Product Market Definition in Online Search and Advertising' (2013) 9(1) *Competition Law Review* 28.

[49] C Smith, 'Facebook Graph Search: how the industry rates it', *Guardian*, 16 January 2013, available at www.theguardian.com/media-network/2013/jan/16/facebook-graph-search.

ceased its partnership with Bing and instead has focussed on internal Facebook content for its search service, thereby removing it from direct competition with Google.

In light of the demise of Facebook's Graph Search, Google still has market power for the foreseeable future in the online search market. Google is highly likely to be monitoring its rivals' developments closely in order to respond to any competition, actual or potential, and ensure that it is doing its utmost to secure its existing dominance. Given that Google's market share in the EU has not varied by any great degree over the last few years, and is not expected to do so any time soon, despite the potential competition, Google still has a dominant position.

Google faces more competitive constraints in online advertising markets, with Facebook gaining market share particularly in mobile advertising markets.[50] However, Google's inclusion of exclusionary terms in contracts with advertisers does suggest that, despite these constraints, Google still has market power in these markets as it is able to operate independently of its competitors.

Thus, while Google experiences competitive constraints from other online platforms such as Facebook, its achievement and maintenance of a dominant position in the EU market for online search (and advertising) over a period of time suggests that Google does have a dominant position in the market for online search at least, and possibly also in the market(s) for online search and advertising.

(iii) Abuse of Dominance?

The core claim of the Commission's investigation is that Google is favouring its own services in how it displays search results and how it organises its paid advertising, and is acting in a way that is prejudicial to the providers of services competing with Google. There is evidence that Google is engaging at least in the first practice, that of prioritising its downstream services over those of competitors in the unpaid or 'organic' search results. There is also evidence of Google's competitors, such as Yahoo and Bing, doing exactly the same thing with their results,[51] although Yahoo and Bing are not dominant entities, and thus do not have the same obligations regarding 'fair play'.[52]

The issue of whether Google is acting anticompetitively in practice questions whether Google should be allowed to control how it organises its search results. If Google is acting abusively in the instances mentioned above, it would be doing

---

[50] 'Driven by Facebook and Google, Mobile Ad Market Soars 105% in 2013', *eMarketer*, 19 March 2014, available at www.emarketer.com/Article/Driven-by-Facebook-Google-Mobile-Ad-Market-Soars-10537-2013/1010690.

[51] B Edelman and B Lockwood, *Measuring Bias in 'Organic' Web Search* (19 January 2011), available at www.benedelman.org/searchbias/.

[52] In competition law, the dominant entity in a market has a special responsibility not to allow its conduct to impair genuine undistorted competition, as stated by the CJEU in Case 322/81 *Michelin v Commission* [1983] ECR 3461. Similar language was used by the US Supreme Court in *Eastman Kodak Co v Image Technical Services, Inc*, 504 US 451 (1991).

so in a way to foreclose competitors horizontally since it is favouring its own upstream or downstream services. Yet, for any finding of anticompetitive behaviour by Google on this count, evidence must be adduced to show that Google is actually downgrading the results of its competitors. However, Google has denied that it does this, and claimed that its vertical search competitors' results in Google's search are not among the high rankings since they themselves copy most of their data from other websites.[53] Looking specifically at existing abuses of a dominant position, it is unclear what 'head' Google's alleged conduct would fall under.

(iv) Discrimination

The cases so far where non-pricing discrimination has been recognised have involved a dominant firm favouring some third party customers over other third party customers, which is not the case with Google.[54] There appears to be no general duty for vertically integrated firms such as Google not to discriminate against downstream competitors of their subsidiaries, especially if the circumstances do not amount to a case of refusal to deal or margin squeeze, and indeed, this kind of discriminatory conduct may well 'more often than not … [constitute] an expression of competition on the merits'.[55]

(v) Refusal to Deal

If Google's conduct can be considered an anticompetitive refusal to deal, then Google's competitors would have to argue that Google's general search engine constitutes an essential facility to which they require access otherwise they would be unable to run their services, and that by refusing them access, Google is harming competition in the vertical search markets and harming consumer welfare by reducing consumer choice.

First, a refusal to deal would need to be established by Google's competitors. According to the Commission, there does not need to be 'actual refusal' on behalf of the dominant entity, and instead 'constructive refusal' will suffice, which can include 'unduly delaying or otherwise degrading the supply of the product or involve the imposition of unreasonable conditions in return for the supply'.[56] Here, Google is not refusing outright to deal with its vertical search competitors: it is including results from their services in its general search results. It could be argued that the placing of Google's competitors' results less favourably than Google's own results could be characterised as 'undu[e] delaying or otherwise degrading the

---

[53] S van Loon, 'The Power of Google: First Mover Advantage or Abuse of a Dominant Position' in A Lopez-Tarruella (ed), *Google and the Law* (Berlin, Springer, 2012) 30.
[54] P Ibanez Colomo, 'Exclusionary Discrimination Under Article 102 TFEU' (2014) 51(1) *Common Market Law Review* 141.
[55] ibid.
[56] ibid para 79.

supply'. However, merely placing competitors' results less prominently on the page than Google's own results may be insufficient to establish an undue delaying or other kind of degradation of the 'supply' of search results, particularly if the competitors' search results are still available on the first page of Google's general search results. If these results appear on page 10 of the results, then the argument would be stronger that Google's treatment of these results is a constructive refusal to deal, especially if they are 'relevant' to the search term entered.

In any event, it seems that what is happening here is that Google is refusing to deal with vertical competitors on the terms they want, not refusing to deal with them entirely, and Google's conduct could only be seen as a constructive refusal to deal if, all things being equal, the vertical search engines' results would be 'relevant' to a particular search term but they are not appearing on the first page of Google's search results.

Nevertheless, even if this can be conceptualised as a constructive refusal to deal, Google's competitors must also fulfil three other criteria:

— the refusal relates to a product or service that is objectively necessary to be able to compete effectively on a downstream market;
— the refusal is likely to lead to the elimination of effective competition on the downstream market; and
— the refusal to likely to lead to consumer harm.[57]

First, regarding the objective necessity or indispensability of inclusion in Google's general search results, this goes beyond a 'mere' dominant position in an upstream market, and the input to which access is sought must be incapable of being duplicated or could only be duplicated with great difficulty.[58] This does not appear to be the case with Google's general search: Google has competitors in online search and advertising markets so there are alternative 'inputs' for Google's vertical search competitors. Furthermore, users can access their sites by typing in their web addresses rather than searching through Google, and it is open to them to advertise their services elsewhere, for instance offline, with information about their web address. In addition, they can create 'apps' for use with tablets and smartphones which entail that users can find their services without going through Google's general web search service.

Furthermore, it seems that in practice Google's conduct has not eliminated competition in the vertical search markets: Google's competitors have remained in operation since the Commission opened the investigation into Google. Whether Google's conduct is 'liable' to eliminate such competition is more debatable,[59] but

---

[57] European Commission, *Guidance on the Commission's Enforcement Priorities in Applying Article 82 EC Treaty to Abusive Exclusionary Conduct by Dominant Undertakings* [2009] OJ C45/7, para 81.
[58] Case C-7/97 *Oscar Bronner v Mediaprint* [1998] ECR I-7791.
[59] Case C-95/04 *British Airways v Commission* [2007] ECR I-2331.

would probably depend upon the actual placing of the rivals' results, ie whether they were still on the front page, or on a later page.

In any event, it is unclear what consumer harm is suffered via Google's conduct, since results from vertical search competitors are still being displayed in Google's general search results. Some degree of competition still exists in these markets and consumers still have a choice of products and services, as far as competition law is concerned. Thus it seems that the conditions for a refusal to deal have not been definitively fulfilled.

It is possible that the 'refusal to deal' may actually concern access to the user data that Google has amassed, with the claim that this itself is an 'indispensable' for Google's competitors such as Microsoft or the vertical search engines to provide their services. Vast accumulations of such data have been recognised as a possible essential facility by the European Data Protection Supervisor, with a refusal to supply access to it constituting a possible abuse of dominance.[60] Yet, even if Google has amassed more user data than its rivals, in practice these other services have not closed down as a result of not having access to this data. Moreover, the other services are also likely to be amassing data about their users. Thus, it seems that the user data here is also not an essential facility.

(vi) Tying

Another line of argumentation would be that Google is abusing its dominance in the market for online search to leverage its dominance into other markets, such as the market for price comparison sites and flight/travel search.

It is certainly true that Google groups its services together and encourages users to use its portfolio of services through default settings and prominent placement of links to these other services. However, for tying to be abusive, certain requirements must be met: the undertaking must be dominant in the tying product market; the tying product and the tied product are two distinctive products; and the tying practice is likely to lead to anticompetitive foreclosure.[61] Here, Google does have a dominant position in the tying product market: general online search (and advertising). The tying and the tied products also appear to be distinctive even if closely related—separate markets can be defined for general search services and specific vertical search services. The third requirement, however, would seem not to be fulfilled, that the tying is likely to lead to anticompetitive foreclosure, since it is still possible for users to use another competing search service through their browser or download another search app on mobile devices, as well as scroll down Google's results to use an alternative vertical search service to those offered by Google. Furthermore, it is unclear whether, assuming Google's vertical search results are identified as being from Google, users are in some way harmed by these results.

---

[60] EDPS, *Privacy and Competitiveness in the Age of Big Data* (n 5) 31.
[61] European Commission, *Guidance on the Commission's Enforcement Priorities* (n 57) para 50.

The *Microsoft* case seemed to add a fourth requirement for tying, which was that the dominant entity did not give consumers a choice to obtain the tying product without the tied product.[62] This potential fourth requirement could prove even more problematic to finding Google has abused its dominant position, since users are not usually obliged to use Google's vertical search services if they use Google's general search. Some results from Google's vertical search services may be displayed when a user searches for particular terms using the general search engine but they are certainly not, for instance, required to click on these results in order to see the general search results, and will also see results from vertical search competitors.

Moreover, even if this conduct amounts to tying, Google may argue that it has an 'objective justification' for what it is going, that through its newer services and its integration of these with its older services it is offering 'richer, more-responsive and varied forms of information', ie a better, improved, more relevant service to its users.[63] If what Google has been doing can be characterised thus, then this may result in Google having an objective justification for its behaviour.

Indeed, one of the conclusions of the FTC's investigation into Google in the US, which ultimately found Google was not abusing its dominant position, was that the FTC found evidence that Google adopted design changes to its search results page (which displayed its vertical search results more prominently and had the effect of pushing the organic search links further down the page) primarily to improve the quality of its search product and the overall user experience,[64] following precedents such as *Kodak*[65] and *IBM*.[66] Although Google's vertical search competitors may have lost sales as a result of this improvement, this was just a normal part of a fierce competitive process, and the outcome for users was more directly relevant information for their search queries.

There is no clear equivalent precedent to *Kodak* and *IBM* on this matter in EU law. Recent CJEU case law is conflicting on the extent to which EU law employs an 'effects-based approach' to exclusionary abuses of dominance coupled with an 'efficiency' defence: such an approach seems apparent in *Post Danmark*,[67] but the subsequent *Intel* decision seems to represent a divergent approach.[68]

---

[62] Commission Decision 2007/53/EC *Microsoft* [2007] OJ L32/23, upheld on appeal Case T-201/04 *Microsoft Corporation v Commission* [2007] ECR II-3601.

[63] G Manne, 'Google isn't "Leveraging Dominance", It's Fighting to Avoid Obsolescence', *Truth on the Market*, 12 March 2012, available at http://truthonthemarket.com/2012/03/12/google-isnt-leveraging-its-dominance-its-fighting-to-avoid-obsolescence/.

[64] Federal Trade Commission, *Statement Regarding Google's Search Practices, In the Matter of Google Inc*, FTC File No 111-0163 (3 January 2013).

[65] *Berkey Photo v Eastman Kodak*, 603 F.2d 263 (2d Cir. 1979).

[66] *California Computer Products v IBM*, 613 F.2d 727 (1979).

[67] Case C-209/10 *Post Danmark A/S v Konkurrenceradet* [2012] ECR I-0000, para 20–22; M Marquis and E Rousseva, 'Hell Freezes Over: A Climate Change for Assessing Exclusionary Conduct under Article 102 TFEU' (2013) 4(1) *Journal of European Competition Law and Practice* 32.

[68] P Nihoul, 'The Ruling of the General Court in Intel: Towards the End of an Effect-based Approach in European Competition Law?' (2014) 5(8) *Journal of European Competition Law and Practice* 521.

Overall, it is unclear whether the conditions for tying have been found regarding Google's general search and its vertical search subsidiaries.

(vii) Sui Generis *Abuse*

It seems highly unclear whether Google's conduct falls into one of the established categories for an abuse of dominance. Yet the examples of abuse given in TFEU, Article 102 are not exhaustive:[69] it is possible that the Commission considers Google's conduct to be a new kind of abuse of dominance. If this is the case, it is unclear from the Commission's public statements so far what this new kind of abuse is. Since the Commission has now opened a formal investigation into Google's practices, more information on possible *sui generis* abuse may be revealed during its course. If so, this may also open up more possibilities for Google to challenge the Commission's application of competition law before the EU courts.

C. Google's Commitments

The saga between Google and the Commission regarding the first two complaints detailed above has been lengthy and drawn out. The Commission has twice rejected offers from Google to change its behaviour before seeming to accept Google's current proposal in early 2014, yet bowing to lobbying pressure later that year in appearing to reject the third proposal.

Google's first proposal to the Commission in early 2013 to remedy its behaviour appeared to include an offer to label its own services in search results in order to distinguish them from its competitors' and to provide links to rival services. The offer was criticised by Foundem because it did not address the deeper problem of how Google determined the 'relevance' of links to search queries, especially when its competitors' services were involved.[70]

The second proposal from Google came later in 2013,[71] which involved more detailed labeling of Google's own services in order that they would not be confused with generic search results, and links to rival services in 'a manner to make users clearly aware of these alternatives'. In response to Google's offer, FairSearch (a lobby group comprising many of Google's search rivals) commissioned a survey with the aim of finding the likely impact of these proposals on actual Internet users, in particular testing the extent to which users were likely to click on any of the three rival links and whether they understood and recognised the

---

[69] Case 6/72 *Continental Can v European Commission* [1973] ECR 215, para 26; Case C-280/08 *Deutsche Telekom v European Commission* [2010] ECR I-9555, para 173.

[70] K Fiveash, 'Google's Euro antitrust offer: Fine! We'll link to our search rivals', *The Register*, 25 April 2013, available at www.theregister.co.uk/2013/04/25/ec_gives_google_rivals_one_month_to_market_test_search_tweaks/.

[71] Google, *Commitments in Case COMP/C-3/39.740 Foundem and others* (21 October 2013), available at www.consumerwatchdog.org/resources/googlesettlment102113.pdf.

different parts of Google's proposed search results page, ie the labeling and descriptions.[72] The survey found that 'only a modest number' of users would click on one of the rival links and that users were confused about the difference between Google's vertical search results and the other results.[73] The conclusion was that if Google presented links to its rivals in a relatively 'neutral' fashion, ie in a comparable way in terms of appearance and placement on the page, then this would result in higher click through rates for the competitors' links. However, the second proposal commitments offered by Google did not achieve this and so were not 'likely to command materially increased consumer attention or restore competition for [Google's] rivals'.[74] In the end, the European Commission again rejected Google's offer.

Google's third and final offer comprised: informing users via a label that Google's own specialised services are promoted; Google separating its specialised service results from the other search results in order to make clear the difference between them and 'normal' results; and Google displaying 'prominent' links to three rival specialised search services from a pool of 'eligible competitors', which would be displayed clearly to users in a 'comparable' way to how Google displays its own services.[75] Screenshots provided by the Commission showed how the search results pages would look, which suggested that rivals' results would be positioned in a way that would encourage more user engagement than the previous commitments offers, on the basis of the FairSearch research.

In contrast to Google's first two proposals, the third proposal was not subject to a rigorous 'market test' during which interested third parties could offer their opinions and research, such as the FairSearch survey evidence mentioned above.

However, in a highly unusual move for the European Commission, it retreated from accepting Google's third proposal, despite initially making comments that would suggest it intended to accept the proposal. This retreat seems due to great dissatisfaction expressed by the original complainants with the terms of the third proposal,[76] but also the 'politicisation' of the case within the EU.[77] The culmination of this politicisation can be seen with an unprecedented vote from the

---

[72] DJ Franklyn and DA Hyman, 'Review of the Likely Effects of Google's Proposed Commitments dated October 21, 2013 ("Second Commitments")', *FairSearch*, 9 December 2013, available at www.fairsearch.org/wp-content/uploads/2013/12/FairSearch-Hyman_Franklyn-Study.pdf.

[73] ibid 2.

[74] ibid 13.

[75] European Commission, *Antitrust: Commission Obtains from Google Comparable Display of Specialised Search Rivals: Frequently Asked Questions*, MEMO/14/87, available at http://europa.eu/rapid/press-release_MEMO-14-87_en.htm.

[76] Initiative for a Competitive Online Marketplace, *ICOMP Response to Commission's Announcement on the Google Antitrust Case* (ICOMP, 5 February 2014), available at www.i-comp.org/blog/2014/icomp-response-commissions-announcement-google-antitrust-case/.

[77] FY Chee, 'Microsoft, publishers try to stop "catastrophic" Google EU deal', *Reuters*, 4 September 2014, available at www.reuters.com/article/2014/09/04/us-eu-google-microsoft-idUSKBN0GZ1NW20140904.

European Parliament in late 2014 which called for EU Member States and the Commission to increase their regulation of Google, including the possibility of breaking the company up into smaller constituent parts.[78]

Thus, it seems that external pressures have brought about this *volte face* by the Commission, which resulted in the Commission issuing Google with a formal Statement of Objections in 2015, claiming that Google is acting anticompetitively 'by systematically favouring its own comparison shopping product in its general search results pages' which Google could remedy by 'treat[ing] its own comparison shopping service and those of rivals in the same way'.[79] Google responded later in 2015, asserting that the Commission's allegations were incorrect and that its conduct was not anticompetitive.[80]

At the time of writing, the outcome of the Commission's investigation is still unknown. However, it seems that at most Google would have to make some changes to how results from its competitors' vertical search services were presented on the general Google search results page in order to satisfy the Commission, regardless of whether not doing so actually does constitute an anticompetitive abuse according to EU law.

IV. Outcome of Competition Investigations and User Concerns

While the outcome of the EU competition investigation against Google remains to be seen, the Commission's Statement of Objections gives some indication of what Google must do to allay its concerns: essentially treating its competitors in the same way as it treats its own comparison services.

Given the problems with Google search enumerated at the beginning of this chapter and the kind of action the European Parliament wants to see, such a remedy may seem rather weak, especially from the user perspective; particularly when the Commission can radically change the way businesses operate if it makes an official finding of abusive conduct, such as obliging certain kinds of business practices vis-à-vis competitors and customers, or even breaking up an entity into smaller constituent parts in extreme circumstances. Google, seemingly, will not have to be a lot more transparent about its inner machinations, including how its secretive algorithm works. More transparency around how Google's algorithm

---

[78] European Parliament Resolution on supporting consumer rights in the digital single market, 2014/2973(RSP) (27 November 2014).

[79] European Commission, *Antitrust: Commission Sends Statement of Objections to Google on Comparison Shopping Services*, MEMO/15/4781 (2015).

[80] K Walker, 'Improving quality isn't anticompetitive', Google Europe blog, 27 August 2015, available at http://googlepolicyeurope.blogspot.co.uk/2015/08/improving-quality-isnt-anti-competitive.html.

works would have positive consequences for user-centric concerns. Furthermore, the problems of user data identified above do not seem to be addressed at all by the Commission at this stage of the investigation. Finally, the breaking-up of Google's conglomeration, while a possible move given the Commission's powers, seems unlikely on the basis of the Statement of Objections, which seems to envisage Google continuing to exist in the way it does currently but giving a 'fair chance' to its competitors' services.

The fact that the Commission has been willing to take, and pursue, this investigatory action against Google seems at first blush to be a departure from the neo-classical, neoliberal approach to competition and regulation. The Commission's investigation seems definitely not to be in the interests of the transnational globalised capital that Google constitutes. In addition, the Commission's willingness to intervene and even push for changes, however minimal, to Google's business practices when it is debatable that Google is behaving in an anticompetitive way would also not seem to accord with the approach of minimising intervention in markets that neoliberalism promotes. Indeed, it seems that the Commission may have gone beyond what is 'necessary' or the bare minimum to address competition concerns.

Yet the Commission's conduct may possibly be attributed to factors such as European protectionism when faced with an American corporation (although some of Google's competitors which have been making the complaints are also American) or its own political concerns, such as being seen by the general public to be a relevant institution by acting in the face of what many perceive as a pernicious monopoly.[81] The Commission, though, has also been the subject of lobbying by a coalition of European 'digital companies' mainly from France and Germany, and some domestic politicians from these countries also urged the Commission to reconsider the commitments offered by Google.[82]

It is clear thus far that the Commission has not been overly 'invasive' of Google's business practices, particularly those which hold the most concern for users. While the Commission's latest views on Google's conduct might suggest a more 'ordo-liberal' approach to preserving the competitive process at the level of comparison shopping, the overall power of Google would not seem to be dramatically weakened as a result. Instead, it may be that it is Google's competitors which benefit in the end, rather than users.

[81] A Lamadrid, 'European Commission v Google', *Chillin'Competition*, 10 December 2010, available at http://chillingcompetition.com/2010/12/10/european-commission-vs-google/.
[82] J Vasagar, 'The news baron battling Google', *Financial Times*, 9 June 2014, available at www.ft.com/cms/s/0/beb7aeae-eb3d-11e3-bab6-00144feabdc0.html#axzz3C77rQzcj.

V. Other Legal Regimes, Ex Ante Regulation and Extra-Legal Solutions

A. Data Protection

The new General Data Protection Regulation has been designed as an update to EU data protection law in order to provide better resolutions for issues arising from the digital economy. Personal data may only be processed in certain situations, prominent among which is the 'data subject' giving consent for the processing to occur for one or more specific purposes.[83] However, the Regulation's original draft text proposed by the Commission actually went further, stating that this consent would not provide a legal basis for processing the data 'where there is a significant imbalance between the position of the data subject and the controller',[84] which would certainly appear to be the case in the relationship between Google and the vast majority of its users. Yet this potentially equalising provision was modified in subsequent versions and did not survive into the final text except as a Recital. It would seem that under the new General Data Protection Regulation, Google will be largely able to continue its practices in the EU of collecting large amounts of user data; it will have to ensure that data collected for one purpose is not used for other purposes, but a carefully worded privacy policy will be sufficient.

It would seem, broadly speaking, that the current configuration of incentives for Google to proliferate data about users is not radically altered by the intervention of data protection law. Due to the large amount of concentration in the market for search, users do not have a real choice either to use Google's services without their data being collected and processed, or to use similarly robust and well-functioning search engines which uphold the protection of their data and privacy. Without more aggressive data protection/privacy-based intervention, or competition enforcement which is also suspicious of such vast accumulations of power for its non-economic as well as economic consequences, it seems the vastly unequal positions of users vis-à-vis Google will persist.

B. Free Expression

Users may claim that their right to free expression is affected by the possibility of Google censoring certain information in its search results, and bias in how those results are presented, since these affect users' abilities to send and receive information.

---

[83] EU Data Protection Regulation, art 6(1)(a).
[84] COM (2012)11 final, art 7(4).

The potential censorship constituted by Google deliberately leaving certain results that would otherwise be 'relevant' out of its results page, and thus producing biased results, might amount to circumstances where a breach of users' free expression could be argued. However, the possibility to receive this information in other ways, for instance via another search engine or directly inputting the web address into a browser, may distinguish these circumstances from those found to infringe European Convention on Human Rights (ECHR), Article 10 in the case law. Google presenting biased results may only be seen as a possible infringement of Article 10 if it implicates media plurality. In any event, restrictions of users' Article 10 rights can be justified 'for the protection of the ... rights of others', which might be considered to include Google's right to carry on its business, even if there is 'bias' in how the results are presented.

The Council of Europe has turned its attention to search engines, and in April 2012 its Committee of Ministers adopted a Recommendation to Member States concerning the protection and promotion of respect for human rights with regard to search engines.[85] The non-binding recommendation recognises the potential challenges from search engines to the right of freedom of expression (Article 10) and the right to a private life (Article 8), which may come from the design of algorithms; de-indexing and/or partial treatment or biased results; concentration in the market; a lack of transparency about how results are selected and ranked; the ability of search engines to gather and index content which may not have been intended for mass communication; general data processing and retention; and the generation of new kinds of personal data such as individual search histories and behavioural profiles. Thus far it does not seem that the recommendation has been followed by Member States.

C. Ex Ante Regulation

There have been various proposals for regulation as well as, or in place of, appeal to other legal regimes for addressing the problems created by a dominant search engine. These proposals appear to be motivated by a mixture of a wish to address a market failure (the asymmetry of information between Google and its users over how Google works), and a desire to pursue certain social goals such as free expression for users.

The Council of Europe's Committee of Ministers advocated a co-regulatory approach to search engines. Member States should cooperate with the private

---

[85] Council of Europe, Recommendation of the Committee of Ministers to Member States on the protection of human rights with regard to search engines, CM/Rec(2012)3 (4 April 2012), available at https://wcd.coe.int/ViewDoc.jsp?id=1929429&Site=CM.

sector and civil society to develop strategies to protect fundamental rights and freedoms pertaining to search engine operation, particularly regarding:

— how the search engines provide information;
— the criteria according to which search results are organised;
— how content not intended for mass communication (although in the public space) should be ranked and indexed;
— transparency as to the collection of personal data;
— empowerment of users to access and modify their personal data held by search engine providers;
— the minimisation of the collection and processing of personal data; and
— the assurance that search engine services are accessible to people with disabilities.

Member States should also consider offering users a choice of search engines, including search outputs based on criteria of public value. This may act as some kind of substitute for competition law inasmuch as the user has options of different search engines to use, including those which may not (wholly) be driven by concerns of profit.

However, as mentioned above, Member States so far have not acted on this recommendation, and as it stands the recommendation is also non-binding. Furthermore, it is difficult to see what incentive search engines would have for such cooperation unless they are 'threatened' by the possibility of new legislation and regulation which would restrict their activities unless they cooperate.

Regulation similar to that advocated for ISPs in the net neutrality debate has been suggested for search engines including Google. An equivalent obligation on Google might encompass non-discrimination rules for its search results, as well as a requirement that Google does not 'block' content which would otherwise be considered a 'relevant' result for a search. However, without knowing more about how Google's search algorithm works, it may be difficult to design such an obligation of neutrality and see that it is effectively put in place. Co-regulation may have a role to play here whereby Google would be 'incentivised' to cooperate in the design of the rules. With ISPs it is easier to determine whether they are acting in a non-neutral fashion due to their technical makeup. Furthermore, truly neutral design for search engines may not even exist since every design choice necessarily reflects certain normative values, in this case around what is 'relevant'.[86]

A transparency obligation may also be considered, either on its own or as part of a broader package of ex ante regulation. This would partially address the design problem for 'search neutrality' and would enable oversight of search engines' activities to ensure they are operating in accordance with such an obligation. Aside from potentially aiding Google's competitors in exposing any 'bias' against them in Google's search results, it may also benefit users at large, giving them the tools

---

[86] Goldman, 'Revisiting Search Engine Bias' (n 15) 107.

to determine 'the appropriate level of cognitive authority to assign to their search results'.[87]

Despite these suggestions for law and regulation to deal with Google's dominance, there has been no attempt to implement any of them. These legislative and regulatory solutions would entail significant intervention and 'interference' with the market for online search and advertising. This is also true of suggestions that Google should be broken up into smaller constituent parts in order to reduce its influence. Given the general environment, it is not surprising that these solutions for Google's dominance may be thought of as idealistic or going too far. Furthermore, the risk remains that even if regulation concerning Google is enacted, it may be difficult to enforce for the reasons discussed above: that understanding how Google works may be a difficult task for regulators; and a co-regulatory solution may run the risk of regulatory capture by Google to a greater extent given the close working relationship that would be likely to ensue between the regulator and the regulated. In any event, given Google's search engine is subject to a great deal of innovation and alternations to how the algorithm works, this fast pace of change may render attempts to regulate obsolete in practice.

Finally, at least in terms of privacy and data protection concerns, in the wake of the Snowden revelations it would seem that states also have an interest in private parties engaging in data collection about Internet users which they can then tap into for their own purposes, and so the now-more-visible 'invisible handshake' may also operate to deter regulation of conduct that gives rise to this data proliferation and collection—as the collection is in both the interests of Google for its business model and nation-states for their own surveillance purposes.

D. Extra-Legal Solutions

If ex ante regulation of search engines along the lines suggested above seems unlikely to be designed and implemented in practice, then attention turns to the possibilities offered by extra-legal solutions.

One suggestion has been for a publicly-funded search engine which would compete with Google and its ilk.[88] Nevertheless, Lewandowski notes that such initiatives have already been trialled, such as the French project Qaero, but this alternative only has an 'insignificant' market share and so can be considered to have 'failed' as an online search tool.[89] He critiques the idea of publicly funding

---

[87] Goldman, 'Search Engine Bias and the Demise of Search Engine Utopianism' (n 11) 117.

[88] ibid 117–18; FA Pasquale, 'Dominant Search Engines: An Essential Cultural and Political Facility' in B Szoka and A Marcus (eds), *The Next Digital Decade: Essays on the Future of the Internet* (Washington DC, TechFreedom, 2011) 416.

[89] D Lewandowski, 'Why We Need an Independent Index of the Web' in R Konig and M Rasch (eds), *Society of the Query Reader* (Amsterdam, Institute of Network Cultures, 2014) 55.

a single alternative search engine to Google as the engine could fail for a number of reasons which may not even be related to the quality of search offered, instead suggesting 'to create a search engine index and make it available to other providers', based on an open structure, access to the index being on a fair and transparent basis, and institutional resilience in the form of state sponsorship (not subject to the unpredictability of the market).[90] This model is similar to that proposed by Pasquale: a non-governmental agency indexing and archiving the Web, using open standards for ranking and rating websites, which might provide 'an important alternative source of information and metadata on ranking processes'.[91] This is also similar to the transparency and interoperability approach to Internet regulation advanced by Brown and Marsden.[92] In any event, this kind of publicly funded search index would enable, it is hoped, the creation of various alternative search engines to provide users with a more substantial choice than they currently have.

A more radical position is taken by Fuchs, specifically in response to the issues around the use and exploitation of user data.[93] Instead he advocates that Google should be 'expropriated and transformed into a public, non-profit non-commercial organization that serves the common good', with its services being run by non-profit organisations such as universities and supported by public funding. Interestingly, Vaidhyanathan has previously identified Google as remedying what he terms 'public failures', the opposite of a 'market failure', when the state cannot satisfy public needs and deliver services effectively, and so Google has 'stepped into voids better filled by the public sector'.[94]

While there seems consensus that an alternative to the status quo brought about by state action of some sort is desirable to remedy the problems identified, the preceding paragraphs present alternative paths to follow in order to achieve this: either the state should set up a new search engine as an alternative to Google, or Google itself should be nationalised. However, Fuchs also admits that despite these suggestions, a truly non-exploitative search engine for the benefit of humanity may only be possible through the general establishment of a commons-based Internet in a commons-based society.

In the interim, creating a strong rival to Google with a public service mandate seems the most realistic extra-legal solution, since the expropriation of Google would require an amount of 'intervention in the market', even if it would provide the advantage of acquiring Google's existing equipment and know-how as

---

[90] ibid 56–58.

[91] Pasquale, 'Dominant Search Engines' (n 88) 416–17.

[92] I Brown and CT Marsden, *Regulating Code: Good Governance and Better Regulation in the Information Age* (Cambridge, MIT Press, 2013).

[93] C Fuchs, 'Google Capitalism' (2012) 12(1) *Triple C Communication, Capitalism and Critique Journal for a Global Sustainable Information Society* 42, 47–48.

[94] S Vaidhyanathan, *The Googlization of Everything (And Why We Should Worry)* (Berkeley, CA, University of California Press, 2011) 44.

opposed to starting from a more preliminary stage with the design of a Google alternative.

Nevertheless, caution is due regarding the state's involvement in creating an alternative to Google from the perspective of protecting and upholding users' rights. The concerns around data protection, privacy and free expression encompassed by users' use of Google's search engine should also be at the forefront of the design of a state-backed alternative to Google. This alternative should not be used as a platform for states to gain even more intrusive information about their citizens.

Thus, it may well be that peer-to-peer (P2P) design is also most appropriate for a true alternative to Google's monopoly, both as a 'radical' and a competition law conceived alternative. Handley advocates P2P search engine YaCy as both a solution to the problems presented by Google and other for-profit data-gathering centralised search engines, and an enabler of users' autonomy online.[95]

VI. Conclusion

This chapter has examined the problem of dominance and Internet search through an interrogation of the practices of the dominant entity, Google, and the concerns that such a dominant entity poses for users and their autonomy, both in terms of undesirable economic consequences encompassed in a standard competition investigation, and the undesirable 'non-economic' consequences of dominance that the use and operation of Google entail, such as the infringement of privacy and data protection, and free expression concerns related to the 'gatekeeper' role Google plays for users wishing to access information on the Web.

The progress and outcomes of the competition investigations into Google have been examined. The European investigation is particularly interesting given the lack of clarity as to whether Google is actually abusing its dominant position in violation of EU competition law rules. Precisely what has driven the Commission to adopt this course of action is unclear, but it actually seems a more 'interventionist' approach than the 'More Economic' approach would normally entail in this situation. Perhaps it is the lobbying from European-based competitors of Google which can account for the Commission's conduct.

However, neither competition law nor its somewhat unusual enforcement by the Commission goes very far in addressing the concerns around Google for users. Thus far, this has produced no greater transparency around how Google conducts searches via its secretive algorithm, transparency which also would have addressed in part at least the concerns already identified around bias and censorship. Whether

---

[95] T Handley, 'P2P Search as an Alternative to Google: Recapturing Network Value through Decentralized Search' (2013) 3 *Journal of Peer Production*.

more transparency regarding the search algorithm will form a part of a possible fourth set of commitments from Google remains to be seen.

Nevertheless, it would seem that ex ante regulation (in theory at least) is a more desirable avenue to protecting and upholding users' rights vis-à-vis Google. This chapter has outlined certain proposals for regulatory reform, which may involve transparency and 'search neutrality' obligations being placed on Google, and it is argued that these would be more effective in achieving the aim of protecting and empowering users than competition law itself. Yet the regulatory inaction in this field, and the lack of prospect of any regulation actually being put in place in the near future despite a 2012 Council of Europe Recommendation along these lines, does not inspire confidence that ex ante regulation is a realistic solution. In addition, there are the usual concerns around the success of any regulation that might be enacted given the practical problems of enforcement, the regulation being 'too little, too late', and the possibility of regulatory capture.

Thus, it is the extra-legal solutions to which attention ought to be turned, which may be in the form of a publicly-funded search engine (or the possible, though unlikely, public expropriation of Google), in order to provide a non-profit alternative to the status quo, given that the market is not providing it. This, however, would also need to be properly designed in order to ensure data minimisation, transparency, neutrality, and so on, and indeed it may be that a P2P equivalent is the most desirable option in practice, again given the untrustworthiness of public power to advance user autonomy, evidenced by its vast surveillance of Internet users.

5

Dominance and Mobile Devices

When the Internet became publicly available, the average user accessed it on a desktop computer, or (less likely) a laptop via a fixed line connection. In the interim, technological developments have given rise to a proliferation of devices, especially mobile, with which users can connect to the Internet via wifi and mobile broadband technologies: smartphones, e-book readers, games consoles, tablets and netbooks as well as laptops and desktops. The development of mobile devices and the move to cloud computing (the subject of the following chapter) has contributed to a more 'closed' Internet experience. Initially, desktop and laptop's software and hardware did not influence how users accessed the Internet but online service providers such as AOL and CompuServe did restrict the Internet experience by offering limited 'walled garden' access in the early 1990s. Yet now it is the devices themselves and their vertical integration with other parts of their manufacturer's business, such as 'app stores', which determine the users' Internet experience.

This move to more 'closed' devices has raised concerns about continued innovation, free expression, privacy, ownership and control, and competition—in other words, user autonomy. The markets for Internet devices are characterised by vertical integration of the device provider and distribution platforms (app stores) to access content and applications for the device. Furthermore, the devices increasingly rely on cloud services (which are usually part of the vertically integrated value chain) to store data as opposed to on the device itself, giving cloud providers a level of control over this data and the device.

Justifications for allowing a more 'reduced' access for mobile devices have been based on the fact that mobile devices engage the use of a scarce resource, the electromagnetic spectrum, to function. However, this argument diminishes with advances in technology which have brought high speed mobile Internet, and even the issue of spectrum scarcity may well be less relevant as spectrum-agile networks and cognitive devices become increasingly prevalent.

Another justification for allowing such reduced Internet access is that of security: device manufacturers and software distribution platform operators ensure that only 'safe' applications are available to users, that is, those with no viruses or illegal content. However, this process gives device manufacturers and software distribution platform operators (almost) complete control over what users can do and view on their devices.

The transition from the open desktop 'culture' to the closed and 'sanitised' mobile device environment has been criticised by Zittrain, who laments this trend to less 'generative' devices.[1] He acknowledges the advantages of a more controlled environment, such as the aforementioned security gains, but warns of the corresponding disadvantages for innovation and progress, especially given the track record of the Internet itself as a system open to widespread change which has produced more innovation and benefits than a 'closed' system which can only be altered by a centralised entity. The transition to the Internet of Things is continuing these trends to more 'closed' and 'controlled' systems.[2]

I. Mobile Device Value Chain

The definition of different kinds of Internet-enabled mobile devices is blurred, but they can be defined in distinction to laptops and desktop computers, and include smartphones, tablet computers and certain e-book readers. These categories of mobile devices converge into each other, especially when the same operating system is used for both tablets and smartphones, as is the case with iPad and iPhone Apple devices which both use Apple's iOS operating system, and Google Nexus smartphone and tablet devices which both use the Android operating system. Here, it is only the size of the device and possibly the ability to make phone calls through the mobile phone network which distinguish a smartphone from a tablet.

One important feature of all mobile devices, though, is the strong level of vertical integration encompassed in their value chain, which is significantly greater than the situation with 'non-mobile' desktop and laptop computers. While PC desktops and laptops may typically be made by a certain manufacturer, they use a different operating system (often Microsoft Windows) which can then run any compatible third party applications and can store any compatible files on the computer itself. Apple desktops and laptops are more vertically integrated since Apple is the manufacturer as well as the operating system owner for these systems, but these devices can also run any compatible third party applications and store any compatible files. However, mobile devices can encompass the same corporation acting as manufacturer, operating system provider and application provider. Furthermore, mobile devices have also been designed to constitute another virtual 'layer' in this value chain in the form of app stores. These app stores offer an extra point of control for their vertically integrated operators, which must approve third party apps before they are available to users in the app stores. Due to the more restricted architecture of mobile device operating systems and device functionality, power is thus concentrated in the app store operators, which are usually

---

[1] J Zittrain, *The Future of the Internet and How to Stop It* (New Haven, CT, Yale University Press, 2008).
[2] See RH Weber, 'Internet of Things: Governance Quo Vadis?' (2013) 29(4) *Computer Law and Security Review* 341.

also vertically integrated with the device manufacturer and/or operating system provider.

II. Problems with Mobile Devices and App Stores

This configuration implicates three broad categories of problems for users and third party app developers: problems concerning anticompetitive conduct from the entities which control the app store; problems of expression and control, that the app store operators can 'censor' certain apps for non-economic reasons or put other restrictions on what users can do with their devices; and problems of privacy and data protection regarding the user data gathered in the course of using these devices and app stores.

A. Competition

The concerns around competition encompass the economic 'gatekeeping' or 'control' function that app store operators exercise over what is available within the store to users. For instance, an app store operator which also makes apps 'in-house' may have an incentive to exclude apps from third parties which compete with its own offerings. The app store operator may also have an incentive to engage in predatory pricing, such as offering its own apps at a low or zero price with the intention of raising the price for users once its competitors have exited the market.

There are also other issues of competition given the high level of vertical integration of the value chain. Users who purchase, for instance, an Apple device are forced to use the Apple app store and operating system unless they 'jailbreak' the device. In order to jailbreak these devices, however, and load on an alternative operating system and/or access an alternative app store, certain digital rights management measures (DRMs)/technical protected measures (TPMs) whose primary purpose is to protect digital copyrighted material may need to be circumvented. Various problems arise here, since the circumvention of these digital 'locks' may be illegal, even if there is no infringement of copyright, and the purpose is to provide users with a choice of operating system or app store. Thus, the vertically integrated provider's control over the value chain and ability to resist competition can be entrenched by the laws concerning circumventing TPMs by restricting users' choice at the various parts of the value chain.

B. Free Expression and Control

These characteristics of mobile device value chains and control also pose other, non-economic problems for users. First, the app store operators can ensure that certain apps are not approved and made available in the store for users for reasons other than competition. The inclusion of apps in the Apple App Store, for instance, is governed by the non-negotiable App Store Review Guidelines (as well as general Terms of Use). Some apps containing 'adult', pornographic or erotic content have not been approved for inclusion in the App Store, even though this content is not necessarily illegal. Other apps with controversial political (but still legal) content have been removed from the App Store.[3] Thus, app store operators can perform a censoring role over what content and applications users can receive and use. Indeed, Hestres considers that the control that Apple and other App Store and operating system providers exercise over what apps are approved or not 'poses a greater barrier to content diversity and freedom of expression than lack of technological generativity'.[4]

This control extends as well to users' ability to use their mobile devices however they wish. The use of DRMs/TPMs to 'lock' users into a particular app store or operating system, and the more limited functionality of these mobile devices via their original design, leaves users much less able to use their devices as they may wish. This is compounded by the degree of legal 'greyness' in certain circumstances when it comes to jailbreaking the devices.

C. Privacy

There are heightened privacy concerns over mobile devices and their app store ecosystems, since the operation of the app stores has implicated the collection of a large amount of data about users. For certain apps to be downloaded to a user's device, the user must agree to the app store itself, and sometimes also the third party developer, having access to certain information about that user and device. Furthermore, there have been allegations that app store operators have passed along personal information about users to third party developers in a less than transparent fashion.[5]

'In-kind' payments by users of their personal data or metadata characterises mobile device ecosystems in a similar way to the user side of search engines, as discussed in chapter 4. Users may be able to download certain apps for free inasmuch as they do not pay a sum of money for the app, but they do 'pay' by handing over information about themselves and their conduct.

Privacy issues for mobile devices may be exacerbated by the greater reliance on the cloud that these devices have, so files may be more easily stored in the cloud

---

[3] See eg A Daly, 'Private Power and New Media: The Case of the Corporate Suppression of Wikileaks and Its Implications for the Exercise of Fundamental Rights on the Internet' in CM Akrivopoulou and N Garipidis (eds), *Human Rights and Risks in the Digital Era: Globalization and the Effects of Information Technology* (Hershey, IGI Global, 2012) 83.

[4] LE Hestres, 'App Neutrality: Apple's App Store and Freedom of Expression Online' (2013) 7 *International Journal of Communication* 1265, 1268.

[5] A Oreskovic and M Sin, 'Google app store policy raises privacy concerns', *Reuters*, 14 February 2013, available at www.reuters.com/article/2013/02/14/us-google-privacy-idUSBRE91D1LL20130214.

rather than on the device itself. This line of control enables a large amount of data to be collected about users. Furthermore, mobile devices involve the collection of new kinds of data due to their transportable nature which entails that a rich supply of information is also collected about the user's location and movements.

While the user may 'consent' when she first buys the device and each time she downloads a new app to use, it may not be clear exactly what is being consented to (in terms of exactly what data is being gathered) and the average user may not understand the language in the privacy policy.[6] Furthermore, there is no real 'choice' on this matter between the different offerings from Apple, Google, and so on, given that none of the main companies provide users with a mobile device which does not invade their privacy. Accordingly, a lack of respect for user privacy when using these devices and applications entails an interference with user autonomy and is exacerbated by the concentration of the market and an absence of true choice.

III. Mobile Devices, Apps and Market Developments

Mobile device markets are characterised by their two-sided nature: the platform is provided which acts as a meeting place for users, on the one side, and app developers and content providers, on the other side. The markets are also characterised by a strong degree of vertical integration, where device manufacturers are integrated with operating systems, app stores, cloud services and applications. Related are the network effects which also characterise these markets, and contribute to their concentration around certain big players, namely Google and Apple. The more users that these platform ecosystems have, the more attractive they are to app developers and content providers as their offerings can reach more potential customers. Accordingly, the more a mobile device ecosystem offers in terms of a variety of content and applications, the more attractive these ecosystems will be to users.

Another characteristic of these mobile device ecosystems is the strong degree of 'lock-in' users experience, which makes switching to competitors' offerings more challenging. This lock-in is achieved in various ways: with smartphones, it can be due to users obtaining the device as part of a long-term contact with a particular network provider with penalties for the user if the contract is terminated early, thus lock-in by legal means. Another significant method of lock-in is the design of the devices and operating systems, which entails that only one app store from which applications for the device can be downloaded is available, and this is usually a vertically integrated offering of the device manufacturer and/or operating system provider. Users are thus 'locked-in' by technical means to using that app

⁶ I Pollach, 'A Typology of Communicative Strategies in Online Privacy Policies: Ethics, Power and Informed Consent' (2005) 62(3) *Journal of Business Ethics* 221.

store and the applications it approves. It is possible for users to choose another app store or operating system via 'jailbreaking' the device and then have a wider selection of apps available, but this is not a simple procedure. If the device is not jailbroken, then the app store operator/operating system provider/device manufacturer exercises ultimate power and control over the content that can be accessed on it and the programs that it can run.

This lock-in is compounded by the legal status of jailbreaking. In addition to jailbreaking devices in order to use other software and applications being a somewhat technically complex procedure, the process involves breaking DRMs/TPMs. These technical locks are intended to protect copyright and prevent infringement by limiting the user's ability to copy/lend/modify files and devices, and they also allow syncing between 'approved' devices; but their practical application often goes much further than this purpose, for instance preventing interoperability of file formats and devices, or preventing the use of copyrighted works that are legal, such as fair use/dealing or copying for private/research purposes.

Hackers have worked out technical measures to get around, remove or 'break' DRMs but such techniques are not necessarily legal, even though they have at least a dual use: they can be used to infringe copyright, but they can be used for legitimate reasons such as to facilitate interoperability. In most jurisdictions, including the EU, it is at least a grey area as to whether breaking DRMs to make a file or device interoperable or to load on different software/content is legal. The US does have a mechanism for exceptions to rules against breaking DRM/TPM, and there is currently one for jailbreaking smartphones, but not for jailbreaking tablets or e-books readers. Different EU Member States have identified different exceptions to the prohibition on circumvention in their domestic laws, but the EU also lacks a similar centralised and methodical exception process to the American one regarding the issuing of exceptions.[7] As a result of this opacity as to the legal situation for users, jailbreaking can be viewed as a 'legally unattractive option', especially when there is no explicit exception.[8]

A. Market Leaders

While precise market definition can prove tricky for mobile devices, given overlapping functionality and use by users, certain large players can be identified as raising dominance concerns, especially Apple and Google.

Apple is active in both the smartphone and tablet markets, pioneering tablet take-up with the introduction of its iPad. As mentioned already, Apple provides its own operating system on its devices, the iOS, and also operates the Apple App

---

[7] V Samartzi, 'Optimal vs Sub-optimal Use of DRM-Protected Works' (2011) 33 *European Intellectual Property Review* 517, 527.

[8] D MacSithigh, 'App Law Within: Rights and Regulation in the Smartphone Age' (2013) 21(2) *International Journal of Law and Information Technology* 154, 170.

Store for these devices, as well as providing its own apps alongside the offerings of third parties.

Google provides its own devices in the form of the Nexus branded tablets and smartphones, but it also offers its Android mobile device operating system to be used by other device manufacturers. Android is an open source operating system: Google releases the source code under an Apache licence, which allows the software to be modified and distributed freely by the device manufacturers and wireless carriers. However, Google has trademarked 'Android' and only permits others to use this trademark and call what they have done 'Android', as well as use the Google Play App Store, apps created by Google and related data, if their version passes Google's certification tests and adheres to various other terms. Nevertheless, Android has undergone a process of fragmentation with 'forked' versions of it emerging; Amazon's Kindle Fire uses a forked version of Android that is not approved by Google, and has its own app store rather than using Google's services.

At the time of writing, precise figures on mobile device market share are difficult to find. Some figures suggest that as regards tablet operating system, Android is the market leader in Europe (EU and non-EU nations) with a share of 68 per cent, followed by Apple's iOS with a share of 31 per cent.[9] There are similar figures for the mobile market: Android has a market share of 65 per cent and Apple's iOS with 28 per cent.[10] These figures have remained fairly constant for the last year, with no significant fluctuations in market share, and Android has a sufficiently high market share which may be considered to constitute a dominant position. However, market share based on device vendor differs: Apple is the leading vendor in Europe for mobiles and tablets, with a market share of 37 per cent, followed by Samsung (whose devices mainly run Android) with a share of 30 per cent.[11] If the mobile and tablet market is separated, then Samsung is the leading mobile device vendor followed by Apple, and vice versa for the tablet market. The tablet market is interesting inasmuch as Apple has the lead market share at 68% per cent compared to Samsung at 16 per cent.[12] Market shares on the combined mobile and tablet markets seem competitive, with no one player likely to occupy a dominant position, but Apple may have a dominant position on the tablet market if it is taken separately.

Nevertheless, even if one player does not have a dominant position in these broader markets, and so there is little cause for concern from a competition

---

[9] StatCounter Global Stats, *Top 7 Tablet OSs in Europe from Jan 2015 to Jan 2016*, available at http://gs.statcounter.com/#tablet+console-os-eu-monthly-201501-201601.

[10] StatCounter Global Stats, *Top 8 Mobile Operating Systems in Europe from Jan 2015 to Jan 2016*, available at http://gs.statcounter.com/#mobile_os-eu-monthly-201501-201601.

[11] StatCounter Global Stats, *Top 10 Mobile and Tablet Device Vendors in Europe from Jan 2015 to Jan 2016*, available at http://gs.statcounter.com/#mobile+tablet-vendor-eu-monthly-201501-201601.

[12] StatCounter Global Stats, *Top 10 Tablet Device Vendors in Europe from Jan 2015 to Jan 2016*, available at http://gs.statcounter.com/#tablet-vendor-eu-monthly-201501-201601.

perspective, the possibility of user lock-in and each brand of device/app store constituting a market in itself can create a situation in which there are problems for competition, and most certainly problems for user autonomy once stuck in such a situation.

B. Allegations of Anticompetitive Conduct

Both Google and Apple have been accused of behaving anticompetitively in the running of their mobile device ecosystems.

(i) Apple

Apple devices have been involved in various competition investigations and proceedings, mainly in the US.

One case involved the alleged anticompetitive tying of the iPod (iPhone predecessor) with Apple's iTunes store, and was triggered by the iPod not supporting a music file format engineered by a competitor via the use of Apple's proprietary DRMs.[13] This entailed that iPod device owners had to obtain their music files via the iTunes store, and music bought through the iTunes store could only be played on iPods and not on competitors' digital music devices. The case was dismissed due to insufficient factual evidence of the monopolisation claims, and a failure by the plaintiff to show that the use of proprietary DRMs constituted an antitrust injury.[14] This suggests that the use of DRMs (or TPMs) will not in itself be anticompetitive; it must also produce an anticompetitive outcome for it to constitute antitrust injury. A class action proceeded with some other plaintiffs, and went to trial again in late 2014.[15] However, the jury at trial found no antitrust violation, due to Apple making legitimate product and security improvements to the iPod devices and the iTunes software, seemingly following the *Kodak* and *IBM* lines of case law.

Apple has also faced other controversies in the US regarding the governance of its App Store. Apple initially blocked Skype and Google Voice as VoIP apps for its iPhone, but Skype was finally made available in 2009, possibly due to some informal regulatory pressure,[16] and Google's Voice app was also eventually included after some pressure from the Federal Communications Commission (FCC).[17]

---

[13] *Apple iPod, iTunes Antitrust Litigation*, C05- 0037JW (ND Cal 2010).

[14] *Somers v Apple*, No 11-16896 (9th Cir 2013).

[15] M Masnick, 'Apple Facing Trial over Whether Its Use of DRM Violated Antitrust Laws', *Techdirt*, 6 October 2014, available at www.techdirt.com/articles/20141003/15453128723/apple-facing-trial-over-whether-its-use-drm-violated-antitrust-laws.shtml.

[16] AT&T, 'AT&T Extends VOIP to 3G Network for iPhone', *AT&T News Room*, 6 October 2009, available at www.att.com/gen/press-room?pid=4800&cdvn=news&newsarticleid=27207.

[17] R Singel, 'Feds Want Apple and AT&T to Explain Google Voice Rejection', *Wired*, 31 July 2009, available at www.wired.com/business/2009/07/feds-want-apple-and-att-to-explain-google-voice-rejection/; JW Croft, 'Antitrust and Communications Policy: There's an App for Just About Anything, Except Google Voice' (2010) 14 *SMU Science and Technology Law Review* 1.

More US litigation against Apple involved allegations that Apple unlawfully stifled competition and consumer choice and artificially increased the prices in the aftermarkets for iPhone voice and data services and iPhone software apps by retaining exclusive control over the iPhone's design, features and operating software; refusing to approve any app by an outside developer which did not agree to Apple's financial terms; and not providing iPhone customers with any means by which they could download third party apps not approved by Apple. A US District Court dismissed the complaint due to standing issues concerning the plaintiffs' ability to bring the antitrust case and the questionable accuracy of some of their allegations.[18] This decision leaves open the possibility of a better-worded complaint being made in which the plaintiffs' standing is established, and certainly does not definitively establish that Apple's conduct is not anticompetitive.

Finally, Apple has been embroiled in litigation regarding anticompetitive conduct vis-à-vis the distribution of e-books.[19] Apple and five of the 'Big Six' book publishers (HarperCollins, Hachette, Simon & Schuster, Penguin and Macmillan) have been investigated for alleged price-fixing in both the EU and US. Apple provides access to e-books on its mobile devices via its iBookstore app, though also allows users to purchase or otherwise obtain e-books from other sources, such as via Amazon's Kindle app, but all content being read outside of an app must be uploaded to Apple's distribution platforms and Apple has also tried to ensure that e-books being sold from other sources are not available for lower prices than via the iBookstore. The particular conduct which was the subject of the competition investigations concerned new 'agency' contracts that Apple entered into with the book publishers which gave them more control over retail prices, and also gave Apple 30 per cent of the final retail prices and an assurance that the e-books would not be sold elsewhere for less than Apple's price for them. The European Commission investigated Apple and the book publishers for alleged price fixing in breach of Treaty on the Functioning of the European Union (TFEU), Article 101, suspecting that the shift to agency contracts may have been the result of collusion between competing publishers with Apple's help and may have had as their goal the increase of retail e-book prices or the prevention of the emergence of lower prices for consumers. Apple and the publishers eventually offered commitments to the Commission that they would terminate the existing agency agreements and not adopt clauses which would prevent them from selling e-books more cheaply via Apple's competitors compared to Apple's prices for five years.

However, in the US, all of the publishers settled with the Department of Justice (DoJ) which filed a civil antitrust suit against them, while Apple opted not to settle and the case went to trial. The District Court judge held that Apple had violated section 1 of the Sherman Act, finding direct and circumstantial evidence

---

[18] *In Re Apple IPhone Antitrust Litigation*, 11-cv-06714-YGR (ND Cal 2013).
[19] This section is based on A Daly, 'E-book Monopolies and the Law' (2013) *Media and Arts Law Review* 350.

that Apple had conspired with the publishers to eliminate retail price competition and raise the price of e-books.[20] The DoJ had proposed a remedy for Apple's illegal conduct that would have had consequences beyond the e-book markets: it wanted Apple to be prohibited from entering into agreements with suppliers of other types of content as well as e-books (eg music, films, TV) that were likely to increase the prices at which Apple's competitors might sell that content too.[21] Furthermore, the DoJ also proposed that Apple must allow competing e-book sellers, such as Amazon and Barnes & Noble, to provide links from their e-book apps for Apple devices to their e-bookstores.[22] Yet neither of these remedies appeared in the final judgment, which concerned only e-books, and stipulated that the agency agreements must be terminated as well as agreements containing clauses which restrict the retailer's ability to set the retail price of an e-book or clauses which attempt to ensure that other retailers will not sell e-books for lower prices.[23]

While the final judgment may benefit consumers through lower prices, the measures initially proposed by the DoJ but left out in the end would have had more wide-ranging consequences, particularly for the operation of Apple's App Store. Similar aspects of the model Apple used to contract with the book publishers are found in Apple's contracts with other entities selling their content/apps through its App Store, including newspaper publishers and software developers. The DoJ's initial proposal would not have prevented Apple from continuing to receive a 30 per cent cut of revenue, but it might have averted the move to agency contracts in other content sectors and have encouraged more competition among content retailers. The initial proposal would also have affected the In-App Purchase rules by allowing third party providers in the form of rival e-book retail distributors to provide direct links to their platforms from inside their apps; while Apple's rules entail that third parties which do not wish to follow the rules and wish to sell content via their own prices must do so through their websites, accessible via iPad and iPhone browsers, or even create a 'web app' in HTML5. However, there have been allegations that certain web apps may run slowly on Apple devices when launched from the home screen, possibly to deter users from these apps and encourage them to use ones available through the Apple App Store.[24]

There are other options for content providers than adhering to Apple's In-App Purchase rules but they are less convenient for users, and attempts to circumvent Apple's App Store rules by creating web apps may provide a lower quality experience for users compared to using Apple-sanctioned apps.

---

[20] *United States v Apple Inc*, 12 Civ 2826 (SD.NY, 10 July 2013).
[21] Department of Justice Press Release, *Department of Justice Proposes Remedy to Address Apple's Price Fixing* (2 August 2013), available at www.justice.gov/opa/pr/2013/August/13-at-877.html.
[22] ibid.
[23] *United States v Apple Inc*, 12 Civ 2826 (SDNY, 6 September 2013).
[24] C Metz, 'Apple handcuffs "open" web apps on iPhone home screen', *The Register*, 15 March 2011, available at www.theregister.co.uk/2011/03/15/apple_ios_throttles_web_apps_on_home_screen/.

(ii) Google

Google and its Android-fronted mobile ecosystem have also been accused of anticompetitive conduct.

The online search-facing side of the European Commission's competition investigation into Google was discussed previously in chapter 4; however, that investigation also has concerned other aspects of Google's business. Indeed, part of Microsoft's complaint to the Commission alleging anticompetitive behaviour from Google included an allegation that Google prevented Microsoft's smartphones from working properly with YouTube, as contrasted with the situation with YouTube and phones using Google's Android operating system (and apparently Apple iPhones as well). Microsoft competes with Google, inter alia, in the search market and the mobile operating system market, initially with Windows Mobile for smartphones, which was succeeded by Windows Phone, and Windows 8 for tablet computers.

Furthermore, the FairSearch coalition of Google's competitors filed another complaint with the European Commission regarding Google's practice of obliging manufacturers which wish to use the Android operating system to 'pre-load an entire suite of Google mobile services and to give them prominent default placement on the phone'.[25] This formulation of the problem somewhat obscures the actual situation with Google's demands; in fact, manufacturers are free to use the Android operating system without pre-loading Google apps, but if they wish to pre-load some Google apps, they must pre-load a whole suite of them as opposed to just the apps which are more prominent or popular. Subsequent information surfaced which suggests that if manufacturers wish to use the *most recent* version of Android, they must pre-load a suite of Google apps and services, although they can use older versions of Android without being obliged to load on these additional Google products.[26]

Simultaneously to its announcement of the Statement of Objections regarding Google's search practices, the European Commission also announced that it was initiating a separate formal investigation of Google's Android business.[27] The investigation is proceeding on the basis of three allegations:

1. Google hindered the development and market access of rival mobile applications by requiring or incentivising device manufacturers to exclusively pre-install Google's own apps and services;

---

[25] FairSearch, *FairSearch Announces Complaint in EU on Google's Anti-Competitive Mobile Strategy* (8 April 2013), available at www.fairsearch.org/mobile/fairsearch-announces-complaint-in-eu-on-googles-anti-competitive-mobile-strategy/. Google's methods are also discussed by B Edelman, *Secret Ties in Google's 'Open' Android* (13 February 2014), available at www.benedelman.org/news/021314-1.html.

[26] FY Chee and A Oreskovic, 'European regulators training sights on Google's mobile software', *Reuters*, 30 July 2014, available at www.reuters.com/article/2014/07/30/us-google-europe-android-insight-idUSKBN0FZ2B220140730.

[27] European Commission, *Antitrust: Commission Opens Formal Investigation Against Google in Relation to Android Mobile Operating System*, MEMO/15/4782 (2015).

2. Google prevented device manufacturers which wish to install Google's applications and services on some of their Android devices from developing and using forked versions of Android on other devices;
3. Google tied or bundled certain Google applications and services distributed on Android devices with other Google applications, services and/or programming interfaces.

The US FTC has also apparently started investigating Google Android for possible antitrust violations along similar lines to the EU proceedings.[28] This follows a decision from the Russian competition authority that Google requiring manufacturers to pre-install apps and services on their devices was a violation of Russian antitrust law.[29]

There are, however, important differences between how Google and Apple operate their mobile device ecosystems. First, unlike Apple, Google permits other app stores beyond its own Google Play to be installed on devices running Android operating systems,[30] except possibly the situation in which a manufacturer wishes to install the latest version of Android. Secondly, bona fide Android apps can be installed and executed on a device without needing to go through Google Play, either via the aforementioned non-Google app stores which Google permits, or directly downloaded from a developer's website; this process is known as 'sideloading'. Finally, 'rooting' the device is another option open to Android users, similar to 'jailbreaking' Apple devices inasmuch as both processes give the user 'superuser' administrative privileges, but distinct from jailbreaking, as using a different operating system or app store is usually permitted on Android devices (while not on Apple ones) by the device vendor.

IV. Is there Anticompetitive Conduct?

A. Relevant Markets and Market Share

There is a high degree of vertical integration in mobile device markets, and also conglomeration inasmuch as the main players in these markets are also active in other information markets as well, most prominently Google.

---

[28] D McLaughlin, 'Google Said to be Under US Antitrust Scrutiny over Android', *Bloomberg*, 25 September 2015, available at www.bloomberg.com/news/articles/2015-09-25/google-said-to-be-under-u-s-antitrust-scrutiny-over-android-iezf41sg.

[29] I Khrennikov, 'Russia Says Google Broke Antitrust Laws', *Bloomberg*, 15 September 2015, available at www.bloomberg.com/news/articles/2015-09-14/russia-says-google-broke-antitrust-laws-sending-yandex-soaring.

[30] A Lamadrid, 'Some Thoughts on the New Anti-Google (Android) Complaint (Post 3/3): Bundling Allegations', *Chillin'Competition*, 9 September 2013, available at http://chillingcompetition.com/2013/09/09/some-thoughts-on-the-new-anti-google-android-complaint-post-33-bundling-allegations/.

(i) Device/Operating System Markets

Certain relevant markets can be defined for identifying possible anticompetitive conduct. First, there is the market for Internet-enabled mobile devices, which can be further subdivided into markets for smartphones and markets for tablets. Secondly, there is the market for operating systems for mobile devices. Apple and Google are active in both of these markets, but Google only has a small presence in the device markets with its Nexus range, which does not even make up a majority of devices using its own Android operating system.[31]

It would seem that Apple may only have a dominant position in the market for tablet devices, based on the figures detailed above. If the market is defined as being based on operating system, then Google may have a dominant position in that market, but not in device markets. Markets defined in other ways, such as a combined mobile-tablet device market, seem competitive.

However, narrower markets around particular branded devices may also be defined: Apple iPhones may be found to constitute their own market, so Apple is the only player in this market and thus dominant. This seemed to be the approach taken in a French case regarding a contract entered into between Apple and Orange for exclusive distribution rights concerning the iPhone in France, Belgium and Romania, which was found to be anticompetitive.[32] Cox considers that the iPhone's 'unique characteristics' gave Apple 'monopolist bargaining power': the iPhone's industrial design combined with its functions rendered it distinct from other smartphones.[33] Yet the question remains as to the extent to which Apple products are substitutable for Android products. The French litigation took place before mobile devices with Android operating systems became widely available. At the time of those French proceedings, iPhones constituted a product market in themselves, but the subsequent launch and take-up of Android-enabled products has provided an equivalent to Apple products in terms of design and functionality. This is belied by the 'patent wars' (litigation between various companies including Apple, Google and Samsung concerning unauthorised use of patented processes and objects in Internet enabled mobile devices) which have included allegations that Android infringed Apple's patents.[34] It would seem now that if Apple did raise its prices then it would likely lose market share to competitors.

---

[31] M Hamblen, 'Google's Nexus Lineup May Not Sell Well, But Still Challenges Android Makers', *Computer World*, 3 December 2013, available at www.computerworld.com/s/article/9244477/Google_s_Nexus_lineup_may_not_sell_well_but_still_challenges_Android_makers.

[32] Unreported case discussed in F Fontaine, 'French Antitrust Law and Strategic Analysis: Apples and Oranges?' (2009) 30(6) *European Competition Law Review* 286.

[33] MB Cox, 'Apple's Exclusive Distribution Agreements: A Refusal to Supply?' (2012) 33(1) *European Competition Law Review* 11.

[34] See G Goggin, 'Google Phone Rising: The Android and the Politics of Open Source' (2012) 26(5) *Continuum: Journal of Media and Cultural Studies* 741; M Carrier, 'A Roadmap to the Smartphone Patent Wars and FRAND Licensing' (2012) 2 *CPI Antitrust Chronicle* 1.

Nevertheless, Apple may be considered to offer a sufficiently 'different' experience to devices running Android operating systems for Apple devices to constitute separate product markets, due to factors such as the perception of quality and security the Apple ecosystem offers compared to that of Android. Furthermore, from the 'demand' side of the market, app developers are likely to make separate apps for the Apple App Store and the Google Play/other Android app stores given the different APIs (application program interfaces) that each ecosystem uses; therefore they may be regarded as separate markets from that side as well.

In any event, even if Apple devices are not considered to constitute their own product markets per se, the Apple App Store or iOS operating system may be considered as a complementary product constituting an 'aftermarket', such that even if Apple does not have power over the smartphone or tablet market, it may have a dominant position in the secondary market for iPhone or iPad app stores or operating systems.

Regarding Google, as mentioned above it may have market power in the operating system market. Nevertheless, Android's 'open' nature may be at odds with a finding of market power since anyone can freely produce a version of Android to 'compete' with Google's.[35]

(ii) App Stores

If mobile app stores can be taken to be another market, then market share can be calculated in two ways: either via revenue for the app store provider, in which case Apple leads the market globally, or in terms of app downloads, in which Google Play leads.[36] It is important to remember that data collected through apps is another way in which Google 'feeds' its overall business model, so even if apps are 'free' in terms of costing no or little money compared to Apple App Store prices, users may be 'paying' instead via the collection of their personal information while they are using the app and device.

The market for mobile app stores may be further subdivided into narrower markets for mobile app stores on Apple/iOS devices (which as mentioned above could also be considered an 'aftermarket' for these devices) and app stores on Android. Google Play is considered to be the leading Android app store in terms of number of apps available and downloads of those apps,[37] but there are other app stores for Android not affiliated to Google, and there are fewer barriers to using these alternatives compared to the situation with Apple devices.

---

[35] Free Software Foundation Europe, 'FSFE Objects to Claims of "Predatory Pricing" in Free Software', Letter to European Commission, 29 July 2013, available at http://fsfe.org/activities/policy/eu/20130729.EC.Fairsearch.letter.en.html.

[36] D Walter, 'Apple Still Rules the App Market', *CMS Wire*, 22 January 2016, available at www.cmswire.com/mobile/apple-still-rules-the-app-market/.

[37] S Hill, 'Tired of Google Play? Check Out These Alternative Android App Stores', *Digital Trends*, 5 December 2013, available at www.digitaltrends.com/mobile/android-app-stores/#!OIQus.

(iii) Markets for Specific Apps

Further markets may be defined for specific types of app, such as for search engine apps or video apps, including those provided by Google.

Search apps may be judged to be also in a separate relevant market to 'desktop' search or 'browser' search, with which the competition investigations into Google detailed in chapter 3 were principally concerned. Whether they constitute a separate market in themselves will depend on their substitutability—the extent to which desktop or browser search is substitutable for search app search. This may well be the case given the different functionality of each, and the 'better experience' that search via a search app may offer on a mobile device compared to via a browser. In any event, even if search apps are judged to constitute a separate market, then it would seem that Google has a dominant position in this market globally and also in the US at least.[38] It is likely that Google would also dominate the search app market in the EU as well.

As for YouTube, the relevant market would need to be defined, which is not clear: it may be the market for online video content aggregators or specific apps for online video content aggregation. How market share might be measured in whatever market is defined is also unclear: it may be measured either by views, downloads and/or advertising revenue. Nevertheless, YouTube has an important position globally as generating a large amount of advertising revenue, as well as being a very popular online resource in terms of total views,[39] so may well be found to have a leading share in that market.

B. Competitive Constraints

The markets for mobile Internet devices are currently reasonably competitive from the consumer perspective. There is competition among Apple devices, Android-enabled devices, devices running Windows Mobiles, etc, and, except in the case of Apple, there is a selection of manufacturers making devices running each operating system, whether Google's Android for which there is no charge, or Windows Mobile operating system for which device manufacturers pay Microsoft for a licence to use. There is not significant buyer power on the part of the device manufacturers given the consolidation of the mobile operating system markets around Apple, Google and (to a lesser extent) Microsoft, and the network effects

---

[38] 'Google's Mobile Division to Fuel Revenue Growth in 2014 and Beyond', *Forbes*, 8 April 2014, available at www.forbes.com/sites/greatspeculations/2014/04/08/googles-mobile-division-to-fuel-revenue-growth-in-2014-and-beyond/.

[39] J Graham, 'YouTube Takes on Netflix with Originals', *USA Today*, 9 February 2016, available at www.usatoday.com/story/tech/news/2016/02/09/youtube-takes-netflix-originals/80023958/#; R Hof, 'Google's Ad Machine is Even More Profitable Than Anyone Knew', *Forbes*, 1 February 2016, available at www.forbes.com/sites/roberthof/2016/02/01/googles-ad-machine-is-even-more-profitable-than-anyone-knew/#2715e4857a0b677929eb7e7a.

each exhibit for users and app developers. As mentioned above, in terms of device provider, there seems to be no one provider with an overall dominant share, unless the market for tablet devices is taken separately, in which case Apple may be considered dominant.

However, it is a different picture if a market specifically for Apple products is found. Apple is completely dominant over these products as it is the only vendor and it does not license its iOS operating system to other manufacturers to use with their devices. This is also the case for any Apple product aftermarkets that may be identified, such as for the Apple App Store or iOS operating system. While it is unclear how many Apple devices have been jailbroken, the scant evidence available suggests that only a very small percentage of Apple products are indeed jailbroken, perhaps 2 per cent of the total,[40] and so the practice of jailbreaking is likely to be insufficient to exercise much of a competitive constraint on Apple in these aftermarkets. In consequence, users experience a high degree of 'lock-in' to Apple's ecosystem when they acquire an Apple device, given the lack of choice offered in terms of operating system and App Store, as well as the difficulty in switching to rivals' offerings, which essentially must be done through jailbreaking—a complex and sometimes unsuccessful process.

The overall situation for app stores in general is likely to be competitive as well, since there are various app stores in circulation exerting competitive constraints on each other. This is especially the case as regards Android devices, on which Google permits a choice of app store, including its own Google Play offering but also the offerings of competitors. Nevertheless, these app stores also exhibit network effects inasmuch as the more users there are, the more attractive developing an app for a specific app store is from the perspective of developers, while conversely the more apps there are available in an app store, the more attractive that store is for users. For Apple devices, the Apple App Store could be considered a specific aftermarket in which Apple is dominant, even if it is not accepted that Apple products themselves form their own relevant market, as discussed above.

Finally, as regards the markets for specific apps, in theory these ought to be competitive given the low entry barriers a priori for creating an app to run on mobile devices. However, in the specific circumstances of search engine apps, this market would seem to mirror the entry barriers in the search engine market, most notably the vast amount of user data over which Google presides which would be difficult to replicate by many potential competitors (except possibly Facebook), which leads to Google having a dominant position in these markets at least in the EU. YouTube as a video content aggregator would seem to experience more competitive constraints, from other video hosting/aggregating sites and apps and possibly also from social networks and other user generated content platforms.

---

[40] AW Kosner, 'What 7 Million Jailbreak are Saying. Is Apple Listening?', *Forbes*, 10 February 2013, available at www.forbes.com/sites/anthonykosner/2013/02/10/what-7-million-jailbreaks-are-saying-is-apple-listening/.

However, YouTube is likely to benefit from network effects inasmuch as the more users upload videos to it, the more attractive it will be to those wishing to watch videos, and the more users it has as an audience, the more attractive it will be to those wishing to upload their videos and have them seen.

C. Abuse of Dominant Position

Three types of potentially anticompetitive conduct in mobile device ecosystems may be considered most injurious to users' autonomy: tying products and services from one market to products and services in another, thus depriving users of choice; the mobile device ecosystem operator locking users into that ecosystem, also depriving them of choice; and a mobile app store blocking apps.

(i) Tying

Two instances of tying will be examined here: Apple's tying of its operating system, app store and possibly also individual Apple apps to the initial purchase of the mobile device; and Google's alleged tying of a pre-loaded suite of its apps either to certain other Google apps or the current version of the Android operating system.

Taking the situation with Apple first, in order to show tying, the relevant market would have to be one specifically for Apple-branded devices or for tablets (excluding smartphones). However, the discussion above shows that the market may not be defined so tightly around Apple products alone, and in the general market for smartphones and tablets Apple will not have a dominant position, although it may be dominant in the tablets market. Assuming the market is defined in a way where Apple would have a dominant position, the anticompetitive conduct would be Apple tying its devices to downstream markets for operating systems, app stores and possibly also certain individual Apple-owned apps. This situation is reminiscent of the *Microsoft* case,[41] where Microsoft engaged in 'technical tying' by physically integrating the tied product into the tying product so that it was impossible to take one product without the other. Here it is impossible (or at least only possible via legally questionable jailbreaking) to take Apple devices (the tying product) without also getting the Apple operating system and the Apple App Store on them (the tied products).

To show anticompetitive tying, there must also be two distinct products being tied as opposed to a single integrated one. Here, that does not seem to pose a problem: as the conduct of other players (particularly Google) in these markets demonstrates, the device is distinct from the operating system which is distinct from the app store. Customers must also be coerced into purchasing both the tying and tied product: in *Microsoft*, the General Court found that there had been coercion

---

[41] *Microsoft*, Commission Decision of 24 March 2004, upheld on appeal Case T-201/04 *Microsoft Corporation v European Commission* [2007] ECR II-3601.

of customers to take the Windows Media Player application with Windows operating system since it was 'technically bundled' and impossible to uninstall from the operating system. Here, unless the device is jailbroken, it would be impossible to uninstall the operating system or app store from the Apple device—an analogous situation to that of *Microsoft*. This is unlikely to be the case with individual Apple apps, however, as it is possible to uninstall them.

Finally, it must be demonstrated that the tie has an anticompetitive foreclosure effect. It would appear that this is the case here, that the market for operating systems on Apple devices and/or app stores on Apple devices is indeed foreclosed as a result of the tie between the device and these other products since no other players are able to compete in these markets as a result. Thus, unless Apple was able to show an objective justification for this tie, or that the tie enhances efficiency, it is likely it would be judged anticompetitive. One justification may be the 'safety' of the experience Apple offers on its devices: that users are sure that they will receive a quality and 'family friendly' product at all stages from the device itself to the applications available on the device. However, a similar justification was rejected by the European Commission in *Hilti*,[42] which was upheld on appeal by the General Court.[43]

If the market is not defined as being a narrow one for Apple products, then the aftermarkets approach could be taken. Apple may not have market power on the wider markets for smartphones and tablets, but does have power in the secondary markets of operating systems and/or app stores for Apple devices. Here, the tying would be between the iOS operating system and the app store, and this scenario would likely be judged anticompetitive if these aftermarkets are found to exist. Thus, the tying claim on this basis would be more likely to succeed than the claim based on Apple products as constituting their own separate market. Yet while this might have been more credible some years ago, the competitive constraint exercised by similar products using other operating systems such as Android would appear to place Apple devices in more general markets for smartphones and tablets. Accordingly, overall it is unlikely that Apple will be found to have the requisite dominant position at the time of writing and so it is unlikely to be found to have engaged in anticompetitive conduct in the form of abuse of dominance.

For Google, the claim would concern Google's alleged tying of certain desirable Google apps to a whole suite of (supposedly less desirable) Google apps if a device manufacturer wants to pre-load any Google apps onto an Android operating system-enabled device. If the claim is true, then this may also constitute tying: the Google app suite is tied to the operating system. Google would have to be found to have a dominant position over the 'tying' apps, ie the desirable ones that devices manufacturers would wish to pre-load. As mentioned above, it is

---

[42] Case IV/30.787 and 31.488 *Eurofix-Bauco/Hilti*, Commission Decision 88/138/EEC [1988] OJ L65/19.
[43] Case C-53/92P *Hilti AG v European Commission* [1994] ECR I-667.

unclear what the relevant markets here are, but supposing that Google did have a dominant position with YouTube, for instance, then it would appear that Google is tying two distinct products: the desirable apps to the less desirable apps. The issue of coercion may be more difficult to establish, and depends upon the truth of the allegation that Google coerces device manufacturers into pre-loading the Google app suite if they wish to use the most recent version of Android. If this is not the case, then the tying situation only arises when the device manufacturers wish to pre-load some apps before the device is sold to the user, in which case they must pre-load the whole suite if they wish to include any of the individual apps. Users are still able to download the apps (including Google's) they wish on their devices once they have bought the device, even if there has been no pre-loading of Google apps. Nevertheless, if this situation is deemed to mount to coercion, then the anticompetitive foreclosure effects must be found: that Google is leveraging its dominance in certain markets into other markets, which may well be the case in practice. Furthermore, there must be no objective justification for the tie; indeed it is difficult to see what objective justification Google could have here beyond attempting to increase its market share in other markets, or increase the amount of data it gathers about users in order to boost the advertising side of its business.

As regards the second situation of Google possibly tying the most recent version of Android to its suite of pre-loaded apps, then Google would have to be demonstrated to have a dominant position in the 'tying' product market, that of operating systems. This may well be the case since Android has around a 70 per cent share of EU smartphone and tablet markets which is sufficient to constitute dominance. The apps also constitute a separate market to the operating system, and coercion is likely to be established if the allegations are true: that manufacturers must take this app suite if they wish to have the latest version of Android. Again, it would be difficult to see what the objective justification is for this conduct. However, one weakness in this claim may lie in the fact that if the allegations are true, it is only the most recent version of Android which is implicated in the tying, while other versions of Android can be used by manufacturers without this obligation to pre-load apps. The most recent version of Android may be viewed to have a much smaller share of the market than Android operating systems taken altogether, and so the dominant position may not be found in the first place, and thus the tying would not be anticompetitive.

In terms of remedies for any anticompetitive conduct found to exist, Apple may be forced to give users a choice of operating system or app store, which would represent a major change to its business practices; although Apple is unlikely to be found to have a dominant position in the requisite market in the first place and so it is unlikely it will be found to have engaged in an anticompetitive abuse of dominance. In Google's case, the remedy is likely to encompass Google being forced to offer certain individual apps for pre-loading onto Android devices rather than forcing device manufacturers to pre-load the app suite, or force Google to offer the latest version of Android without forcing device manufacturers to pre-load apps.

However, these remedies are unlikely to alter fundamentally how Google conducts its mobile device business from the user perspective, particularly with regard to Google's data gathering, but then Google's mobile ecosystem is decidedly more 'open' than Apple's and gives the users more control (although not total control) over their devices.

(ii) Lock-in

Another scenario which may constitute an abuse of dominance is the use of DRMs and TPMs in mobile device ecosystems to 'lock' users technically into that ecosystem, for instance, by preventing them from accessing a choice of app store (in the case of Apple devices), a choice of cloud service or certain other apps, content and services, and possibly also preventing users from engaging in data portability to a rival's service.

These DRMs and TPMs usually involve certain standards protected by intellectual property, and the exclusive rights of the intellectual property holder (the device ecosystem operator) are usually to be respected notwithstanding the restrictions on portability and interoperability the operations of these standards can involve. However, in certain, exceptional circumstances, a dominant player preventing interoperability of such standards may be viewed as an abuse of dominance.[44] Indeed, this was one of the findings in the European *Microsoft* case, that Microsoft had to give its competitors full access to the information which would allow them to interoperate with its services, otherwise they would not be able to compete viably with Microsoft.

In mobile device markets, a dominant position must be found, and whether this is so has been discussed above. Google may be the most likely candidate to be considered to have a dominant position in EU smartphone and tablet markets, regarding its Android operating system and certain apps, but it generally engages in less lock-in than Apple. Apple may only be considered to have this dominant position if its devices are taken to be markets in themselves, or if aftermarkets are found. Even in these scenarios, it is unclear whether the requisite 'exceptional circumstances' would be found in mobile device markets, particularly where there does seem to be competition overall in the markets.

(iii) Blocking Apps

The practice of blocking apps created by third party developers by app store operators may also be subjected to competition scrutiny as constituting a possible abuse of a dominant position in the form of a refusal to deal.

However, it would have to be demonstrated that entry into the particular app store was an essential facility or 'indispensable' for a developer wishing to

---

[44] I Graef, J Vershakelen and P Valcke, 'Putting the Right to Data Portability into a Competition Law Perspective' (2013) *Law: Journal of the Higher School of Economics Annual Review* 53.

compete in the downstream apps markets.[45] There are various other app stores which the developer could use to distribute the app, as well as 'web apps' such as the *Financial Times* approach,[46] and then of course distribution of that information via the web browsers on these devices. Although jailbreaking the device may not be attractive for many users due to a lack of technical knowledge and the risks involved with doing so, accessing information through the web browser is likely to be attractive and accessible even to users without much technical knowledge, even if the contents may not be fully optimised for mobile devices. Furthermore, the app store operator may well have objective justifications for not including certain apps, such as that they contain prohibited content in accordance with its guidelines for developers, content which may be prohibited by the app store even if it is not prohibited eg by the law on pornography.

Thus in the absence of a finding of essential facility, an app store, even one with a dominant position, is unlikely to be acting anticompetitively in blocking apps.

(iv) Summary

Competition law's abuse of dominance prohibition is unlikely in practice to do much to alleviate users' concerns with private economic power exercised over mobile device ecosystems. Apple may not be judged to have a dominant position, even though its business practices in its mobile device ecosystem are the most restrictive of user freedom and choice. It may be more likely that Google is engaging in anticompetitive conduct, particularly tying. Yet, from the user perspective, Google's conduct is less limiting of user choice, and remedies for anticompetitive conduct are more likely to benefit device manufacturers. Lock-in using DRMs and TPMs and app stores blocking apps are unlikely to be anticompetitive due to the intellectual property rights involved in the former case, and the high threshold that needs to be reached in order for a refusal to deal to be found.

V. Other Legal Regimes

A. Free Expression

A lack of free expression for users was identified earlier as one of the problems posed by mobile devices due to the higher level of control over them that their vendors exercise, particularly Apple. Previous chapters have detailed how laws

---

[45] Case C-7/97 *Bronner v Mediaprint* [1998] ECR I-7817.

[46] S Dredge, 'Financial Times: "There is no drawback to working in HTML5"', *Guardian*, 29 April 2013, available at www.theguardian.com/media/appsblog/2013/apr/29/financial-times-html5-no-drawbacks.

protecting freedom of expression may apply to scenarios where it is another private party restricting users' free expression. This discussion will not be repeated here, suffice it to say that in Europe, European Convention on Human Rights (ECHR), Article 10 has been found to have some horizontal effect in disputes between two private parties and it has also been found to apply to restrictions on the freedom to receive information on the Internet, yet whether it has been infringed is highly dependent on the facts of the situation at hand. Internet users being blocked from receiving some expression can constitute a violation of Article 10, which is relevant here given that Apple (for instance) can block certain classes of content or apps. Although these apps may be blocked or restricted, if the content is still available on the device via the browser or web apps then it is highly unlikely that there would be an Article 10 infringement. If the information is available by other means, although not via a mobile device, then this is probably sufficient to ensure that Article 10 has not been violated. One other avenue may be if Apple's App Store management practices had a sufficiently adverse effect on media plurality, as this has been another scenario about which the European Court of Human Rights (ECtHR) has been particularly concerned in its jurisprudence. However, it would seem that if the material that Apple is blocking from its App Store is still available via the web browser, then Apple's prohibition is unlikely to amount in practice to being a threat to media plurality in a particular territory.

In addition, mobile device ecosystem operators may well be able to use their intellectual property rights in order to fend off users' free expression claims. Since intellectual property, and particularly TPMs protecting this intellectual property, are used at each stage of Apple's device value chain, then Apple may argue that its exclusive rights granted under this regime permit it to decide how its property is used and by whom.

Thus, due to a combination of the high barriers that must be traversed to find an Article 10 infringement, and the intellectual property protections that mobile device vendors enjoy which allow them to lock users into their particular mobile device ecosystems, it is unlikely that free expression laws can aid users in addressing the problems that Internet mobile device vendors pose for their free expression and free flow of online information.

B. Data Protection and Privacy

The data protection and privacy problems are not addressed at all by any potential competition intervention in mobile device markets. Again, the EU data protection regime has already been explained earlier in this book, so a detailed account will not be repeated here.

The British Information Commissioner's Office issued more specific guidance to mobile app developers as to how they can comply with data protection law, which emphasises data minimisation and privacy by design as desirable traits for apps collecting user data.[47] While data minimisation and privacy by design are laudable goals for mobile apps and the systems on which they run, the option for users not to have their data gathered in the first place while using these devices and applications is usually not present. Users who may wish to preserve their privacy either must agree to standard term contracts when using the devices and apps, or not agree and thus not use the apps. Data protection law will not mandate these companies to give users another option, that they can use the services and not have their data collected, even if they may have to pay an additional fee. This lack of real choice for users is compounded by the fact that all mobile ecosystems are engaging in this data-gathering conduct, so even if users opt out eg of the Android ecosystem, they do not encounter a significant qualitative difference in this regard when using eg the Apple ecosystem.

The forthcoming General Data Protection Regulation entails that app developers and mobile device vendors must seek user consent more actively than under the previous Directive. The Regulation's original text, in which user consent would not provide a legal basis for processing data where there is a significant imbalance between the data subject's and controller's position, may have entailed that large corporations such as Google and Apple providing mobile devices and apps would not have been permitted to process user data, given the imbalance between them and users. However, this provision did not survive into the Regulation's final version (except by way of a Recital), which states that consent must be 'purpose-limited', such that these corporations would only be permitted to process users' personal data for a specific purpose and would have to seek users' consent again to process it for another purpose. While this would put some restrictions on what these corporations could do with the data they collect, it is not as restrictive (and protective of user privacy) as the original formulation of the text. Moreover, the Regulation would not prevent this user data being collected in the first place assuming its conditions are met, which is effectively the strongest way to protect user privacy.

The configuration of popular mobile device ecosystems ensures a much greater intrusion into user privacy than previous desktop/laptop computers entailed, or even pre-smartphone mobile phones. The grouping of computer facilities with connectivity over telecoms infrastructure, GPS tracking, built-in cameras and the development of high-speed mobile Internet ensures that a large amount of data about an individual's movements can now be gathered, such as real-time location, images, and so on.[48] The portable nature of such devices also has spillover effects in other, hitherto offline, areas of life, raising concerns about privacy in public places. Previously, CCTV was perhaps the main threat to data protection and

---

[47] UK Information Commissioner's Office, *Privacy in Mobile Apps: Guidance for App Developers* (December 2013), available at http://ico.org.uk/for_organisations/data_protection/topic_guides/online/mobile_apps.

[48] See Y Welinder, 'Facing Real-Time Identification in Mobile Apps and Wearable Computers' (2013) 30 *Santa Clara Computer and High Technology Law Journal* 89.

individual privacy in public spaces, whereas now other citizens are equipped with machines that perform similar functions, with a large amount of the data generated being collected and stored. Here, even if individual mobile device users agree to terms and conditions which outline privacy protections, other citizens circulating in public places may become incidental data subjects yet not have expressed any consent for their image to be taken or other data to be gathered about them. Thus, the portability of these devices demonstrates one limitation of the current data protection regime, which is not remedied in the new Regulation. This trend is likely to be exacerbated with the rise of the Internet of Things adding many more data-gathering Internet-enabled objects to the network.

Nevertheless, one aspect of new Regulation that may be of benefit to users, given the lock-in they experience in these mobile device ecosystems, is the right to data portability, whereby users would be able to obtain their personal data held by a particular entity 'in a structured and commonly used and machine-readable format', in order to move to a competitor, for instance.[49] However, this right to data portability only applies where the data is being processed by automated means based on the data subject's consent. Data portability does not represent a particularly strong right for users, since entities processing user data on a basis which is not consent or a contract could sidestep some of its stipulations.[50] Furthermore, even if users 'port' their data to another provider, it will not necessarily be deleted from the repository where it was originally held, and it will only be that user's 'personal data' which is ported.

C. Regulation

Some kind of ex ante regulation mandating 'openness' or 'neutrality' in how app stores' function may address the free expression and competition concerns that arise in mobile device ecosystems. Mac Sithigh has suggested that electronic programming guides (EPGs) regulation in the EU may provide a possible model for app stores to adopt. Fair, reasonable and non-discriminatory access terms are imposed under EPGs, regardless of whether there is significant market power or a dominant position, although these do not amount to a right to be included or price regulation as such, but requirements to conduct themselves in a particular way when entering into dealings with other parties, which are publicly available, unlike Apple's opaque review guidelines for developers.[51] Certainly app stores, especially those with more prescriptive terms for inclusion such as Apple, would

---

[49] Data Protection Regulation, art 18(2).
[50] P Swire and Y Lagos, 'Why the Right to Data Portability Likely Reduces Consumer Welfare: Antitrust and Privacy Critique' (2013) 72 *Maryland Law Review* 335, 340.
[51] MacSithigh, 'App Law Within' (n 8) 172. See also C Cowie and CT Marsden, 'Convergence, Competition and Regulation' (1998) 1 *International Journal of Communications Law and Policy* 1.

benefit consumers and the competitive process by being more transparent about how they accept or reject third party apps, and in this way would uphold the interests of developers on their side of the market.

However, this process would still not necessarily guarantee users' freedom to receive information via app stores. To do this, Hestres suggests a more 'invasive' regulatory approach to that effect in the form of 'app neutrality':

— The app store operator would reject apps that contain universally accepted illegal content or facilitate/incite universally accepted illegal behaviour, such as child pornography/paedophilia.
— Apps that violate national laws, which themselves conflict with internationally recognised human rights laws and standards, would not be rejected.
— Apps could be rejected for technical reasons, such as the potential damage they may cause to devices.
— There must be clear, unambiguous, publicly available developer guidelines.
— When rejecting apps, the app store operator would provide clear reasons for doing so, which refer to the specific guidelines allegedly breached by the developer.
— A transparent appeals process for rejected apps would be established.
— If an app which was initially approved is now rejected, clear reasons referring explicitly to the guidelines would be provided.[52]

The adoption of guidelines akin to these would allay the free expression concerns regarding which apps are included in app stores, especially the Apple App Store, which is controlled in a top-down manner. In this way, a less paternalistic approach would be taken to users, giving them more autonomy over the content they access, as well as possibly having spillover effects as regards competition in the app store offerings.

However, this approach only concentrates on app stores themselves, and does not address the technical issue of interoperability and a lack of choice of app store and operating system. A lack of interoperability or access to competitors' products in itself is not an infringement of competition law: there must be a dominant position, and even then 'exceptional circumstances' may be necessary for access to be granted. Yet this does not aid users who are locked into these particular proprietary mobile device ecosystems. Thus, some form of mandated interoperability with other systems, and the presenting of users with a choice of operating systems and/or app store when they first purchase a mobile device, would be welcome. The right to data portability included in the forthcoming General Data Protection Regulation may go some way towards facilitating users switching their data from one provider to another, but it does not prevent this data being collected in the first place, nor does it ensure interoperability at all levels of the mobile device ecosystem.

---

[52] Hestres, 'App Neutrality' (n 4) 1725–26.

Thus, some kind of app neutrality regulation is needed to address the expression problems inherent in how Apple in particular operates its App Store and deals with third party apps. Some kind of interoperability/data portability regulation, such as a stronger version of the right to data portability, would address the problems around user lock-in to particular branded mobile device ecosystems and programs. Yet the deeper privacy problems still remain and perhaps can only be solved at a more socio-cultural level than current legal conceptions of the problem. For instance, data protection laws and privacy contracts focus on the device user and her consent, yet these devices can also constitute an infringement of others' privacy given their near-constant Internet connectedness, their geolocation revelations and their capacity to collect data about other people, such as photographs or audio in public places. Given advancements in technology whereby facial or voice recognition is possible, there is a profound problem in how these devices facilitate near-constant surveillance of peers. Of course, this is convenient for Elkin-Koren and Salzberger's invisible handshake, thus there is little incentive for government to reduce the privacy-invading impact of these devices by laws and regulation if that will affect its own surveillance activities. This status quo also suits corporations whose business models are based on or aided by gathering data about users. Thus, a broader paradigm shift is necessary in order to ensure an adequate level of non-interference with private persons and their behaviour, and the current legal, political and economic climate is otherwise unlikely to facilitate that level of protection.

D. Extra-Legal Options

While Apple and Google represent a radical monopoly or oligopoly of centralisation and control over mobile device ecosystems, some user-autonomy-friendly (or -friendlier) devices have begun to emerge. One such device is the Blackphone, a smartphone launched in 2014 which prioritises user privacy, and runs a forked version of Android called PrivatOS which comes with a number of security tools.[53] Blackphone seems to prioritise privacy and security at the expense of consumer convenience, and arguably is not particularly 'generative' of user innovation, nor operated on a commons basis in any respect, but it does represent a privacy-protecting alternative to Apple and Google's smartphone offerings. Blackphone's creators seem to be in the process of developing a tablet with similar privacy and security features but it is not yet available to purchase.[54]

---

[53] J Rigg, 'Blackphone Review: Putting a Price on Privacy', *Engadget*, 10 March 2014, available at www.engadget.com/2014/10/03/blackphone-review/.

[54] M Moon, 'Privacy-focused Blackphone 2 is Ready for Pre-Order', *Engadget*, 19 August 2015, available at www.engadget.com/2015/08/19/blackphone2-preorder/.

VI. Conclusion

This chapter has explored issues of dominance in mobile Internet devices, looking at the familiar combination of competition, free expression and privacy. At best, the anticompetitive abuses taking places in these scenario are abusive tying of one level of the mobile device ecosystem to another (in Apple's case) or certain desirable apps to other less desirable apps (in Google's case). Yet the remedies for these potential abuses are likely to be no more severe than users being given a choice of offerings from competitors along with the hitherto tied product. The remedies are unlikely to be so invasive as to change fundamentally the operation of the app store, for instance, or ensure users are given the choice to use certain services without their personal data being gathered, even for an extra fee.

Other areas of law have been explored to discern whether they can offer more protection to users and their interests when engaging in these mobile device ecosystems. Free expression laws are unlikely to facilitate this greater protection of users unless certain content is blocked entirely from them (including via web browsers and possibly not available at all via any other means) or there is a threat to media plurality—highly specific circumstances that may not arise in practice. The data protection regime in the EU does little to stop these services gathering vast amounts of data about users, which are usually governed by standard terms and conditions to which users must 'agree' and abide by the stated rules on data gathering, or disagree and not use the services at all.

Ex ante regulation would address the main competition and free expression concerns that arise, through 'app neutrality' rules at the app store level, by which app store operators would have to include apps that contain otherwise legitimate material and are not harmful to the network or device (eg such as being sufficiently secure and not introducing viruses). This would address problems around app store operators not including apps made by rivals and apps that may be 'ideologically awkward' but otherwise legal. Furthermore, a strong right to data portability for users may well ensure that they are not 'locked-in' to the entire Apple ecosystem when they buy an Apple product, further stimulating competition and giving them more freedom over their own devices.

However, the issue of privacy in these mobile ecosystems and outside of the systems remains, and is only likely to be exacerbated by the onward march of the Internet of Things and the norm of sustained data gathering from any source possible, promoted by Big Data evangelists yet coopted by governments for their 'political' surveillance programmes and large information corporations for their 'economic' surveillance programmes. This unholy marriage of state and corporate interests in advancing data-maximising and data-collecting technologies is unlikely to be subject to sufficient pressure to reform from the law, architecture, market and norms as they currently are. A socio-cultural change is necessary in order to preserve individual privacy and autonomy from this technocorporatist alliance. The solitary Blackphone demonstrates what this change might look like in the marketplace, by offering a privacy-enhancing alternative to the current status quo, and opens the possibility for more and better technical options for enhancing user autonomy.

6

Dominance and the Cloud

Cloud computing, broadly speaking, is the storage of data and processing in a location which is not the user's own computer,[1] or the provision of computer resources on-demand over the Internet.[2] The programs and applications run on an external server, and data is stored on this external server, rather than on the user's own device. Even if the term 'cloud computing' was not coined until recently, users have been storing their data in 'the cloud' at least since they have been using web-based email clients. Yet 'cloud computing' became the mainstream term to describe the remote programs, applications and data storage services with the launch of Amazon Web Services (AWS) in 2005.[3]

Cloud facilities offer many advantages to users such as remote storage, easy and ubiquitous accessibility, the storage or processing of (very) large amounts of data which would not be possible on a user's device, the opportunity to collaborate with other users privately and remotely, and so on. However, cloud computing also poses problems for users, including for competition given a lack of inter-operability and data portability, along with other issues regarding the control of information, data protection and privacy. In addition, surveillance is heightened with the placing of yet more user data in the cloud, accompanied by the trends observed earlier with mobile devices to store data, especially content, in the cloud rather than on the users' devices.

There is no one type of cloud or cloud computing. There are 'public' clouds, 'private' clouds, 'community' clouds, hybrid clouds (encompassing a mixture of private and public for instance) and even distributed clouds. The major deploy-ment models for cloud computing are public, private and hybrid. Public clouds encompass services rendered over a network open for use by the general pub-lic and usually only offer access to the cloud via the Internet. Examples of pub-lic cloud providers include Amazon, Microsoft and Google. Private clouds are operated solely for a single organisation which may be managed internally or by a third party provider and can be hosted either internally or externally. They

---

[1] J Cave and others, 'Regulating the Cloud: More, Less or Different Regulation and Competing Agendas', 40th Research Conference on Communication, Information and Internet Policy, Arlington, September 2012, at 1.
[2] P De Filippi and S McCarthy, 'Cloud Computing: Centralization and Data Sovereignty' (2012) 3(2) *European Journal of Law and Technology*.
[3] ibid.

usually are subject to more security settings and protections than public clouds. Community clouds occupy a position between public and private clouds, in which infrastructure is shared among a few organisations with common interests, with costs shared between fewer users than public clouds yet more users than private clouds. Hybrid clouds encompass a mixture of services typical of private, public and community clouds.

This chapter will concentrate on dominance and public cloud services, since these cloud services directly use the Internet for users' connections, and thus directly implicate online information flows (as opposed to data flows in closed private networks).

I. Problems with the Cloud

There are various issues that arise from use of the cloud by users, encompassing the now-familiar trio of privacy/data protection, free expression/control and competition. Despite the name, public clouds are another sector in which the main players are private corporations providing these services for profit.

A. Privacy and Data Protection

Privacy and data protection are engaged by use of cloud services since users usually have to provide credentials to access these services, as well as the high likelihood of confidential, personal and otherwise sensitive information being divulged through their use, and the rich contextual picture that can be also built of these users and their habits through use of the cloud.

While users may be able to minimise the risk of privacy and data protection breaches by not storing sensitive data in cloud services, or by relying on more than one provider, the metadata about their conduct in interacting with cloud services could still be collected by the cloud provider. Metadata can be conceptualised as the data 'about' a communication as opposed to the content of that communication, such as IP address of the sender/receiver, time, date, place of connection, etc. However, the theoretical distinction between metadata and communications content cannot be sustained so neatly in practice. Metadata can paint a highly detailed picture of an individual and in some circumstances can be 'even more revealing than the content of our communications'.[4]

This collection of data about users, whether via the content of their communications with the cloud or the metadata that these communications generate, fuels

---

[4] BC Newell and JT Tennis, 'Me, My Metadata, and the NSA: Privacy and Government Metadata Surveillance Programs', iConference 2014, Berlin, March 2014, at 2.

the business models of some cloud providers, which may provide data storage space in the cloud for no monetary cost to users, but may harvest and aggregate this data as 'recompense' for the 'free' service, which can then be sold on to advertisers (or accessed by governments for surveillance purposes).

Perhaps unsurprisingly, Google is a major cloud services provider to individual users with its Google Drive cloud data storage service, and this forms one of the portfolio of Google services from which it gathers data, as mentioned in the previous chapters. Apple also operates the iCloud for use with its stable of Apple devices.

Furthermore, there are often jurisdictional issues concerning cloud providers which provide services to customers geographically located in other countries, and may have their servers geographically located in a third country. Such a scenario may exacerbate privacy concerns given the differing privacy and data protection standards in different countries and their practical enforceability abroad, as well as the possibility of data being accessed by the governments of countries of which a user is not a citizen.[5]

B. Free Expression and Control

The issue of users' control of data resurfaces here as well: by moving their data to the cloud either in terms of storing files in the cloud or using applications in the cloud from which data about them is gathered, they give the cloud provider more effective control over the management of their data.[6] There are implications for data ownership in cloud storage,[7] and for freedom of expression, given the surveillance role that the data storage provider has over the information uploaded to it and the power it has to censor that information.[8]

Indeed, Lametti sees the move to the cloud as not only potentially rendering the concept of user privacy meaningless, but also reducing the possibilities for users to participate in the Internet as 'creators, collaborators and sharers', contributing to a reduction of user autonomy online, compounded by the fact devices are also decreasingly 'generative', as seen in the previous chapter.[9] Cloud providers thus

---

[5] D Svantesson and R Clarke, 'Privacy and Consumer Risks in Cloud Computing' (2010) 26(4) *Computer Law and Security Review* 391; WK Hon, J Hornle and C Millard, 'Which Law(s) Apply to Personal Data in Clouds?' in C Millard (ed), *Cloud Computing Law* (Oxford, Oxford University Press, 2013); I Walden, 'Law Enforcement Access to Data in Cloud' in C Millard (ed), *Cloud Computing Law* (Oxford, Oxford University Press, 2013).

[6] See WK Hon and C Millard, 'Control, Security, and Risk in the Cloud' in C Millard (ed), *Cloud Computing Law* (Oxford, Oxford University Press, 2013).

[7] See C Reed and A Cunningham, 'Ownership of Information in Clouds' in C Millard (ed), *Cloud Computing Law* (Oxford, Oxford University Press, 2013).

[8] P De Filippi, 'Ubiquitous Computing in the Cloud: User Empowerment vs. User Obsequity' in JE Pelet and P Papadopoulou (eds), *User Behavior in Ubiquitous Online Environments* (Hershey, PA, IGI Global, 2013) 46.

[9] D Lametti, 'The Cloud: Boundless Digital Potential or Enclosure 3.0?' (2012) 17(3) *Virginia Journal of Law and Technology* 190, 197.

have a greater capacity to manage and control what users do within the cloud, weakening users' online autonomy, and arguably also their free expression.[10] While this is not the fault of the cloud per se, its implementation along with its entwinement with mobile devices leads to this loss of user privacy, leaving users without a means of using such devices (with the notable exception of the Blackphone) or using the cloud in ways in which their privacy is preserved.

In addition, the use of digital rights management measures (DRMs) and technical protection measures (TPMs) to control content and applications in the cloud is often done in a way which is more restrictive of users than the law entails. As mentioned in the previous chapter, these 'digital locks' are used to protect content and software subject to intellectual property rights, but they often do not reflect the permitted user exceptions to these rights that exist in the law and have the effect of reducing data portability and interoperability. Users may not be able to remove the content or applications which they have legally bought from one cloud ecosystem to another as a result of DRMs/TPMs. In addition, interoperability can also be limited by contractual terms which oblige users to use certain cloud services when purchasing a certain device.

C. Competition and Dominance

Similarly to other Internet markets already examined, in theory some of the privacy, data protection and data control concerns would be addressed by a competitive market for cloud data storage services, in which users would switch provider if they were dissatisfied with the terms and conditions, and consumer demand for services with privacy protection etc would be met by providers.

Nevertheless, the cloud promotes centralisation, since it has become profitable for large-scale data storage (along with other computing services) to move from a local computer and server to the resources of a non-local centralised system.[11] Furthermore, the move to the cloud has also facilitated vertical integration, with cloud providers competing with each other for users by offering cloud storage for free or for a small cost, and integrating other services with their cloud services in order to make their cloud services more attractive. Once users choose the particular cloud provider, they usually experience lock-in due to a lack of interoperability and high switching costs to other providers (and perhaps even the inability to access their data in cloud storage on the devices of competitors) or experience restriction in the content that is available to them depending on the vertically integrated cloud provider's 'commercial and ideological interests'.[12]

[10] De Filippi and McCarthy, 'Cloud Computing: Centralization and Data Sovereignty' (n 2) 47.
[11] Lametti, 'The Cloud: Boundless Digital Potential or Enclosure 3.0?' (n 9) 208.
[12] S Zizek, 'Corporate Rule of Cyberspace', *Inside Higher Ed*, 2 May 2011, available at www.insidehighered.com/views/2011/05/02/slavoj_zizek_essay_on_cloud_computing_and_privacy#sthash.B8DVfwFj.04ssAm14.dpbs.

In addition, there are various features of cloud markets which facilitate dominance. First, the market for data storage in the cloud can be characterised as being two-sided with the presence of network effects. The network effects and the associated accumulation of user data by platforms (whose revenue is based on selling this information to advertisers) can constitute a barrier to entry for potential competitors which wish to enter the market. This is particularly so when these cloud services are not interoperable with each other (as is often the case in practice), limiting users' mobility and ability to switch between competing platforms. Potential cloud competitors in these circumstances would have to make large investments in technical infrastructure, software and advertisement to provide a service of sufficient quality and sufficiently popular to compete with what already exists, highlighting the economies of scale and scope in the operation of data centres. Data portability does not appear to be a problem that will be solved by the market since providers currently have no incentive to facilitate it. Furthermore, since the provision of cloud services to individual users tend to be governed by standard form contracts, and given the unequal bargaining power between these parties in favour of the cloud provider, users often face terms that can raise switching costs and lead to consumer lock-in.

A further feature of cloud markets is the possibility of leveraging dominance from one market into another, either a dominant position in a cloud market into a non-cloud market, or a dominant position in a non-cloud market (mobile devices, mobile device operating systems, etc) into a cloud market. Indeed, as will be seen below, given that a dominant position is unlikely to be found in cloud markets, the leveraging of dominance from a non-cloud market into the cloud may constitute the most likely finding of abusive conduct.

II. Cloud Computing and Market Developments

Overall, markets for cloud computing seem relatively competitive. Cloud computing is a broad and vague term, and so encompasses a variety of functions: software as a service, infrastructure as a service, platform as a service, etc. Thus an overall market for cloud computing would be defined in a very broad fashion and would likely not exhibit dominance. Indeed, Sluijs, Larouche and Sauter noted in 2006 that markets for cloud computing were quite competitive.[13] This seems still to be the case, with various large vertically integrated providers such as Google, Amazon, and Apple, as well as other cloud-only players, all vying with each other to provide cloud services. It seems unlikely that in a generalised market for cloud computing services any one of these players could be deemed to have a dominant position. Even if the market is defined more narrowly, such as for data storage

---

[13] J Sluijs, P Larouche and W Sauter, 'Cloud Computing in the EU Policy Sphere' (2012) 3(1) *Journal of Intellectual Property, Information Technology and e-Commerce Law* 12.

in the cloud, then it is still likely that this market would also be found to be sufficiently competitive not to have given rise to a dominant player.

Nevertheless, as mentioned above, certain cloud providers are vertically integrated with other Internet services, in whose markets they may be dominant. A prime candidate is Google, which has a dominant position in the European online search market. Thus cloud providers could be implicated in anticompetitive conduct in other markets, such as an attempt to tie a cloud service to use of search, or a particular mobile device.

Furthermore, the net neutrality debate detailed in chapter 3 has a bearing on competition in cloud computing markets. If priority access to the network is permitted (and thus there is a deviation from the principles of net neutrality), then incumbents may well pay for such priority access to ensure the connection with their users is as quick and of as high a quality as possible. This will increase entry barriers for potential entrants since they will require an even greater investment in order to enter the cloud market. There is also the possibility for cloud providers to merge with Internet Service Providers (ISPs) and become vertically integrated, with the potential for the newly vertically integrated player to discriminate in favour of its own cloud services. Thus, competition and openness in the network layers has a direct bearing on cloud computing since the cloud depends directly on these layers to function.[14]

At the time of writing, markets for cloud computing per se are probably insufficiently mature for substantial competition issues to emerge. However, it is possible to see that the ways in which they are developing already raise prospective competition concerns, aside from the privacy and control issues mentioned above.[15] Thus, this chapter is shorter in length and more forward-looking in style than its predecessors which are 'reactive' to concrete events, in particular alleged abuses of dominance. Instead, this chapter considers the extent to which current laws are able to address the problems caused by accumulations of private power in cloud computing. This is not an overly theoretical endeavour given the trends towards moving more and more content and data storage, platforms and applications to the cloud as opposed to running on users' own devices, and thus the control that cloud providers will increasingly possess.

III. Effectiveness of Competition Law in Addressing Cloud Concerns

Dominance as recognised by competition law is unlikely to be found in cloud markets as they currently stand nor does there seem to be the requisite conditions

---

[14] I Walden and LDC Luciano 'Facilitating Competition in the Clouds' in C Millard (ed), *Cloud Computing Law* (Oxford, Oxford University Press, 2013).
[15] ibid.

for collective dominance or collusion. Nevertheless, problems for competition are already emerging in these markets, particularly the locking-in of users to particular branded cloud ecosystems and the leveraging of dominance from external markets into cloud markets. The problem with competition law, though, is that it can only act reactively to deal with these problems once they blossom into full-blown infringements, rather than nip them in the bud as they emerge.[16]

A. Market Definition

Given cloud computing markets overall are probably competitive, a broadly drawn market definition is unlikely to lead to a finding that a particular player is dominant. Thus, narrower markets would need to be defined to arrive closer to that finding of dominance. Since cloud computing services often exhibit features including consumer lock-in, it is possible that very narrow markets might be defined for a particular cloud service, such as a market for Google Drive or a market for Dropbox, in which either of these players would be found to be dominant as they are the only player in that very narrowly-defined market.

B. Competitive Constraints

Competitive constraints in the form of entry barriers and switching costs exist in cloud computing markets. As already mentioned, there is already a degree of user lock-in. Other barriers to new entrants in cloud markets include the costs in providing cloud infrastructure such as data centres, software and a sufficiently large bandwidth connection such that users do not experience interruptions in service. The net neutrality debate is also of relevance here since if 'prioritised' or 'special' services are permitted, then this could pose a further barrier to new entrants. Leading cloud services are likely to want to guarantee a certain quality of service for their users and take advantage of the possibility to pay for a prioritised service for their data packets to users, thus raising the costs of an entity which wished to enter the market to compete.

Furthermore, cloud operators' offerings may be protected by intellectual property, mainly copyright and patents, giving the cloud operator exclusive rights. If 'proprietary' and 'closed' standards are adopted by cloud computing operators for their services, then this will contribute to a lack of interoperability between their services and their rivals' services, which is not anticompetitive per se but will contribute to users' switching costs.

---

[16] ibid.

C. Operation of Abuse of Dominance

Only if the market is sufficiently narrowly defined is dominance likely to be found and thus trigger the application of competition law. So if the market is defined more broadly, a finding of dominance is less likely and cloud computing players' conduct towards users such as stymying data portability and locking them into a particular cloud system is unlikely to be found to be anticompetitive.

A dominant cloud provider will have incentives to retain as many users (and their data) as possible, so will be incentivised to restrict data portability and may also be incentivised to restrict the interoperability of their ecosystem with those of rivals, lest it lose users to these other services. Restricting interoperability and data portability per se will not constitute an abuse of dominance; there is usually intellectual property protection of the standards used by the dominant player, and these exclusive rights are generally to be respected.

However, in certain, exceptional circumstances, a dominant player preventing interoperability of such standards may be viewed as an abuse of dominance.[17] Indeed, this was one of the findings in the European *Microsoft* case, that Microsoft had to give its competitors full access to the information which would allow them to interoperate with its services, otherwise they would not be able to compete viably with Microsoft. Such a finding, and its remedy, may have positive spillover effects for users, such as increasing the possibility of them being able to engage in data portability. Yet, it is unlikely that these exceptional circumstances will exist in cloud markets, even if dominance is found, and so it is unlikely that a lack of interoperability will constitute an abuse of dominance. Also, the circumstances of the *Microsoft* case were that Microsoft was leveraging its dominance from one market (for operating systems) into another (for work group server operating systems) and so it may also have to be shown that a cloud operator is leveraging its dominance from one market into another by refusing to interoperate with rivals' services. In the scenario where a user stores files in the cloud and wants to move them to another cloud operator's service which competes in the same market, then if the first, original operator refused to interoperate this would not be an attempt to leverage dominance from one market into another, as the entities are competing in the same market. While it is possible that a cloud operator would refuse interoperability in order to leverage its dominant position in one cloud market (eg for file storage) into another market (eg the provision of a certain software service for those files already stored in the cloud), this would only seem to be one criterion for the lack of interoperability to be found to be an abuse of this dominant position.

A dominant cloud provider may also have an incentive to leverage its dominant position from one market into another, such as that for a mobile app, which could prevent users having a choice of mobile app as the leveraging of dominance

---

[17] I Graef, J Vershakelen and P Valcke, 'Putting the Right to Data Portability into a Competition Law Perspective' (2013) *Law: Journal of the Higher School of Economics Annual Review* 53.

involves the tying of the cloud service to this particular mobile app, or vice versa. Although it is unlikely that a cloud provider would have a dominant position in a cloud market (unless it is very tightly drawn eg around one provider's particular offering), it is possible that cloud services may be tied to another product or service in which the same owner has a dominant position, ultimately depriving users of choice. If such a tie is found to constitute anticompetitive conduct, then remedying this situation could ensure users are given choices when it comes to which cloud service they use in conjunction with other online services.

Moreover, even if primary cloud computing markets are competitive, it is possible that a particular cloud operator may attempt to impose the use of that operator's software on users already using the cloud service, thus constituting a possible example of abusive conduct in an aftermarket. Whether there are primary and secondary markets comprised in a particular combination of products and services is highly context-dependent. Distinctness of the two claimed products or services is important, and a key question will be whether consumers take into account the prices and other features of the secondary market, eg software in the cloud, when making their initial purchase/decision in the primary market for cloud provision: did the consumer take the view that they were acquiring a 'package'?

As more content and applications are being moved to the cloud or being accessible via cloud services, Renda recognises that cloud operators constitute another online gatekeeper, and in theory similar competition issues may arise as have done with the physical network infrastructure discussed in chapter 3: refusals to deal with certain content or applications with the result that they are inaccessible or blocked to cloud users; preferential treatment to certain content and applications via agreements; and vertical integration leading to discrimination against upstream or downstream competitors.[18] Indeed, the operation of competition law here links back to the discussion in chapter 3 on the operation of competition law (and existing ex ante regulation) in Internet provision markets. There, a finding of dominance was pivotal as to whether competition law operates to sanction this kind of conduct by an ISP. If there is no dominant position, then accordingly and perhaps obviously, these behaviours will not be found illegal under competition law's abuse of dominance. Given the lack of specific regulation of cloud computing, conduct which may be harmful to users, such as restricting what they can access in the cloud and not permitting them to take their data with them to other services, is likely to be unaddressed if done by non-dominant providers, and, as seen above, even a dominant player restricting interoperability may not be abusing that dominance.

Thus, unless a dominant position can be found, either by a very tight market definition or through finding a dominant position in a cloud computing aftermarket, it is unlikely that competition law's abuse of dominance mechanism will aid users in the problems they face with cloud computing. However, these

---

[18] A Renda, 'Competition, Neutrality and Diversity in the Cloud' (2012) 85 *Communications and Strategies* 23, 39.

problems are already emerging from cloud markets, and include a lack of inter-operability of services, an inability for users to take their data with them from one service to a rival's (or take it out of the cloud and offline completely), and a lack of choice for users when a cloud service is tied to another product or service. However, absent any merger in this sector which would enable competition authorities to consider some of these user-harming tendencies in cloud markets, or evidence of collusive conduct or collective dominance among cloud providers, European competition authorities must wait for the achievement of a position of dominance by one player before they can potentially intervene to address any possible abuses.

From the user perspective, this seems highly inadequate—there are already threats to their autonomy by cloud service operators in terms of a restriction of their choice, a lack of interoperability and an absence of data portability. Yet as it stands competition law is unlikely to provide solutions to these problems. As this conduct without dominance is unlikely to be anticompetitive, and as the achievement of dominance itself is likely to be permitted, competition law seems impotent: one must wait for the worst to happen even if it was already predicted and current conduct and conditions could be observed to lead in that direction.

IV. Other Legal Regimes

Given the unlikelihood of competition law being effective in practice vis-à-vis cloud computing providers to address the concerns identified at the beginning of this chapter, other legal regimes are considered.

A. Data Protection and Privacy

In the EU, data protection law will apply prima facie to the processing of personal data in the cloud when the data controller is based in the EU, and personal data should not be transferred out of the EU to third countries which do not provide an adequate level of protection.

The Article 29 Data Protection Working Party issued an Opinion on Cloud Computing in which it identified concerns surrounding the lack of control by users over the personal data they commit to the cloud, specifically due to a lack of interoperability and lack of confidentiality (given the possibility of law enforcement requests for the data, including from agencies outside of the EU), and a lack of transparency over how precisely the personal data is being processed, including it being transferred to countries outside the EU.[19]

---

[19] Article 29 Data Protection Working Party, Opinion 05/2012 on Cloud Computing, 1 July 2012.

Certain problems have also been identified regarding how EU data protection law applies to the cloud, including the issue of what precisely constitutes 'personal data' in the cloud, such as the extent to which encrypting or anonymising data moves it outside of the 'personal data' category.[20]

The applicability of the EU data protection regime, however, will become more complicated if the controller is not based in the EU. The current Directive's rules will apply if the controller uses equipment located in the territory of a Member State (except only for purposes of transit), even if the controller is established elsewhere. However, at the moment it appears that a data controller based outside of the EU with no equipment (or only transit equipment) physically in the EU's territory will not fall under the data protection laws, even if that entity is processing the personal data of EU citizens. This is modified in the forthcoming General Data Protection Regulation, whose provisions apply to controllers or processors established in the EU processing personal data (although it is not necessary for the processing itself to occur within the EU), and also to controllers or processors not established within the EU but which are processing EU citizens' data.[21] This should provide greater safeguards for the personal data of EU citizens by making this the focus of the jurisdiction question, rather than the location of the processor or controller.

Nevertheless, the problem remains of effectively enforcing these laws vis-à-vis non-EU entities processing the data outside the EU, particularly if they have no assets in the EU, and the possibility of foreign law enforcement access to this data when stored offshore. This issue has been discussed and raised as a concern for some time by commentators, but the recent decision of the Court of Justice of the European Union (CJEU) in the *Schrems* case has brought it to the fore.[22] The decision invalidates the EU-US 'Safe Harbor' agreement facilitating personal data transfers from the EU to the US due to US data protection practices, in light of the National Security Agency (NSA)'s surveillance and data accessing activities (revealed by Edward Snowden) not being consistent with assuring the appropriate level of protection of EU citizens' personal data being transferred to the US. At the time of writing, the EU and US have been negotiating a new agreement, 'Privacy Shield', in order to refacilitate such personal data transfers, although it seems unclear what final shape it may take and whether it would be legally valid vis-à-vis EU data protection law and the Charter of Fundamental Rights. Yet even prior to the *Schrems* decision, there had been some moves away from US cloud providers and towards EU-based alternatives, so as to avoid US law enforcement

---

[20] WK Hon, C Millard and I Walden 'What is Regulated as Personal Data in Clouds?' in C Millard (ed), *Cloud Computing Law* (Oxford, Oxford University Press, 2013).

[21] Data Protection Regulation, art 3.

[22] Case C-362/14 *Schrems v Data Protection Commissioner*, CJEU, 6 October 2015. See N Ni Loidean, 'The End of Safe Harbor: Implications for EU Privacy and Data Protection Law' (2016) 19(8) *Journal of Internet Law* 1.

agency interference and to ensure the applicability of EU data protection rules to EU citizens' personal data.[23]

The Regulation's right to data portability may remedy some of the lock-in users experience in using the cloud.[24] As discussed in the previous chapter, this right entails that users will be able to obtain their personal data held by a particular entity 'in a structured and commonly used and machine-readable format'.[25] However, as highlighted earlier, the right to data portability has various limitations and does not represent a particularly strong right for users. A stronger response to the competition, control and privacy concerns surrounding the cloud would entail a right to the portability of all data, and not just that which is personal, along with interoperability requirements on cloud providers.

B. Free Expression

Competition law and data protection law (particularly that forthcoming in the Regulation) would go some way to addressing the free expression concerns raised at the beginning of this chapter, namely the increased control over what users access and upload that cloud providers have; the increased possibility of surveillance of user activity; and the increased lock-in users experience when using cloud services (either via technical means or contractual terms). If an entity is found to have a dominant position in a particular cloud market, then actions such as preventing interoperability between its services and those of others, or forbidding users to port their data stored with that player, may amount to anticompetitive abuses of dominance. Furthermore, a dominant player restricting the content and services users can access in or via the cloud may also amount to an abuse of that dominant position via tying its different products and services together. The right to data portability may alleviate some of the concerns around user lock-in.

Nevertheless, the problems for free expression that cloud computing presents are not fully addressed by these other legal regimes. Competition is only triggered where there is a finding of dominance or collusion (or if a merger is proposed), so the users of cloud players that are not dominant in their particular market nor exhibit collusive conduct will not be able to seek remedies from this area of law. While the right to data portability will apply to non-dominant players as well as those with a dominant position, in its current formulation it is not a particularly strong right since it only applies to personal data.

Chapter 3's discussion on free expression laws' application to the net neutrality debate is relevant to how free expression laws might be applied in the cloud context. The law is unlikely to address the lack of interoperability or data portability,

---

[23] 'Europe Pushes Own Digital "Cloud" in Wake of US Spying Scandal', *EurActiv*, 29 August 2013, available at www.euractiv.com/infosociety/prism-cloud-european-silver-lini-news-530004.
[24] Data Protection Regulation, art 18.
[25] ibid art 18(2).

but if cloud providers are restricting users' access to content via the cloud, then this restriction may be found to be an infringement of European Convention on Human Rights (ECHR), Article 10. As already mentioned in chapter 3, a finding of infringement is highly context-dependent, and previous case law has tended to set a high bar as to whether this kind of conduct will amount to an infringement. It may be that it will only amount to an infringement if it is not possible for users to access this content in any other way (including offline). Furthermore, it may be necessary that a whole class of content is blocked by the cloud provider. An alternative route to finding an infringement of Article 10 may be if the cloud provider's conduct in some way affects media plurality, and in the increasing move towards online 'walled gardens' this may be less of a fanciful thought than it was during the height of the 1990s cyberliberterian utopianism. Indeed, given the profit-motivation of commercial cloud providers, they have incentives to disseminate 'popular content which attracts a greater number of users and thus generates higher advertising revenues ... at the detriment of less popular, but not necessarily less important content which receives less visibility'.[26]

It is true that state-mandated online mass surveillance facilitated by private parties has been recognised in recent CJEU jurisprudence to pose problems for users' right to free expression.[27] However, such surveillance being carried out for private parties' own business purposes and not obliged by law does not seem to be illegal, provided that private parties abide by EU data protection law and their own contractual arrangements, especially privacy policies.

Thus, it seems that the application of the right to free expression in Europe to cloud providers will be highly context-dependent, and is only likely to apply if a cloud provider is restricting users' access to content via the cloud; and even then, probably only if this restriction means that users are not able to access this content via any other means. The right is unlikely to entail changes to cloud providers' other business practices, such as surveillance, the locking-in of users and prevention of interoperability and data portability.

V. Regulation

The current laws in the form of competition, data protection and free expression laws only go some small way to protecting users' interests in cloud computing but do not protect and promote all of them, and not necessarily in every set of circumstances. Accordingly, regulation or other government action can be considered, which might encompass the implementation of some kind of privacy by

---

[26] De Filippi and McCarthy, 'Cloud Computing: Centralization and Data Sovereignty' (n 2) 50.
[27] See eg Case C-70/10 *Scarlet Extended v Societe belge des auteurs, compositeurs et editeurs (SABAM)* [2012] ECDR 4.

default/design when it comes to new technologies and promoting international standards on privacy and data protection in the cloud.

However, governments themselves have an interest in ensuring users' communications are available to them for their own law enforcement purposes and so are unlikely to promote strong privacy protections which could stymie their own surveillance efforts. Indeed, it is the judiciary at both the domestic and EU levels, rather than governments, who have been pushing back surveillance laws in cases such as *Digital Rights Ireland*.[28] It also seems highly unlikely that an international consensus could be reached on these issues. This is particularly the case given the divergence in data protection and privacy standards between the US and EU (as highlighted by the *Schrems* decision), let alone other global powers. If global standardisation of norms is to occur, then pragmatically it may result in norms being agreed that are not particularly strong protections of individual privacy (and free expression) so the whole exercise may produce unwelcome outcomes. The regional and global trade agreements currently under negotiation, including the Transatlantic Trade and Investment Partnership, the Trans Pacific Partnership (which has been signed), and the Trade in Services Agreement, do not bode well for increased user autonomy online.[29]

At the national or regional level, some more regulation of cloud services could be achievable. This might include obligations on cloud providers to facilitate interoperability with each other, to allow data portability, and not to interfere with users' right to receive and impart information which is otherwise legal. Nevertheless, the problems with jurisdiction in the cloud may persist unless there is more invasive regulation here too, for instance obliging cloud operators providing services to EU citizens to be entirely geographically based in the EU's territory.

The EU adopted a 'strategy' for cloud computing in 2012 which so far has focussed on standardising contractual terms for cloud services, facilitating cloud standards and creating common public procurement mechanisms for cloud services.[30] However, this initiative is premised on the move to the cloud being something positive and to be encouraged when from the preceding discussion it is far from clear that this is the case, and aspects of user autonomy such as privacy and increased control do not appear to feature in the initiative's language. This Commission cloud strategy is also categorised as being related to the 'economy' rather than 'society', framing the cloud as an economic 'consumer' issue rather than a socio-economic 'user' issue.

---

[28] Joined Cases C-293/12 and C-594/12 *Digital Rights Ireland and Seitlinger and Others* (CJEU, 8 April 2014).

[29] See G Greenleaf, 'The TPP Agreement: An Anti-Privacy Treaty for Most of APEC' (2015) 138 *Privacy Laws and Business International Report* 21; S Aaronson, 'Why Trade Agreements are Not Setting Information Free: The Lost History and Reinvigorated Debate over Cross-Border Data Flows, Human Rights, and National Security' (2015) 14(4) *World Trade Review* 671.

[30] European Commission, *European Cloud Computing Strategy*, available at https://ec.europa.eu/digital-single-market/en/european-cloud-computing-strategy.

VI. Extra-Legal Solutions

If privacy and free expression-enhancing regulation is not a realistic prospect, users may turn to certain extra-legal solutions in order to uphold their autonomy vis-à-vis the cloud.

One option for users may be encrypting their data, so that even if it goes into the cloud they retain more protection over the information that they put into it. Yet encryption does not address the fundamental power imbalances in the cloud in favour of the cloud provider, and just means that the cloud provider cannot see exactly what the information is, or may just need to employ decryption services.

Using 'community clouds' is another option, whereby groups of individuals set up their own cloud services, without a profit motive and independent of the state apparatus in accordance with a commons-based peer production model. These community clouds might use peer to peer technologies in order to protect user interests,[31] such as the Freedom Box (a small device comprising a server) which provides a decentralised architecture for users to exchange information and communicate securely,[32] or ownCloud which is a free software alternative to commercial cloud providers that includes encryption and can be installed on a private server. The mesh networks discussed in chapter 3 may also facilitate the setting up of community cloud services on a peer to peer basis.

While De Filippi and McCarthy acknowledge the problems with peer to peer technologies, especially for 'normal' Internet users who may not be so technically adept, their 'mere existence' provides a safeguard for users eager to retain autonomy and freedom of communication, or who are no longer satisfied with the growing encroachments on privacy and civil liberties implemented by cloud operators[33]—and thus should be encouraged as a 'third way' between private, for-profit clouds and state-controlled clouds.

However, the proliferation of data about users in the cloud is not limited to direct interactions of the user with cloud services, but also includes government and corporate use of the cloud via contracting out services, so there will also be data held in the cloud by a third party about an individual collected by the public services of her country or her bank, credit card company, etc. Thus, strong legal and regulatory responses to cloud autonomy problems are also desirable and complementary to any of these extra-legal solutions.

---

[31] De Filippi and McCarthy, 'Cloud Computing: Centralization and Data Sovereignty' (n 2) 51.
[32] Freedom Box Foundation, https://freedomboxfoundation.org/.
[33] De Filippi and McCarthy, 'Cloud Computing: Centralization and Data Sovereignty' (n 2) 53.

VII. Conclusion

Although this chapter may be viewed as more 'speculative' than the others when it comes to issues of private economic power over online information flows to the detriment of user autonomy, it addresses cloud services at a stage before they have been the subject of competition investigations, but when issues of dominance are emerging. Given the move towards placing more content, services and infrastructure in the cloud, this chapter provides a forward-looking consideration of the problems for users that arise, and recommends 'nipping them in the bud' before they become fully blown competition issues. In any event, cloud services already present problems for the effective enforcement of what data protection law there currently is, as well as represent a 'gatekeeping' point for users accessing certain content and services online (with the associated surveillance and censorship capacities that status brings).

Existing competition laws may address some of the concerns identified in the initial part of this chapter, such as a lack of interoperability between one provider's products/services and those of others, but only if dominance is found. The only other triggers for competition investigation here would be a suspicion of collusion among cloud providers, or possibly a planned merger, which do not appear to be the case in practice. Otherwise, competition law will not intervene to promote choice, interoperability, portability and free access to content and services. Users may find that even if there is not dominance in the competition law sense, they still do not have a 'real' choice among cloud providers' offerings, either because they are all offering similar services even if there are many players in the market, or because users are locked-in to a particular cloud service via contracts or technical measures and so are unable to switch providers, thus with no choice but to stay with the original cloud provider.

EU data protection law, particularly the reforms brought by the Regulation, would go some way to addressing user concerns, particularly via the right to data portability. However, as has been discussed above, this right to data portability is not a very strong right nor does it cover all data that users may have in the cloud.

The problem remains, in any event, of jurisdiction and the enforceability of whatever laws that may already be in existence with regard to the cloud, given the lack of transparency over where information 'in the cloud' is actually hosted physically, the ability of that information to be transferred very easily between data centres in different parts of the world, and the differing norms that different countries apply to data being held in the cloud when it is being hosted in their geographical territory.

Pragmatically, a regional or national initiative to impose more regulation on cloud providers in the interests of users may be desirable. This regulation could comprise obligations on cloud providers to facilitate interoperability with each other, to allow data portability, and not to interfere with users' right to receive and impart information which is otherwise legal. Regulation may also be required to address the problem of enforceability of law, for instance obliging cloud providers to be entirely geographically based within a particular jurisdiction. Nevertheless, the practical problems with regulation have already been recognised earlier in this book: the influence of lobbying on the regulatory process as well as the time taken to get to the stage of regulation being contrasted against the often-much-quicker rate of technological development. Given the trajectory of the General Data Protection Regulation, whose formation was years in the making and attracted intense lobbying from (especially US-based) corporations, it seems highly likely that any further attempts to regulate cloud services would be subject to a high level of resistance by the industry, except possibly European-based cloud operators which might be likely to benefit in part at least from such regulation. Furthermore, the problem remains of convincing regulators to make an intervention in the market given the general 'light touch' trend, even though larger problems can be anticipated. The net neutrality example in chapter 3 demonstrates that in practice, if regulators intervene at all, it can be many years afterwards, by which time conditions have changed—and not necessarily for the better.

Thus, as immediate solutions to the problems that cloud services present for users' autonomy online, technical and other extra-legal methods emerge again as the most expedient. Users should be encouraged to encrypt data they send to the cloud, as well as participate in 'community cloud' schemes based on peer to peer technologies. These seem to be the only methods by which users' privacy and freedom of communication—in other words, users' autonomy—can be retained in the cloud.

7

Conclusion

This book has considered the rise and manifestation of private economic power wielded by for-profit corporations over online information flows in the EU, to the detriment of user autonomy, and the legal and regulatory framework which applies to these scenarios. The four case studies through which this inquiry has been held exist along a spectrum or continuum of regulatory intervention, ranging from new ex ante net neutrality regulation being introduced in the case of Internet provision in chapter 3, to the prospective inquiry in chapter 6 on the cloud. Yet each of these case studies (Internet provision, search engines, mobile devices and the cloud) encompass the examination of a 'choke-point' over online information flows to and from users controlled by gatekeepers which are large private entities. Some of these gatekeepers have a recognised dominant position in accordance with EU competition law, while others form part of markets whose main (if not all of whose) participants are large, often transnational, for-profit corporations.

In each case study it can be seen that the law and regulation which does apply to the given situation—competition law and telecoms regulation, supplemented by fundamental rights to free expression and privacy and EU data protection law—fall short of fully protecting and promoting user autonomy in this context of corporate dominance over online information flows. Thus, there are 'gaps' in the existing EU legal framework when it comes to protecting and promoting user autonomy from online private economic power.

The influence of neoliberalism over EU law, policy and regulation vis-à-vis private economic power in Internet markets (if not in other markets as well) can explain, at least in part, this state of affairs. EU competition law's contemporary neoliberal influence and 'More Economic' approach has entailed that values aside from those currently encompassed by the nebulous goal of consumer welfare and which do not fit well into the quantitative analysis competition authorities employ cannot be promoted easily within the competition analysis to limit private economic power. Furthermore, authorities' forbearance from introducing ex ante regulation in situations where there are already or foreseeable problems for user autonomy can also be explained by the influence of neoliberal trends promoting minimalist 'light touch' regulation of private economic power, preferring a more 'reactive' approach when 'market failures' actually occur. In addition, fundamental rights are also caught up in this neoliberal conception of the world given their application is mainly vis-à-vis the nation-state. Data protection law, while exceptional in its application of certain aspects of privacy rights vis-à-vis private entities, is narrow in its scope ('personal data') and not always well-enforced. It also is unable to stop the continuing vast proliferation of data about individuals being collected and used by private, and public, power.

Net neutrality regulation as discussed in chapter 3 represents an exception to this trend of *avoiding* ex ante regulation of information gatekeepers, but can also be critiqued for being too little, too late: many years have passed since net neutrality was first raised as a problem for both competition and digital rights, which has entailed that technology and business methods have moved on, which is not clearly addressed in the regulation. The situation seems similar with the forthcoming General Data Protection Regulation, which does have aspects that represent an improvement on the existing situation for user autonomy such as the right to data portability, but could also be criticised for being too little, too late given it has come years after vast data gathering and analysing initiatives have become mainstream and does not do much to impede these practices.

The European Commission's competition investigation into Google is another exception to neoliberal trends of forbearing from intervention, given it is not clear that Google has actually abused its dominant position. While it is unclear precisely what is motivating the Commission in its actions, in any event so far they are still fairly 'light touch' when it comes to tackling the myriad problems posed for users by the large concentration of corporate power which Google encapsulates. The progress of the Commission's investigation and its aftermath can only be speculated on at the current time, and so the extent to which they uphold user autonomy remains to be seen.

In light of these developments, alternative, usually technical, 'self-help' methods for users in the form of alternatives to the corporate information gatekeepers have been proposed. These alternatives often involve peer to peer design as a means of re-establishing decentralisation, eroding the gatekeeping potential, and providing better protection and promotion of user autonomy in terms of facilitating free speech, more user control over infrastructure, and enhanced user privacy. These alternatives have specifically been chosen not on a technodeterministic basis, but because they embody the normative values of free expression, privacy and decentralisation advanced by the idea of user autonomy.

This book is limited inasmuch as it does not consider in great detail conceptual reforms to EU competition law to promote user autonomy, which may be possible but would be a longer term project. Instead, a realistic and immediate approach is taken to the problems that exist now with these large concentrations of private power online manifesting in commodified information gatekeepers and how they may be resolved in the short term with existing law, regulation and extralegal methods. Nevertheless, as mentioned in the Introduction, the reform of the law, particularly competition law and regulation, in ways which would promote user autonomy online, and perhaps autonomy for citizens in other areas of life as well, may be a much larger project, part of a broader and more profound societal change. As the implications of the EU's Charter for Fundamental Rights for competition and economic regulation become more apparent, the 'constitutionalisation' of these parts of the legal framework will be a more pressing issue, and one ripe for further research at the intersection of economic considerations and human rights, both vis-à-vis new technologies and other areas of life, such as health, energy and the environment. The European Data Protection Supervisor's comments on this topic are thus to be welcomed as starting this discussion in the EU, and the final outcome of the Google search investigation may be instructive as to other institutions' views on the matter.

In addition, a further area of law not considered in detail here is consumer protection, for reasons already detailed in the Introduction. A more thorough consideration of consumer protection's role in advancing user autonomy online would be a worthy subject of further study, particularly possible conceptual reform to the area to take into account the productive as well as consuming attributes of users in spaces such as the Internet, but also increasingly other domains such as 3D printing and renewable energy generation. What might move 'consumer' protection law to 'prosumer' protection law would be an interesting subject for further exploration.

Another limitation to the discussions in this book is its concentration on private economic power, which accordingly excludes a thorough consideration of the exercise of state power over online information flows to the detriment of user autonomy. While there is some acknowledgement of the coupling of state and private economic power in the form of the 'invisible handshake', a detailed consideration of this relationship is outside this book's scope due to considerations of length. The state has very much re-asserted itself (if it ever was truly absent) in recent years, including states of a so-called 'liberal democratic' persuasion, as evidenced in particular by the mass surveillance and data gathering programmes operated by the US and its allies in different parts of the world. The state interest in surveillance of Internet users, whether directly or indirectly via third parties, as has been acknowledged, may entail that reform to privacy and data protection law which would promote optimal conditions for user autonomy online is unlikely to be achieved in practice any time soon. Nevertheless, the peer to peer alternatives offered to the status quo ought to serve to promote and protect user autonomy vis-à-vis the state, as well as vis-à-vis private economic power. In any event, how the state interest in surveillance, the co-option of private providers for this end, and the War on Terror justifications given for these alliances, accord with neoliberal ideology, and how and whether the law including communications regulation and fundamental rights can effectively manage and oversee these relationships for the benefit of users, form other avenues for future research.

In the meantime, short-term reform of EU Internet law and policy should proceed on a basis in which users' autonomy is recognised, celebrated and promoted to the greatest extent possible within the current legal, economic and regulatory framework. Yet, given the challenges to this happening in practice, technical solutions designed with privacy, free expression and the decentralised resistance to control in mind may be for users the most realistic means of protecting and promoting their autonomy online. The least, then, that EU law and policy in this area should be doing is not stopping the emergence of these solutions.

REFERENCES

Aaronson, S, 'Why Trade Agreements are Not Setting Information Free: The Lost History and Reinvigorated Debate over Cross-Border Data Flows, Human Rights, and National Security' (2015) 14(4) *World Trade Review* 671

Acquisti, A, 'Privacy and Market Failure: Three Reasons for Concern, and Three Reasons for Hope' (2012) 10 *Journal on Telecommunications and High Technology Law* 227

Akman, P, '"Consumer Welfare" and Article 82EC: Practice and Rhetoric' (2009) 32(1) *World Competition* 71

—— '"Consumer" versus "Customer": The Devil in the Detail' (2010) 37(2) *Journal of Law and Society* 315

Albert, M and Hahnel, R, *The Political Economy of Participatory Economics* (Princeton, NJ, Princeton University Press, 1991)

Albors-Lorens, A and Jones, A, 'The Images of the "Consumer" in EU Competition Law' in D Leczykiewicz and S Weatherill (eds), *The Images of the 'Consumer' in EU Law* (Oxford, Hart Publishing, 2016)

Alemanno, A and Sibony, AL, *Nudge and the Law: A European Perspective* (Oxford, Hart Publishing, 2015)

Andreangeli, A, *EU Competition Enforcement and Human Rights* (Berlin, Edward Elgar, 2008)

Andriychuk, O, 'Rediscovering the Spirit of Competition: On the Normative Value of the Competitive Process' (2010) 6(3) *European Competition Journal* 575

ARCEP, *Neutralite de l'internet et des reseaux: propositions et orientations* (2010), available at www.arcep.fr/uploads/tx_gspublication/net-neutralite-orientations-sept2010.pdf

AT&T, 'AT&T Extends VOIP to 3G Network for iPhone', *AT&T News Room*, 6 October 2009, available at www.att.com/gen/press-room?pid=4800&cdvn=news&newsarticleid=27207

Bakardjieva, M, *Internet Society: The Internet in Everyday Life* (Thousand Oaks, CA, Sage, 2005)

Baldwin, R and others, 'Introduction: Regulation, the Field and the Developing Agenda' in R Baldwin and others (eds), *The Oxford Handbook of Regulation* (Oxford, Oxford University Press, 2010)

Barendt, E, *Freedom of Speech*, 2nd edn (Oxford, Oxford University Press, 2005)

Barkhuysen, T and Lindenbergh, SD, *Constitutionalisation of Private Law* (Leiden, BRILL, 2006)

Barlow, JP, 'A Declaration of the Independence of Cyberspace', *Electronic Frontier Foundation*, 8 February 1996, available at https://projects.eff.org/~barlow/Declaration-Final.html

Barratt, N and Shade, LR, 'Net Neutrality: Telecom Policy and the Public Interest' (2007) 32(2) *Canadian Journal of Communication* 295

Barzilai-Nahon, K, 'Toward a Theory of Network Gatekeeping: A Framework for Exploring Information Control' (2007) 59(9) *Journal of the American Society for Information Technology* 1493

Bauwens, M, 'From the Theory of Peer Production to the Production of Peer Production Theory' (2012) 1 *Journal of Peer Production*

Benkler, Y, 'From Consumers to Users: Shifting the Deeper Structures of Regulations Towards Sustainable Commons and User Access' (2000) 52 *Federal Communications Law Journal* 561

——— *The Wealth of Networks: How Social Production Transforms Markets and Freedom* (New Haven, CT, Yale University Press, 2006)

——— 'Practical Anarchism: Peer Mutualism, Market Power and the Fallible State' (2013) 41(2) *Politics and Society* 213

Bernal, P, *Internet Privacy Rights: Rights to Protect Autonomy* (Cambridge, Cambridge University Press, 2014)

Bernhard, S, 'From Conflict to Consensus: European Neoliberalism and the Debate on the Future of EU Social Policy' (2010) 4(1) *Work Organisation, Labour and Globalisation* 175.

Biddle, P and others, 'The Darknet and the Future of Content Protection' in E Becker and others (eds), *Digital Rights Management: Technological, Economic, Legal and Political Aspects* (Berlin, Springer, 2003)

Birnhack, MD and Elkin-Koren, N, 'The Invisible Handshake: The Reemergence of the State in the Digital Environment' (2003) 8 *Virginia Journal of Law and Technology* 6

Black, O, *Conceptual Foundations of Antitrust* (Cambridge, Cambridge University Press, 2010)

Blue, L, 'Internet and Domain Name Governance Antitrust Litigation and ICANN' (2014) 19(1) *Berkeley Technology Law Journal* 387

Boas, T and Gans-Morse, J, 'Neoliberalism: From New Liberal Philosophy to Anti-Liberal Slogan' (2009) 44(2) *Studies in Comparative International Development* 137

Bork, R, *The Antitrust Paradox*, 1st edn (Free Press, 1978)

Boyd, D and Crawford, K, 'Six Provocations for Big Data', 'A Decade in Internet Time', Symposium on the Dynamics of the Internet and Society, Oxford, September 2011

Braithwaite, J, 'Responsive Regulation for Australia' in P Grabosky and J Braithwaite, *Business Regulation and Australia's Future* (Griffith, Australian Institute of Criminology, 1993)

Brodley, JF, 'Economic Goals of Antitrust: Efficiency, Consumer Welfare and Technological Progress' (1987) 62 *New York University Law Review* 1020

Brown, I and Marsden, CT, *Regulating Code: Good Governance and Better Regulation in the Information Age* (Cambridge, MA, MIT Press, 2013)

Bruner, CM, 'States, Market, and Gatekeepers: Public-Private Regulatory Regimes in an Era of Economic Globalization' (2008) 30 *Michigan Journal of International Law* 125

Bruns, A, *Blogs, Wikipedia, Second Life, and Beyond: From Production to Produsage* (Bern, Peter Lang, 2008)

Buch-Hansen, H and Wigger, A, *The Politics of European Competition Regulation: A Critical Political Economy Perspective* (Abingdon, Routledge, 2011)

Budzinski, O and Wacker, K, *The Prohibition of the Proposed Springer-Prosiebensat. 1-Merger: How Much Economics in German Merger Control?*, University of Marburg Papers on Economics (2007), available at http://ssrn.com/abstract=976861

Carrapico, H and Farrand, B (eds), *The Governance of Online Expression in a Networked World* (Abingdon, Routledge, 2015)

Carrier, M, 'A Roadmap to the Smartphone Patent Wars and FRAND Licensing' (2012) 2 *CPI Antitrust Chronicle* 1

Cave, J and others, 'Regulating the Cloud: More, Less or Different Regulation and Competing Agendas', 40th Research Conference on Communication, Information and Internet Policy, Arlington, September 2012

Cave, M and Williams, HP, 'Google and European Competition Law', 39th Research Conference on Communication, Information and Internet Policy, Arlington, September 2011

Center for a Stateless Society, *Entrepreneurial Anti-Capitalism: Radical Mesh Networks* (29 May 2014), available at http://c4ss.org/content/27704

Chee, FY, 'Microsoft, publishers try to stop "catastrophic" Google EU deal', *Reuters*, 4 September 2014, available at www.reuters.com/article/2014/09/04/us-eu-google-microsoft-idUSKBN0GZ1NW20140904

Chee, FY and Oreskovic, A, 'European regulators training sights on Google's mobile software', *Reuters*, 30 July 2014, available at www.reuters.com/article/2014/07/30/us-google-europe-android-insight-idUSKBN0FZ2B220140730

Claassen, RJG and Gerbrandy, A, 'Rethinking European Competition Law: From a Consumer Welfare to a Capability Approach' (2016) 12(1) *Utrecht Law Review* 1

Clark, D and others, 'Interconnection in the Internet: Policy Challenges', 39th Research Conference on Communication, Information and Internet Policy, Arlington, September 2011

Clarke, S, 'The Neoliberal Theory of Society' in A Saad-Filho and D Johnston (eds), *Neoliberalism: A Critical Reader* (London, Pluto Press, 2005)

Coase, R, 'The Economics of Broadcasting and Government Policy' (1966) 56(1/2) *American Economic Review* 440

Cohen, J, 'The Place of the User in Copyright Law' (2005) 74 *Fordham Law Review* 347

—— *Configuring the Networked Self: Law, Code and Everyday Practice* (New Haven, CT, Yale University Press, 2012)

Colander, D, *Neoclassical Political Economy: The Analysis of Rent-Seeking and DUP Activities* (Cambridge, MA, Ballinger, 1984)

Coleman, G, *Coding Freedom: The Ethics and Aesthetics of Hacking* (Princeton, NJ, Princeton University Press, 2013)

Comanor, WS, 'Vertical Price-Fixing, Vertical Market Restrictions, and the New Antitrust Policy' (1985) 98 (5) *Harvard Law Review* 983.

Corporate Europe Observatory, *The Record of a Captive Commission: The 'Black Book' on the Corporate Agenda of the Barroso II Commission* (Brussels, 2014), available at http://corporateeurope.org/power-lobbies/2014/05/record-captive-commission

Costa-Cabral, F and Lynskey, O, *The Internal and External Constraints of Data Protection on Competition Law in the EU*, LSE Legal Studies Working Paper 25/2015, available at http://ssrn.com/abstract=2703655

Cowie, C and Marsden, CT, 'Convergence, Competition and Regulation' (1998) 1 *International Journal of Communications Law and Policy* 1.

Cox, MB, 'Apple's Exclusive Distribution Agreements: A Refusal to Supply?' (2012) 33(1) *European Competition Law Review* 11

Crandall, RW and Winston, C, 'Does Antitrust Policy Improve Consumer Welfare? Assessing the Evidence' (2003) 17(4) *Journal of Economics Perspectives* 3

Croft, JW, 'Antitrust and Communications Policy: There's an App for Just About Anything, Except Google Voice' (2010) 14 *SMU Science and Technology Law Review* 1.

Curran, J, 'Rethinking Internet History' in J Curran, N Fenton and D Freeman (eds), *Misunderstanding the Internet* (Abingdon, Routledge, 2012)

—— 'Reinterpreting the Internet' in J Curran, N Fenton and D Freedman (eds), *Misunderstanding the Internet* (Abingdon, Routledge, 2012)

Daly, A, 'Private Power and New Media: The Case of the Corporate Suppression of Wikileaks and Its Implications for the Exercise of Fundamental Rights on the Internet' in CM Akrivopoulou and N Garipidis (eds), *Human Rights and Risks in the Digital Era: Globalization and the Effects of Information Technology* (Hershey, PA, IGI Global, 2012)

—— 'Free Software and the Law: Out of the Frying Pan and into the Fire—How Shaking Up Intellectual Property Suits Competition Just Fine' (2013) 3 *Journal of Peer Production*

—— 'E-book Monopolies and the Law' (2013) *Media and Arts Law Review* 350

—— 'Dominating Search: Google Before the Law' in R Konig and M Rasch (eds), *Society of the Query Reader* (Amsterdam, Institute of Network Cultures, 2014)

'Data, Data Everywhere', *The Economist*, 25 February 2010, available at www.economist.com/node/15557443

De Filippi, P, 'Ubiquitous Computing in the Cloud: User Empowerment vs. User Obsequity' in JE Pelet and P Papadopoulou (eds), *User Behavior in Ubiquitous Online Environments* (Hershey, PA, IGI Global, 2013)

—— 'Bitcoin: A Regulatory Nightmare to Libertarian Dream' (2014) 3(2) *Internet Policy Review*

—— 'It's Time to Take Mesh Networks Seriously (And Not Just for the Reasons You Think)', *Wired*, 2 January 2014, available at www.wired.com/opinion/2014/01/its-time-to-take-mesh-networks-seriously-and-not-just-for-the-reasons-you-think/

De Filippi, P and McCarthy, S, 'Cloud Computing: Centralization and Data Sovereignty' (2012) 3(2) *European Journal of Law and Technology*

De Filippi, P and Treguer, F, 'Expanding the Internet Commons: The Subversive Potential of Wireless Community Networks' (2015) 6 *Journal of Peer Production*

De Nardis, L, 'Governance at the Internet's Core: The Geopolitics of Interconnection and Internet Exchange Points (IXPs) in Emerging Markets', 40th Research Conference on Communication, Information and Internet Policy, Arlington, September 2012

De Streel, A, 'Remedies in the Electronic Communications Sector' in D Geradin (ed), *Remedies in Network Industries: EC Competition Law vs. Sector-Specific Regulation* (Mortsel, Intersentia, 2004)

Deva, S, 'Human Rights Violations by Multinational Corporations and International Law: Where from Here?' (2003) 19 *Connecticut Journal of International Law* 1

Devine, KL, 'Preserving Competition in Multi-sided Innovative Markets: How Do You Solve a Problem Like Google?' (2008) 10(1) *North Carolina Journal of Law and Technology* 59

Diamond, L, *Developing Democracy: Towards Consolidation* (Baltimore, MD, John Hopkins University Press, 1999)

D'Ignazio, A and Giovannetti, E, 'Antitrust Analysis for the Internet Upstream Market: A Border Gateway Protocol Approach' (2006) 2(1) *Journal of Competition Law and Economics* 43

Diker Vanberg, A, 'From Archie to Google: Search Engine Providers and Emergent Challenges in Relation to EU Competition Law' (2012) 3(1) *European Journal for Law and Technology*

Doctorow, C, 'Phone Company Blocks Access to Telecoms Union's Website', *Boing Boing*, 24 July 2005, available at http://boingboing.net/2005/07/24/phone-company-blocks.html

Dredge, S, 'Financial Times: "There is no drawback to working in HTML5"', *Guardian*, 29 April 2013, available at www.theguardian.com/media/appsblog/2013/apr/29/financial-times-html5-no-drawbacks

'Driven by Facebook and Google, Mobile Ad Market Soars 105% in 2013', *eMarketer*, 19 March 2014, available at www.emarketer.com/Article/Driven-by-Facebook-Google-Mobile-Ad-Market-Soars-10537-2013/1010690

Ducklin, P, 'How Effective are Data Breach Penalties? Are Ever-Bigger Fines Enough?', *Nakedsecurity*, 26 April 2013, available at http://nakedsecurity.sophos.com/2013/04/26/how-effective-are-data-protection-regulations/

Dulong de Rosnay, M, 'Peer to Peer as a Design Principle for Law: Distribute the Law' (2015) 6 *Journal of Peer Production*

Dyson, E and others, *Cyberspace and the American Dream: A Magna Carta for the Knowledge Age* (Progress and Freedom Foundation, August 1994), available at www.pff.org/issues-pubs/futureinsights/fi1.2magnacarta.html

Economides, N, 'Chapter 9: The Economics of the Internet Backbone' in S Majumdar and others (eds), *Handbook of Telecommunications Economics* (Amsterdam, Elsevier, 2005) vol 2

—— '"Net Neutrality", Non-Discrimination and Digital Distribution of Content Through the Internet' (2008) 4(2) *I/S: A Journal of Law and Policy for the Information Society* 209

Edelman, B, *Hard-Coding Bias in Google Algorithmic Search Results* (15 November 2010), available at www.benedelman.org/hardcoding/

—— *Secret Ties in Google's 'Open' Android* (13 February 2014), available at www.benedelman.org/news/021314-1.html

Edelman, B and Lockwood, B, *Measuring Bias in 'Organic' Web Search* (19 January 2011), available at www.benedelman.org/searchbias/

Edwards, L, 'Pornography, Censorship and the Internet' in L Edwards and C Waelde (eds), *Law and the Internet* (Oxford, Hart, 2009)

—— 'The Rise and Fall of Online Intermediary Liability' in L Edwards and C Waelde (eds), *Law and the Internet* (Oxford, Hart, 2009)

Elkin-Koren, N and Salzberger, EM, *Law and Economics of Cyberspace: The Effects of Cyberspace on the Economic Analysis of Law* (Berlin, Edward Elgar, 2004)

Endicott, T, 'Law is Necessarily Vague' (2001) 7(4) *Legal Theory* 379

EurActiv, Europe Pushes Own Digital "Cloud" in Wake of US Spying Scandal (29 August 2013), available at www.euractiv.com/infosociety/prism-cloud-european-silver-lini-news-530004

European Digital Rights Initiative, US Privacy Groups Believe US Officials Lobby to Weaken EU Privacy (13 February 2013), available at http://history.edri.org/book/export/html/3215

European Digital Rights Initiative and Access, *Comments to the Consolidated Text on Net Neutrality in the Regulation Concerning the Open Internet Proposed by the Latvian Presidency on February 25th 2015*, available at https://edri.org/files/20150225TSM.pdf

Evans, DS, 'Antitrust Economics of Free' (2011) *Competition Policy International* 17

FairSearch, *FairSearch Announces Complaint in EU on Google's Anti-Competitive Mobile Strategy* (8 April 2013), available at www.fairsearch.org/mobile/fairsearch-announces-complaint-in-eu-on-googles-anti-competitive-mobile-strategy/

Farrand, B, 'Lobbying and Lawmaking in the European Union: The Development of Copyright Law and the Rejection of the Anti-Counterfeiting Trade Agreement' (2015) 35(3) *Oxford Journal of Legal Studies* 487

Feretti, F, *Competition, the Consumer Internet, and Data Protection* (Berlin, Springer, 2014)

Fiveash, K, 'Google's Euro Antitrust Offer: Fine! We'll Link to Our Search Rivals', *The Register*, 25 April 2013, available at www.theregister.co.uk/2013/04/25/ec_gives_google_rivals_one_month_to_market_test_search_tweaks/

Fontaine, F, 'French Antitrust Law and Strategic Analysis: Apples and Oranges?' (2009) 30(6) *European Competition Law Review* 286

Forbes, *Google's Mobile Division to Fuel Revenue Growth in 2014 and Beyond* (8 April 2014), available at www.forbes.com/sites/greatspeculations/2014/04/08/googles-mobile-division-to-fuel-revenue-growth-in-2014-and-beyond/

Fox, EM, 'US and European Merger Policy, Fault Lines and Bridges: Mergers that Create Incentives for Exclusionary Practices' (2002) 10 *George Mason Law Review* 471

Fox, S and Do, T, 'Getting Real about Big Data: Applying Critical Realism to Analyse Big Data Hype' (2013) 6(4) *International Journal of Managing Projects in Business* 739

Franklyn, DJ and Hyman, DA 'Review of the Likely Effects of Google's Proposed Commitments dated October 21, 2013 ("Second Commitments")', *FairSearch*, 9 December 2013, available at www.fairsearch.org/wp-content/uploads/2013/12/FairSearch-Hyman_Franklyn-Study.pdf

Freedman, D, 'Web 2.0 and the Death of the Blockbuster Economy' in J Curran, N Fenton and D Freedman (eds), *Misunderstanding the Internet* (Abingdon, Routledge, 2012)

Freyer, TA, *Antitrust and Global Capitalism, 1930–2004* (Cambridge, Cambridge University Press, 2006)

Frieden, R, 'Internet Packet Sniffing and Its Impact on the Network Neutrality Debate and the Balance of Power Between Intellectual Property Creators and Consumers' (2008) 18(3) *Fordham Intellectual Property, Media and Entertainment Law Journal* 633

Frischmann, B, *Infrastructure: The Social Value of Shared Resources* (Oxford, Oxford University Press, 2012)

Fuchs, C, 'Critique of the Political Economy of Web 2.0 Surveillance' in C Fuchs and others (eds), *Internet and Surveillance: The Challenges of Web 2.0 and Social Media* (Abingdon, Routledge, 2011)

—— 'A Contribution to the Critique of the Political Economy of Google' (2011) 8(1) *Fast Capitalism*

—— 'Google Capitalism' (2012) 12(1) *Triple C Communication, Capitalism and Critique Journal for a Global Sustainable Information Society* 42

Fukuyama, F, *The End of History and the Last Man* (New York, Free Press, 1992)

Gal, MS and Rubinfeld, DL, *The Hidden Costs of Free Goods: Implications for Antitrust Enforcement*, UC Berkeley Public Law Research Paper 2529425, NYU Law and Economics Research Paper 14-44 (2015), available at http://ssrn.com/abstract=2529425

Gandal, N, *The Dynamics of Competition in the Internet Search Engine Market*, University of California Berkeley Competition Policy Center Working Paper CPC01-17 (2001), available at http://papers.ssrn.com/sol3/papers.cfm?abstract_id=502823

Geroski, PA, 'Competition in Markets and Competition for Markets' (2003) 3(3) *Journal of Industry, Competition and Trade* 151

Ginsburg, DH and Haar, DE, 'Resolving Conflicts Between Competition and Other Values: The Roles of Courts and Other Institutions in the US and the EU' in P Lowe and M Marquis (eds), *European Competition Law Annual 2012: Public Policies, Regulation and Economic Distress* (Oxford, Hart Publishing, 2014)

Goggin, G, 'Google Phone Rising: The Android and the Politics of Open Source' (2012) 26(5) *Continuum: Journal of Media and Cultural Studies* 741

Goldfarb, A and Tucker, C, 'Search Engine Advertising: Channel Substitution When Pricing Ads to Content' (2011) 57(3) *Management Science* 458

Goldman, E, 'Search Engine Bias and the Demise of Search Engine Utopianism' (2006) *Yale Journal of Law and Technology* 111

—— 'Revisiting Search Engine Bias' (2011) 38(1) *William Mitchell Law Review* 96

Goldschmidt, N and Rauchenschwandtner, H, *The Philosophy of Social Market Economy: Michel Foucault's Analysis of Ordoliberalism*, Freiburg Discussion Papers on Constitutional Economics 07/4 (2007)

Goldsmith, JL, 'Unilateral Regulation of the Internet: A Modest Defence' (2000) 11(1) *European Journal of International Law* 135

Goldsmith, JL and Wu, T, *Who Controls the Internet? Illusions of a Borderless World* (Oxford, Oxford University Press 2006)

Graeber, D, *Fragments of an Anarchist Anthropology* (Chicago, IL, Prickly Paradigm Press, 2004)

Graef, I, Vershakelen, J and Valcke, P, 'Putting the Right to Data Portability into a Competition Law Perspective' (2013) *Law, Journal of the Higher School of Economics Annual Review* 53

Graham, A, 'Broadcasting Policy and the Digital Revolution' (1998) 69B *Political Quarterly* 30

Graham, J, 'YouTube Takes on Netflix with Originals', *USA Today*, 9 February 2016, available at www.usatoday.com/story/tech/news/2016/02/09/youtube-takes-netflix-originals/80023958/#

Greenleaf, G, 'Global Data Privacy in a Networked World' in I Brown (ed), *Research Handbook on Governance of the Internet* (Berlin, Edward Elgar, 2012)

—— 'The TPP Agreement: An Anti-Privacy Treaty for Most of APEC' (2015) 138 *Privacy Laws and Business International Report* 21

Grewal, DS and Purdy, JS, 'Introduction: Law and Neoliberalism' (2014) 77(4) *Law and Contemporary Problems* 1

Griffen-Foley, B, 'From Tit-Bits to Big Brother: A Century of Audience Participation in the Media' (2004) 26(4) *Media, Culture and Society* 533

Grundmann, S (ed), *Constitutional Values and European Contract Law* (Alphen aan den Rijn, Kluwer Law International, 2008)

Gunningham, N and Rees, J, 'Industry Self-Regulation: An Institutional Perspective' (1997) 19(4) *Law and Policy* 364

Ha, I, Wildman, SS and Bauer, JM, 'P2P, CDNs and Hybrid Networks: The Economics of Internet Video Distribution' (2010) 17(4) *International Telecommunications Policy Review* 1

Hamblen, M, 'Google's Nexus Lineup May Not Sell Well, But Still Challenges Android Makers', *Computer World*, 3 December 2013, available at www.computerworld.com/s/article/9244477/Google_s_Nexus_lineup_may_not_sell_well_but_still_challenges_Android_makers

Hamburger, T and Gold, M, 'Google, once disdainful of lobbying, now a master of Washington influence', *Washington Post*, 13 April 2014, available at www.washingtonpost.com/politics/how-google-is-transforming-power-and-politicsgoogle-once-disdainful-of-lobbying-now-a-master-of-washington-influence/2014/04/12/51648b92-b4d3-11e3-8cb6-284052554d74_story.html

Hamilton, J, 'Historical Forms of User Production' (2014) 36(4) *Media Culture Society* 491

Handley, T, 'P2P Search as an Alternative to Google: Recapturing Network Value through Decentralized Search' (2013) 3 *Journal of Peer Production*

Harvey, D, *A Brief History of Neoliberalism* (Oxford, Oxford University Press, 2005)

Haucap, J and Heimeshoff, U, 'Google, Facebook, Amazon, eBay: Is the Internet Driving Competition or Market Monopolization?' (2014) 11 *International Economics and Economic Policy* 49

Heemsbergen, LJ, 'Designing Hues of Transparency and Democracy After Wikileaks: Vigilance to Vigilantes and Back Again' (2015) 17(8) *New Media and Society* 1340

Helberger, N and others, 'Digital Content Contracts for Consumers' (2013) 36(1) *Journal of Consumer Policy* 37

Hermann, C, *Neoliberalism in the European Union*, DYNAMO Thematic Paper (2005)

Hestres, LE, 'App Neutrality: Apple's App Store and Freedom of Expression Online' (2013) 7 *International Journal of Communication* 1265

Hill, S, 'Tired of Google Play? Check Out These Alternative Android App Stores', *Digital Trends*, 5 December 2013, available at www.digitaltrends.com/mobile/android-app-stores/#!OIQus

Hof, R, 'Google's Ad Machine is Even More Profitable Than Anyone Knew', *Forbes*, 1 February 2016, available at www.forbes.com/sites/roberthof/2016/02/01/googles-ad-machine-is-even-more-profitable-than-anyone-knew/#2715e4857a0b677929eb7e7a

Hon, WK, Hornle, J and Millard, C, 'Which Law(s) Apply to Personal Data in Clouds?' in C Millard (ed), *Cloud Computing Law* (Oxford, Oxford University Press, 2013)

Hon, WK, Millard, C and Walden, I, 'What is Regulated as Personal Data in Clouds?' in C Millard (ed), *Cloud Computing Law* (Oxford, Oxford University Press, 2013)

Horkheimer, M and Adorno, TW, *Dialectic of Enlightenment: Philosophical Fragments* (Palo Alto, CA, Stanford University Press, 2002)

Hou, L and others, 'Can Open Internet Access be Imposed upon European CATV Networks?' (2013) 37(10) *Telecommunications Policy* 970

Ibanez Colomo, P, 'Exclusionary Discrimination Under Article 102 TFEU' (2014) 51(1) *Common Market Law Review* 141

IHS Technology, *Broadband Internet Penetration Deepens in US; Cable is King* (9 December 2013), available at https://technology.ihs.com/468148/broadband-internet-penetration-deepens-in-us-cable-is-king

Illich, I, *Tools for Conviviality* (New York, Harper & Row, 1973)

Initiative for a Competitive Online Marketplace, *ICOMP Response to Commission's Announcement on the Google Antitrust Case* (ICOMP, 5 February 2014), available at www.i-comp.org/blog/2014/icomp-response-commissions-announcement-google-antitrust-case/

Introna, LD and Nissenbaum, H, 'Shaping the Web: Why the Politics of Search Engines Matter' (2000) 16(3) *Information Society* 169

Jarvinen, H, *Net Neutrality: The European Parliament has Decided Not to Decide* (EDRi, 27 October 2015), available at https://edri.org/net-neutrality-european-parliament-decided-not-to-decide/

Jones, CA, 'Foundations of Competition Policy in the EU and USA: Conflict, Convergence and Beyond' in H Ulrich (ed), *The Evolution of European Competition Law: Whose Regulation, Which Competition?* (Cheltenham, Edward Elgar, 2006)

Karppinen, K, 'Rethinking Media Pluralism and Communicative Abundance' (2009) 11 *Observatorio (OBS*) Journal* 151

Khrennikov, I, 'Russia Says Google Broke Antitrust Laws', *Bloomberg*, 15 September 2015, available at www.bloomberg.com/news/articles/2015-09-14/russia-says-google-broke-antitrust-laws-sending-yandex-soaring

King, S, 'Governing the Ungovernable: The Market, Technology and You' (2014) 15 *Insights* 55

Kinley, D, *Civilising Globalisation: Human Rights and the Global Economy* (Cambridge, Cambridge University Press, 2009)

Kinley, D and Tadaki, J, 'From Talk to Walk: The Emergence of Human Rights Responsibilities for Corporations at International Law' (2004) 44(4) *Virginia Journal of International Law* 931

Koops, BJ, 'The Trouble with European Data Protection Law' (2014) 4(4) *International Data Privacy Law* 250

Koops, BJ and Sluijs, J, 'Network Neutrality and Privacy According to Art 8 ECHR' (2012) 3(2) *European Journal for Law and Technology*

Kosner, AW, 'What 7 Million Jailbreak are Saying: Is Apple Listening?', *Forbes*, 10 February 2013, available at www.forbes.com/sites/anthonykosner/2013/02/10/what-7-million-jailbreaks-are-saying-is-apple-listening/

Kuner, C and others, 'When Two Worlds Collide: The Interface Between Competition Law and Data Protection' (2014) 4(4) *International Data Privacy Law* 247

Lamadrid, A, 'European Commission v Google', *Chillin'Competition*, 10 December 2010, available at http://chillingcompetition.com/2010/12/10/european-commission-vs-google/

—— 'Some Thoughts on the New Anti-Google (Android) Complaint (Post 3/3): Bundling Allegations', *Chillin'Competition*, 9 September 2013, available at http://chillingcompetition.com/2013/09/09/some-thoughts-on-the-new-anti-google-android-complaint-post-33-bundling-allegations/

Lametti, D, 'The Cloud: Boundless Digital Potential or Enclosure 3.0?' (2012) 17(3) *Virginia Journal of Law and Technology* 190

Lang, A, *World Trade Law After Neoliberalism* (Oxford, Oxford University Press, 2011)

Lao, M, *'Neutral' Search as a Basis for Antitrust Action?*, Harvard Journal of Law and Technology Occasional Paper Series (2013)

Leiner, BM and others, 'A Brief History of the Internet' (2009) 39(5) *ACM SIGCOMM Computer Communication Review* 22.

Lepp, JT, 'ICANN's Escape from Antitrust Liability' (2012) 89(4) *Washington University Law Review* 931

Lewandowski, D, 'Why We Need an Independent Index of the Web' in R Konig and M Rasch (eds), *Society of the Query Reader* (Amsterdam, Institute of Network Cultures, 2014)

Liang, B and Lu, H, 'Internet Development, Censorship and Cyber Crimes in China' (2010) 26(1) *Journal of Contemporary Criminal Justice* 103

Liebenau, J and others, *European Internet Traffic: Problems and Prospects of Growth and Competition*, London School of Economics White Paper (2013), available at http://eprints.lse.ac.uk/50930/

Liu, J, 'Copyright Law's Theory of the Consumer' (2003) 44 *Boston College Law Review* 397

Lomas, N, 'Google Pays Another Tiny Fine -n Europe, $1.4M, for Street View Privacy Concerns', *TechCrunch*, 4 April 2014, available at http://techcrunch.com/2014/04/04/google-street-view-fine/

Loos, M and Luzak, J, 'Wanted, a Bigger Stick: On Unfair Terms in Consumer Contracts with Online Service Providers' (2016) 39(1) *Journal of Consumer Policy* 63

Lynskey, O, 'Control over Personal Data in a Digital Age: *Google Spain v AEPD and Maria Costeja Gonzalez*' (2015) 78(3) *Modern Law Review* 522

—— *The Foundations of EU Data Protection Law* (Oxford, Oxford University Press, 2015)

Lyon, D, 'Surveillance, Snowden and Big Data: Capacities, Consequences, Critique' (2014) *Big Data and Society* 1

MacKinnon, R, 'Flatter World and Thicker Walls? Blogs, Censorship and Civic Discourse in China' (2008) 134 *Public Choice* 31

MacSithigh, D, 'App Law Within: Rights and Regulation in the Smartphone Age' (2013) 21(2) *International Journal of Law and Information Technology* 154

Mak, C, *Fundamental Rights in European Contract Law: A Comparison of the Impact of Fundamental Rights on Contractual Relationships in Germany, the Netherlands, Italy and England* (Alphen aan den Rijn, Kluwer Law International, 2008)

Manne, G, 'The Problem of Search Engines as Essential Facilities: An Economics and Legal Assessment' in B Szoka and A Marcus (eds), *The Next Digital Decade: Essays on the Future of the Internet* (Washington DC, TechFreedom, 2011)

—— 'Google isn't "Leveraging Dominance", It's Fighting to Avoid Obsolescence', *Truth on the Market*, 12 March 2012, available at http://truthonthemarket.com/2012/03/12/google-isnt-leveraging-its-dominance-its-fighting-to-avoid-obsolescence/

Manolea, B 'Google was Fined by French and Spanish Data Protection Authorities', *European Digital Rights Initiative*, 15 January 2014, available at http://edri.org/google-fined-french-spanish-data-protection-authorities/

Marquis, M and Rousseva, E, 'Hell Freezes Over: A Climate Change for Assessing Exclusionary Conduct under Article 102 TFEU' (2013) 4(1) *Journal of European Competition Law and Practice* 32

Marsden, CT, 'Net Neutrality and Consumer Access to Content' (2007) 4(4) *SCRIPTed* 407

—— *Net Neutrality: Towards a Co-Regulatory Solution* (London, Bloomsbury, 2010)

—— 'Net Neutrality Regulation in the UK: More Transparency and Switching' (2014) *Journal of Law and Economic Regulation*

Masnick, M, 'Apple Facing Trial over Whether Its Use of DRM Violated Antitrust Laws', *Techdirt*, 6 October 2014, available at www.techdirt.com/articles/20141003/15453128723/apple-facing-trial-over-whether-its-use-drm-violated-antitrust-laws.shtml

Mayer Schonberger, V, 'Demystifying Lessig' (2008) *Wisconsin Law Review* 713

McDonald, BP, 'The First Amendment and the Free Flow of Information: Towards A Realistic Right to Gather Information in the Information Age' (2004) 65(2) *Ohio State Law Journal* 249

McIntyre, TJ, 'Child Abuse Images and Cleanfeeds: Assessing Internet Blocking Systems' in I Brown (ed), *Research Handbook on Governance of the Internet* (Cheltenham, Edward Elgar, 2012)

McLaughlin, D, 'Google Said to be Under US Antitrust Scrutiny over Android', *Bloomberg*, 25 September 2015, available at www.bloomberg.com/news/articles/2015-09-25/google-said-to-be-under-u-s-antitrust-scrutiny-over-android-iezf41sg

Meese, J, 'User Production and Law Reform: A Socio-Legal Critique of User Creativity' (2015) 37(5) *Media Culture Society* 753

Metz, C, 'Apple Handcuffs "Open" Web Apps on Iphone Home Screen', *The Register*, 15 March 2011, available at www.theregister.co.uk/2011/03/15/apple_ios_throttles_web_apps_on_home_screen

Mitar, 'Net Neutrality in Slovenia', *Wlan Slovenia*, 16 June 2013, available at https://wlan-si.net/en/blog/2013/06/16/net-neutrality-in-slovenia/

Monteleone, S, *Ambient Intelligence and the Right to Privacy: The Challenge of Detection Technologies*, EUI Law Working Papers No 2011/13 (2011)

Moon, M, 'Privacy-Focused Blackphone 2 is Ready for Pre-Order', *Engadget*, 19 August 2015, available at www.engadget.com/2015/08/19/blackphone2-preorder/

Morozov, E, *The Net Delusion: How Not to Liberate the World* (New York, Public Affairs, 2011)

Moyn, S, 'A Powerless Companion: Human Rights in the Age of Neoliberalism' (2015) 77 *Law and Contemporary Problems* 147

Mueller, M, *Networks and States: The Global Politics of Internet Governance* (Cambridge, MA, MIT Press, 2010)

Newell, BC and Tennis, JT, 'Me, My Metadata, and the NSA: Privacy and Government Metadata Surveillance Programs', iConference 2014, Berlin, March 2014

Newman, N, *The Cost of Lost Privacy: Search, Antitrust and the Economics of the Control of User Data* (2013), available at http://ssrn.com/abstract=2265026

—— 'Search, Antitrust and the Economics of the Control of User Data' (2014) 30(3) *Yale Journal on Regulation* 10

Nihoul, P, 'The Ruling of the General Court in Intel: Towards the End of an Effect-based Approach in European Competition Law?' (2014) 5(8) *Journal of European Competition Law and Practice* 521

Nihoul, P and Skoczny, T (eds), *Procedural Fairness in Competition Proceedings* (Berlin, Edward Elgar, 2015)

Ni Loidean, N, 'The End of Safe Harbor: Implications for EU Privacy and Data Protection Law' (2016) 19(8) *Journal of Internet Law* 1

Nissenbaum, H, *Privacy in Context: Technology, Policy and Integrity of Social Life* (Redwood City, CA, Stanford University Press, 2009)

Oreskovic, A and Sin, M, 'Google app store policy raises privacy concerns', *Reuters*, 14 February 2013, available at www.reuters.com/article/2013/02/14/us-google-privacy-idUSBRE91D1LL20130214

Page, WH, 'Ideological Conflict and the Origins of Antitrust Policy' (1991) 66(1) *Tulane Law Review* 1

Palacin, M and others, 'The Impact of Content Delivery Networks on the Internet Ecosystem' (2013) 3 *Journal of Information Policy* 304

Pasquale, F, 'Dominant Search Engines: An Essential Cultural and Political Facility' in B Szoka and A Marcus (eds), *The Next Digital Decade: Essays on the Future of the Internet* (Washington DC, TechFreedom, 2011)

Pasquale, F, 'Symbiotic Law and Social Science: The Case for Political Economy in the Legal Academy, and Legal Scholarship in Political Economy', Jotwell 5th Anniversary Conference, Miami, 2014

—— *The Black Box Society: The Secret Algorithms that Control Money and Information* (Cambridge, MA, Harvard University Press, 2015)

Peters, MA, 'Foucault, Biopolitics and the Birth of Neoliberalism' (2007) 48(2) *Critical Studies in Education* 165

Petersmann, EU, 'Time for a United Nations "Global Compact" for Integrating Human Rights in the Law of Worldwide Organizations: Lessons from European Integration' (2002) 13 *European Journal of International* Law 621

—— 'Human Rights and International Trade Law: Defining and Connecting the Two Fields' in T Cottier, J Pauwelyn and E Burgi (eds), *Human Rights and International Trade* (Oxford, Oxford University Press, 2005)

Pollach, I, 'A Typology of Communicative Strategies in Online Privacy Policies: Ethics, Power and Informed Consent' (2005) 62(3) *Journal of Business Ethics* 221

Ramirez Perez, SM and van de Scheur, S, 'The Evolution of Law on Articles 85 and 86 EEC [Articles 101 and 102 TFEU]: Ordoliberalism and its Keynesian Challenge' in KK Patel and H Schweitzer (eds), *The Historical Foundations of EU Competition Law* (Oxford, Oxford University Press, 2013)

Raz, J, *The Morality of Freedom* (Oxford, Oxford University Press, 1988)

Renda, A, 'Competition, Neutrality and Diversity in the Cloud' (2012) 85 *Communications and Strategies* 23

Rigg, J, 'Blackphone Review: Putting a Price on Privacy', *Engadget*, 10 March 2014, available at www.engadget.com/2014/10/03/blackphone-review/

Rigi, J, 'Peer Production as an Alternative to Capitalism: A New Communist Horizon' (2012) 1 *Journal of Peer Production*

Robles, G and others, 'Corporate Involvement of Libre Software: Study of Presence in Debian Code over Time' in J Feller and others (eds), *Open Source Development, Adoption and Innovation* (Berlin, Springer, 2007)

Rosenzweig, R, 'Wizards, Bureaucrats, Warriors and Hackers' (1998) 103(5) *American Historical Review* 1530

Rothchild, KW, 'Neoliberalism, EU and the Evaluation of Policies' (2009) 21(2) *Review of Political Economy* 213

Rule, J, *Privacy in Peril: How We are Sacrificing a Fundamental Right in Exchange for Security and Convenience* (Oxford, Oxford University Press, 2009)

Ryan, V, 'The Internet of Things: Data Goldmine and Social Nightmare', *CTO*, 20 May 2014, available at ww2.cfo.com/it-value/2014/05/internet-things-data-goldmine-social-nightmare/

Samartzi, V, 'Optimal vs Sub-optimal Use of DRM-Protected Works' (2011) 33 *European Intellectual Property Review* 517

Sartor, G and Viola de Azevedo Cunha, M, 'The Italian Google-Case: Privacy, Freedom of Speech and Responsibility of Providers for User-Generated Content' (2010) 18(4) *International Journal of Law and Information Technology* 356

Sayer, P, 'Google Must Defend Privacy Policies to 6 European Agencies', *TechHive*, 7 April 2013, available at www.techhive.com/article/2033375/google-must-defend-privacy-policies-to-6-european-agencies.html?tk=rel_news

Scholz, T (ed), *Digital Labor: The Internet as Playground and Factory* (Abingdon, Routledge, 2013)

Schroeder, R, 'Big Data and the Brave New World of Social Media Research' (2014) 1(2) *Big Data and Society* 1.

Schweighofer, E, 'A Review of the Uniform Dispute Resolution Policy of the Internet Corporation for Assigned Names and Numbers (ICANN)' (2001) 6 *Austrian Review of International and European Law* 91

Scott, A, "The Evolution of Competition Law and Policy in the United Kingdom' in P Mehta (ed), *The Evolution of Competition Laws and their Enforcement: A Political Economy Perspective* (Abingdon, Routledge, 2011)

Sidak, G, 'A Consumer-Welfare Approach to Network Neutrality Regulation of the Internet' (2006) 2(3) *Journal of Competition Law and Economics* 349

Simpson, S, 'Pervasiveness and Efficacy in Regulatory Governance: Neo-Liberalism as Ideology and Practice in European Telecommunications Reorganisation', European Consortium for Political Research Standing Group on Regulatory Governance, Second Biennial Conference, '(Re)Regulation in the Wake of Neoliberalism: Consequences of Three Decades of Privatization and Market Liberalization', Utrecht, June 2008

Singel, R, 'Feds Want Apple and AT&T to Explain Google Voice Rejection', *Wired*, 31 July 2009, available at www.wired.com/business/2009/07/feds-want-apple-and-att-to-explain-google-voice-rejection/

Singer, HJ and Litan, RE, 'Unintended Consequences of Net Neutrality Regulation' (2007) 5(3) *Journal on Telecommunications and High Technology Law* 533.

Sluijs, J, 'From Competition to Freedom of Expression: Introducing Art 10 ECHR in the European Network Neutrality Debate' (2012) 12(3) *Human Rights Law Review* 509

Sluijs, J, Larouche, P and Sauter, W, 'Cloud Computing in the EU Policy Sphere' (2012) 3(1) *Journal of Intellectual Property, Information Technology and e-Commerce Law* 12

Smith, C, 'Facebook Graph Search: how the industry rates it', *Guardian*, 16 January 2013, available at www.theguardian.com/media-network/2013/jan/16/facebook-graph-search

Solove, D and Hartzog, W, 'The FTC and the New Common Law of Privacy' (2014) 114 *Columbia Law* Review 583.

Solum, L, 'Models of Internet Governance' in LA Bygrace and T Michaelsen (eds), *Internet Governance: Infrastructure and Institutions* (Oxford, Oxford University Press, 2009)

Speta, J, 'An Appropriate Interconnection Backstop' (2014) 12 *Journal on Telecommunications and High Technology Law* 113

StatCounter Global Stats, *Top 5 Desktop, Tablet and Console Search Engines in Europe from 2013 to 2016*, available at http://gs.statcounter.com/#search_engine-eu-yearly-2013-2016

StatCounter Global Stats, *Top 7 Tablet OSs in Europe from Jan 2015 to Jan 2016*, available at http://gs.statcounter.com/#tablet+console-os-eu-monthly-201501-201601

StatCounter Global Stats, *Top 8 Mobile Operating Systems in Europe from Jan 2015 to Jan 2016*, available at http://gs.statcounter.com/#mobile_os-eu-monthly-201501-201601

StatCounter Global Stats, *Top 10 Mobile and Tablet Device Vendors in Europe from Jan 2015 to Jan 2016*, available at http://gs.statcounter.com/#mobile+tablet-vendor-eu-monthly-201501-201601

StatCounter Global Stats, *Top 10 Tablet Device Vendors in Europe from Jan 2015 to Jan 2016*, available at http://gs.statcounter.com/#tablet-vendor-eu-monthly-201501-201601

Stigler, GJ, 'The Theory of Economic Regulation' (1971) 2 *Bell Journal of Economics and Management* 3

Stucke, M, 'Reconsidering Antitrust's Goals' (2012) 53 *Boston College Law Review* 551

Svantesson, D and Clarke, R, 'Privacy and Consumer Risks in Cloud Computing' (2010) 26(4) *Computer Law and Security Review* 391

Swire, P and Lagos, Y, 'Why the Right to Data Portability Likely Reduces Consumer Welfare: Antitrust and Privacy Critique' (2013) 72 *Maryland Law Review* 335

Tapscott, D, *Digital Economy: Promise and Peril in the Age of Networked Intelligence* (New York, McGraw Hill, 1997)

Tene, O and Polonetsky, J, 'A Theory of Creepy: Technology, Privacy and Shifting Social Norms' (2013) 16 *Yale Journal of Law and Technology* 59

Terranova, T, 'Free Labor: Producing Culture for the Digital Economy' (2000) 18(2) *Social Text* 33

Thepot, F, 'Market Power in Online Search and Social Networking: A Matter of Two-Sided Markets' (2013) 36(2) *World Competition* 195

Tkacz, T, *Wikipedia and the Politics of Openness* (Chicago, IL, University of Chicago Press, 2015)

Townley, C, *Article 81 EC and Public Policy* (Oxford, Hart Publishing, 2009)

—— 'Which Goals Count in Article 101 TFEU?: Public Policy and Its Discontents' (2011) 9 *European Competition Law Review* 441

Trautman, LJ, 'Virtual Currencies: Bitcoin and What Now after Liberty Reserve, Silk Road, and Mt Gox?' (2014) 20(4) *Richmond Journal of Law and Technology* 1

Turner, S, 'Anarchist Theory and Human Rights' in N Jun and S Wahl (eds), *New Perspectives on Anarchism* (Lanhan, Lexington Books, 2010)

Twining, W, 'Law in Context Movement' in P Cane and J Conaghan (eds), *The New Oxford Companion to Law* (Oxford, Oxford University Press, 2008)

UK Information Commissioner's Office, *Privacy in Mobile Apps: Guidance for App Developers* (December 2013), available at http://ico.org.uk/for_organisations/data_protection/topic_guides/online/mobile_apps

Vaidhyanathan, S, *The Googlization of Everything (And Why We Should Worry)* (Berkeley, CA, University of California Press, 2011)

Van Couvering, E, *New Media? The Political Economy of Internet Search Engines* (International Association of Media and Communications Researchers, Porto Alegre, July 2004)

Van der Kroft, D, 'Net Neutrality in the Netherlands: State of Play', *Bits of Freedom*, 15 June 2011, available at www.bof.nl/2011/06/15/net-neutrality-in-the-netherlands-state-of-play/

Van Dijck, J, 'Users Like You? Theorizing Agency in User-Generated Content' (2009) 31(1) *Media, Culture and Society* 41

Van Loon, S, 'The Power of Google: First Mover Advantage or Abuse of a Dominant Position' in A Lopez-Tarruella (ed), *Google and the Law* (Berlin, Springer, 2012)

Van Schewick, B, *Internet Architecture and Innovation* (Cambridge, MA, MIT Press, 2010)

Vasagar, J, 'The news baron battling Google', *Financial Times*, 9 June 2014, available at www.ft.com/cms/s/0/beb7aeae-eb3d-11e3-bab6-00144feabdc0.html#axzz3C77rQzcj

Vatiero, M, 'The Ordoliberal Notion of Market Power: An Institutionalist Reassessment' (2010) 6(3) *European Competition Journal* 689

Vaughan, L and Thelwall, M, 'Search Engine Coverage Bias: Evidence and Possible Causes' (2004) 40(4) *Information Processing and Management* 693

Vega, T and Wyatt, E, 'US agency seeks tougher consumer privacy rules', *New York Times*, 26 March 2012, available at www.nytimes.com/2012/03/27/business/ftc-seeks-privacy-legislation.html?pagewanted=all&_r=0

Vezzoso, S, 'The Interface Between Competition Policy and Data Protection' (2012) 3(3) *Journal of Competition Law and Practice* 225

Volokh, E, 'Cheap Speech and What It Will Do' (1995) 104(7) *Yale Law Journal* 1805

Voss, WG, 'Looking at European Union Data Protection Law Reform Through a Different Prism: The Proposed EU General Data Protection Regulation Two Years Later' (2014) 17(9) *Journal of Internet Law* 1

Walden, I, 'Law Enforcement Access to Data in Cloud' in C Millard (ed), *Cloud Computing Law* (Oxford, Oxford University Press, 2013)

Walker, K, 'Improving quality isn't anticompetitive', Google Europe blog, 27 August 2015, available at http://googlepolicyeurope.blogspot.co.uk/2015/08/improving-quality-isnt-anti-competitive.html

Walter, D, 'Apple Still Rules the App Market', *CMS Wire*, 22 January 2016, available at www.cmswire.com/mobile/apple-still-rules-the-app-market/

Weber, RH, 'Internet of Things: Governance Quo Vadis?' (2013) 29(4) *Computer Law and Security Review* 341

Welinder, Y, 'Facing Real-Time Identification in Mobile Apps and Wearable Computers' (2013) 30 *Santa Clara Computer and High Technology Law Journal* 89

Werbach, KD, 'Only Connect' (2007) 22(4) *Berkeley Technology Law Journal* 1233

Whittaker, Z, 'Germany Fines Google for "Unprecedented" Street View Wi-Fi Data Breach', *ZDNet*, 22 April 2013, available at www.zdnet.com/germany-fines-google-for-unprecedented-street-view-wi-fi-data-breach-7000014337/

Wu, T, 'Network Neutrality, Broadband Discrimination' (2003) 2 *Journal of Telecommunications and High Technology Law* 141

—— *The Master Switch: The Rise and Fall of Information Empires* (New York, Knopf, 2010)

Yoo, CS, 'Network Neutrality and the Economics of Congestion' (2006) 94 *Georgetown Law Journal* 1847

Zalnieriute, M and Schneider, T, *ICANN's Procedures and Policies in the Light of Human Rights, Fundamental Freedoms and Democratic Values* (Council of Europe DGI, 2014)

Zeno-Zencovich, V, *La Libertà d'espressione Media, mercato, potere nella società dell'informazione* (Bologna, Il Mulino, 2004)

Zingales, N, 'Product Market Definition in Online Search and Advertising' (2013) 9(1) *Competition Law Review* 28

Zittrain, J, *The Future of the Internet and How to Stop It* (New Haven, CT, Yale University Press, 2008)

Zizek, S, 'Corporate Rule of Cyberspace', *Inside Higher Ed*, 2 May 2011, available at www.insidehighered.com/views/2011/05/02/slavoj_zizek_essay_on_cloud_computing_and_privacy#sthash.B8DVfwFj.04ssAm14.dpbs

Zook, MA and Graham, M, 'The Creative Reconstruction of the Internet: Google and the Privatization of Cyberspace and DigiPlace' (2007) 38(6) *Geoforum* 1322

INDEX